OLD HAUNTS

OLLIE MASTERS & ROB WILLIAMS
WRITERS

LAURENCE CAMPBELL
ARTIST & COVER ARTIST

LEE LOUGHRIDGE
COLORIST & COVER COLORIST

SAL CIPRIANO
LETTERER

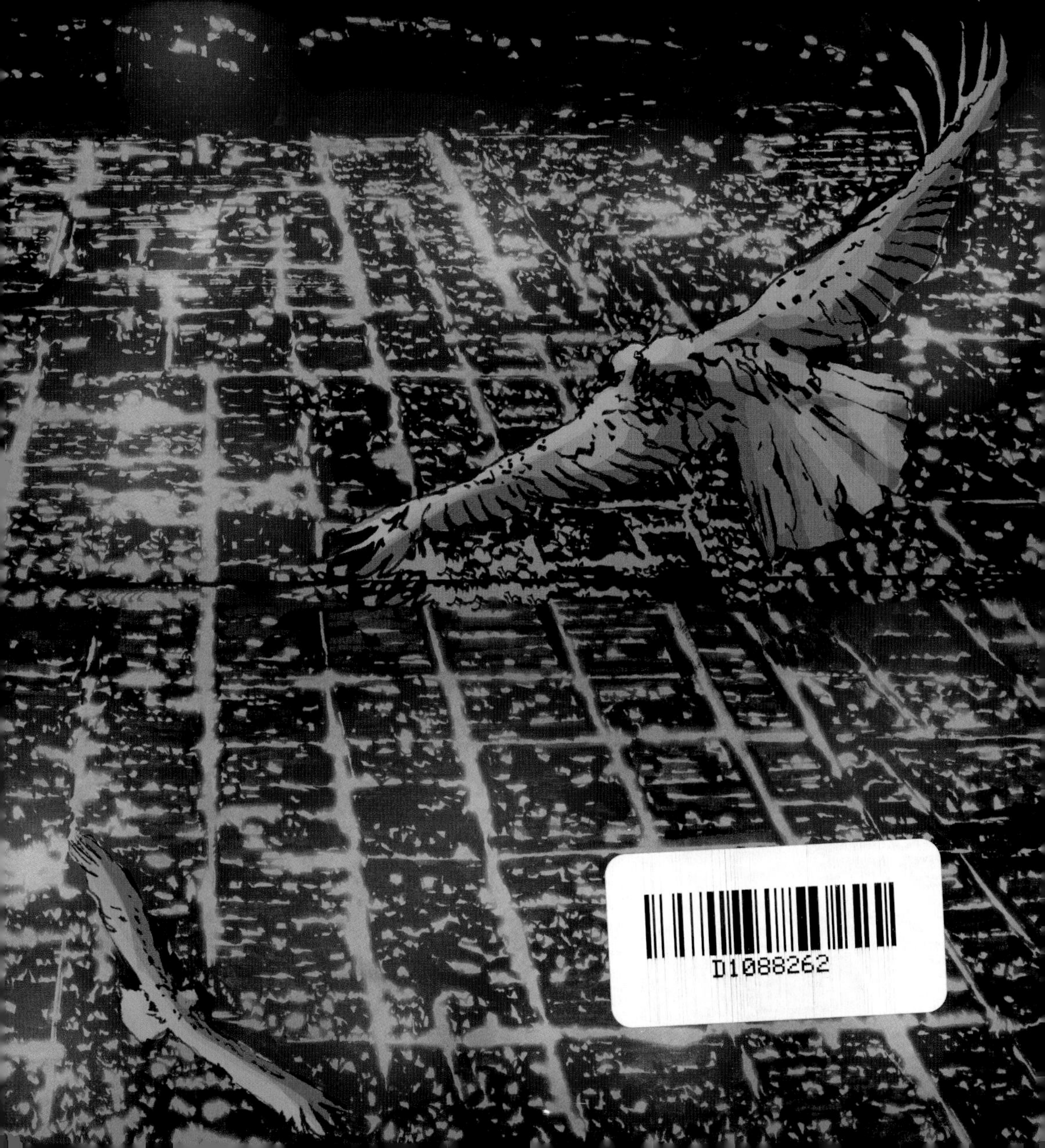

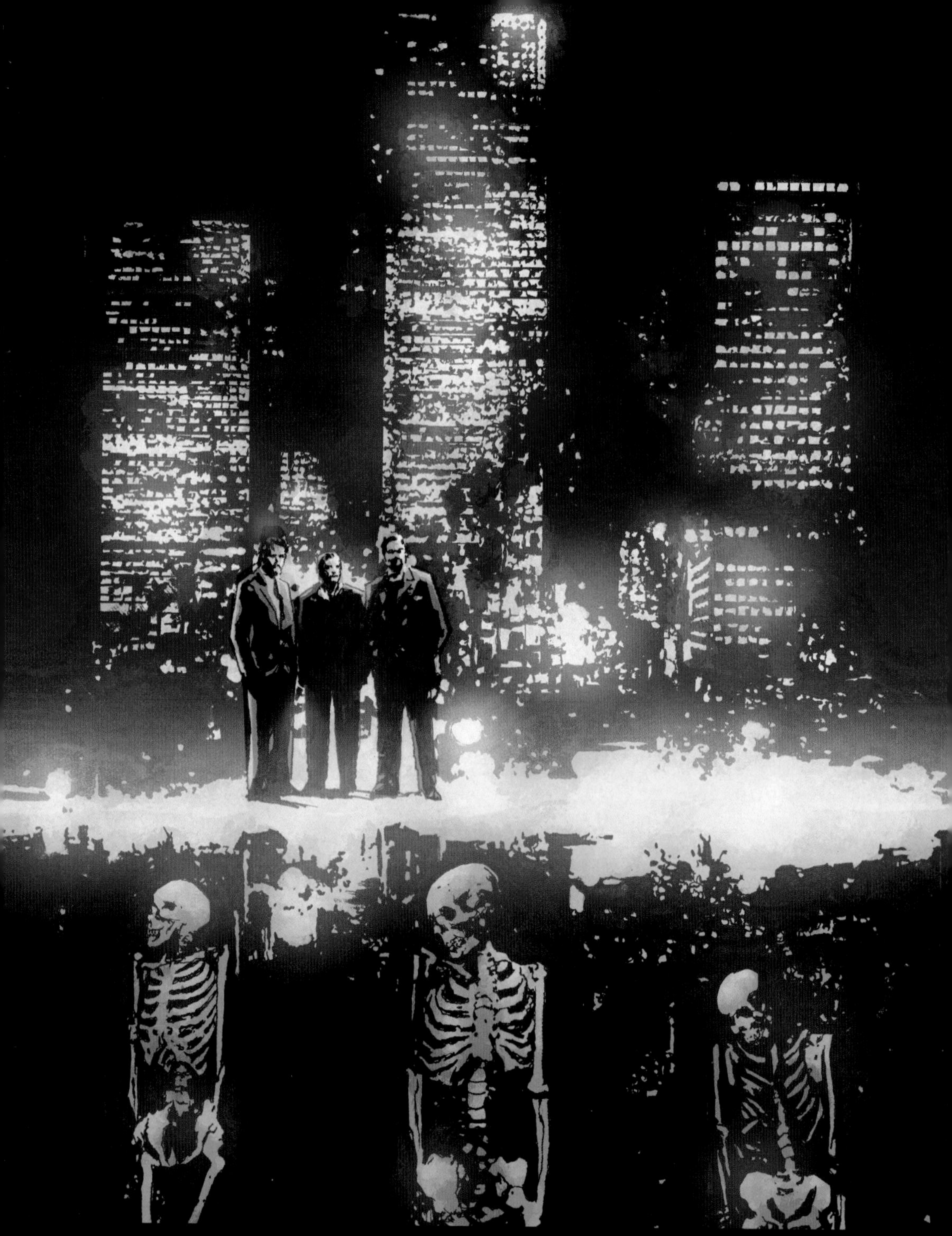

AWA UPSHOT AWA_studios AWAstudiosofficial UPSHOT_studios UPSHOTstudiosofficial

Axel Alonso Chief Creative Officer
Ben Buckley EVP, Revenue and Operations
Chris Burns Production Editor
Stan Chou Art Director & Logo Designer
Michael Coast Senior Editor
Jaime Coyne Associate Editor
Meryl Federman Accounting & Finance Associate
Frank Fochetta Senior Consultant, Sales & Distribution
William Graves Managing Editor
Bill Jemas CEO & Publisher
Amy Kim Events & Sales Associate
Bosung Kim Production & Design Assistant
Allison Mase Executive Assistant
Dulce Montoya Associate Editor
Kevin Park Associate General Counsel
Lisa Y. Wu Marketing Manager

OLD HAUNTS, VOLUME 1. February 2021. Published by Artists Writers & Artisans, Inc. Office of publication: 150 West 28th Street, 4th Floor, Suite 404, New York, NY 10010. **Printed in Canada.**

10 9 8 7 6 5 4 3 2 1

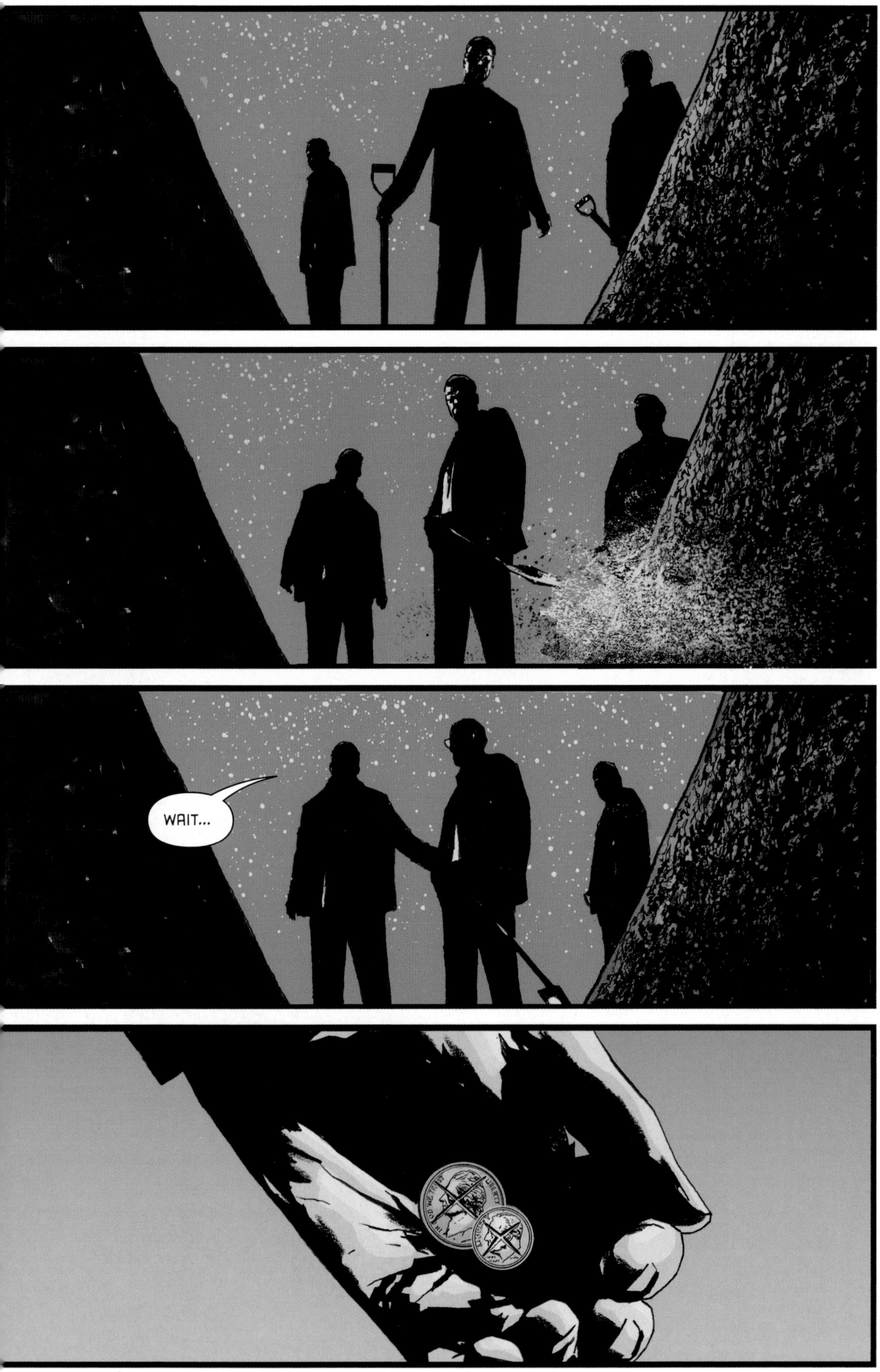
WAIT...

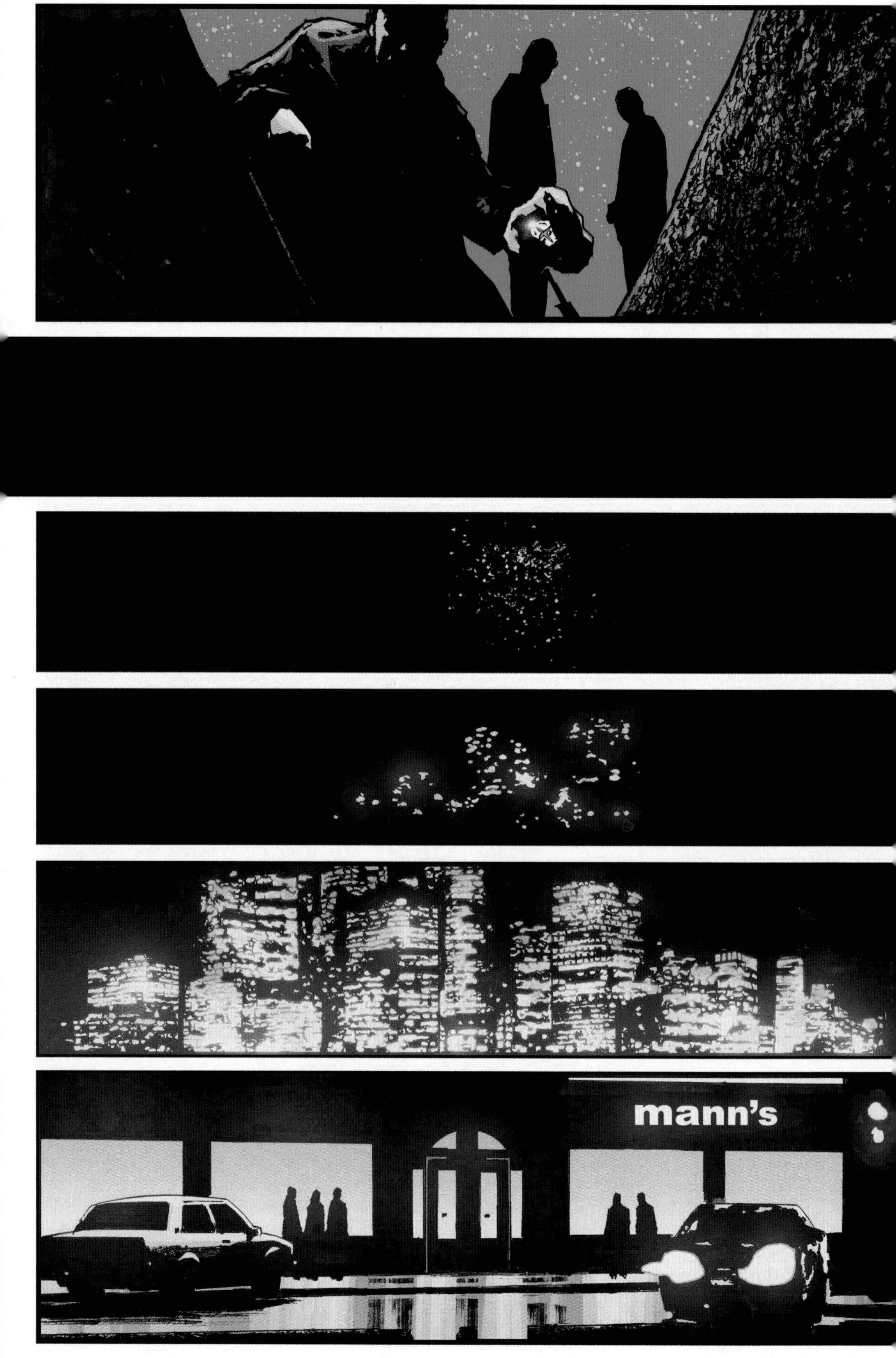
mann's

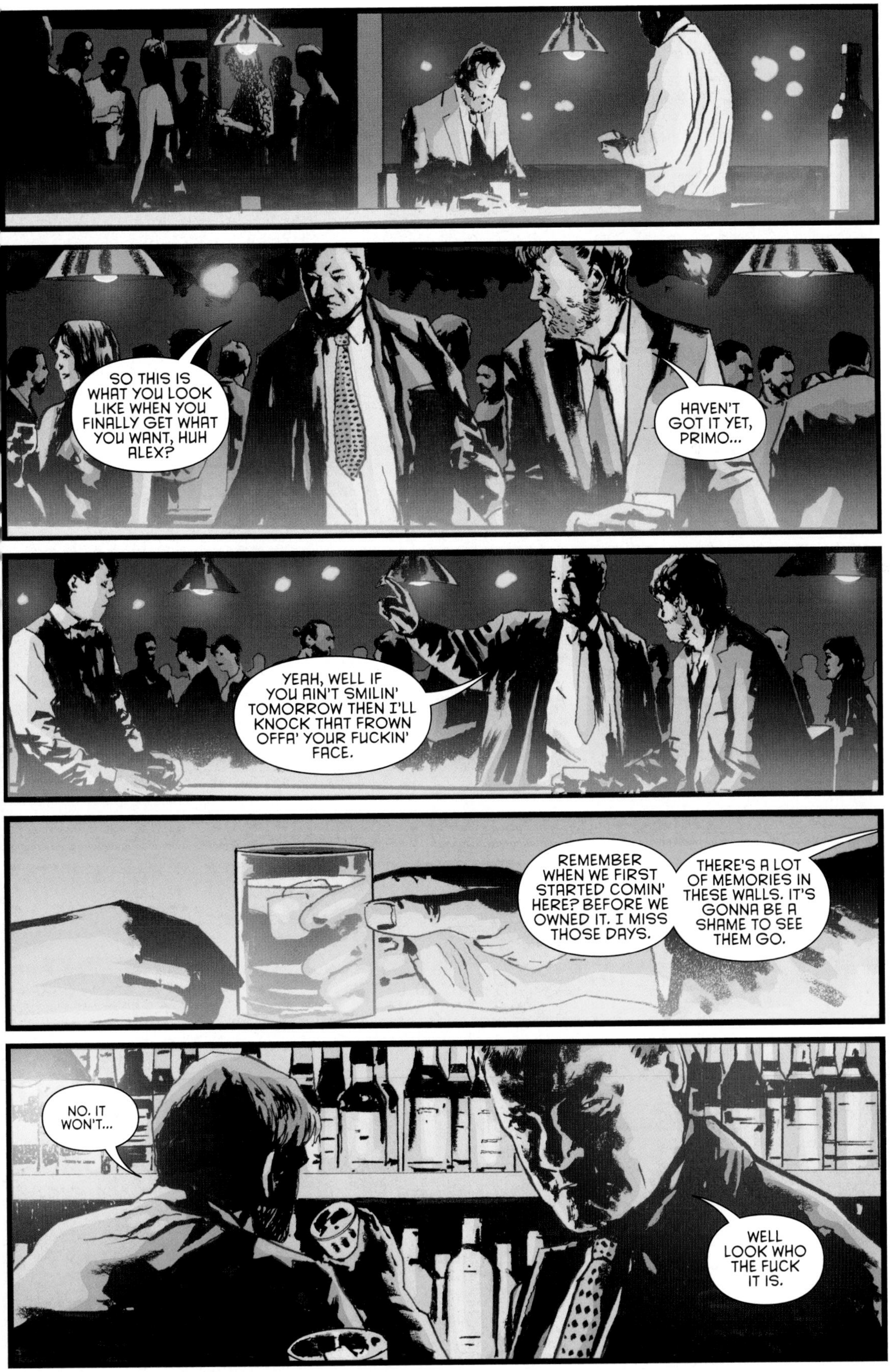

SO THIS IS WHAT YOU LOOK LIKE WHEN YOU FINALLY GET WHAT YOU WANT, HUH ALEX?
HAVEN'T GOT IT YET, PRIMO...
YEAH, WELL IF YOU AIN'T SMILIN' TOMORROW THEN I'LL KNOCK THAT FROWN OFFA' YOUR FUCKIN' FACE.
REMEMBER WHEN WE FIRST STARTED COMIN' HERE? BEFORE WE OWNED IT. I MISS THOSE DAYS.
THERE'S A LOT OF MEMORIES IN THESE WALLS. IT'S GONNA BE A SHAME TO SEE THEM GO.
NO. IT WON'T...
WELL LOOK WHO THE FUCK IT IS.

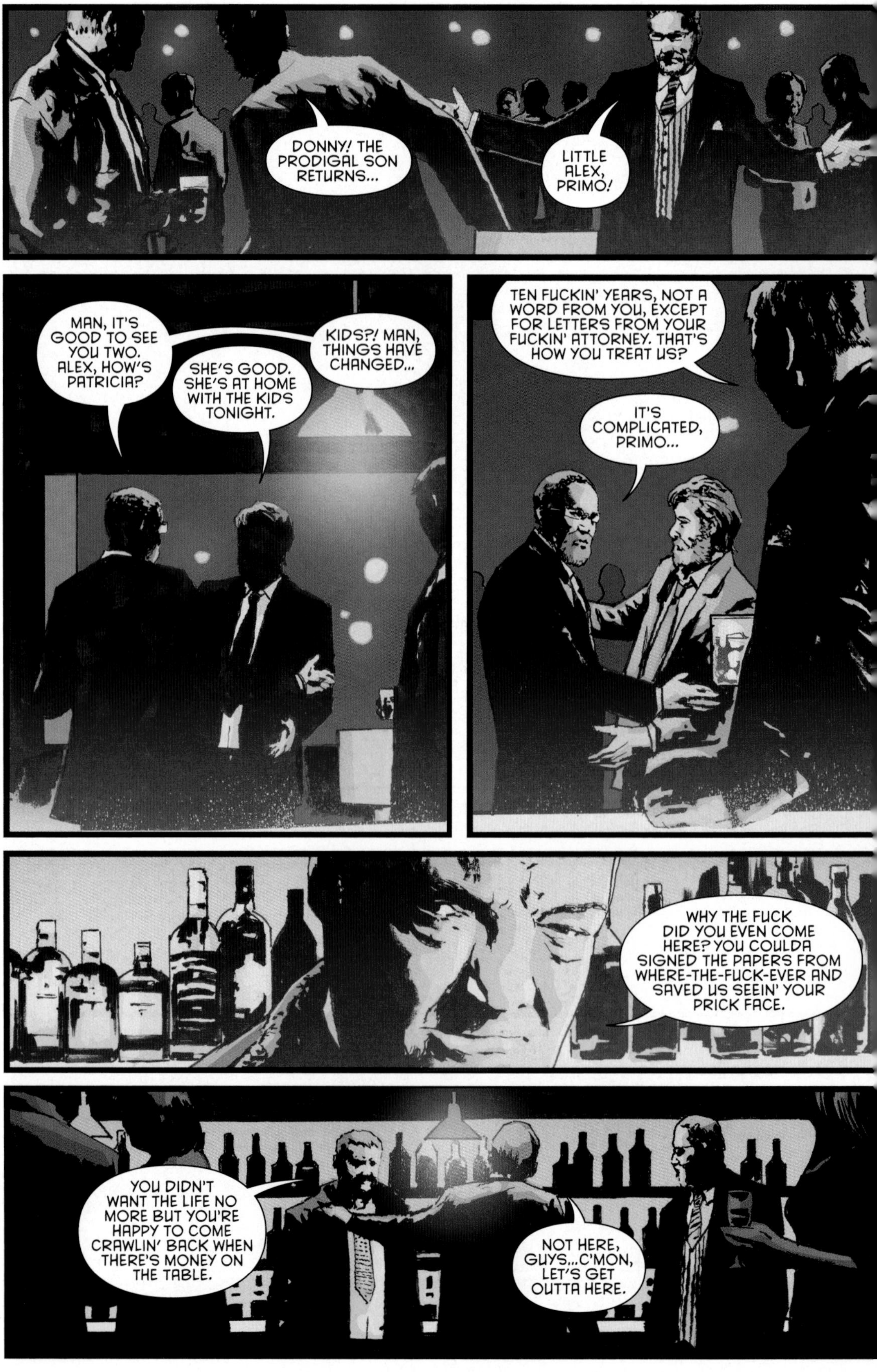
DONNY! THE PRODIGAL SON RETURNS...
LITTLE ALEX, PRIMO!
MAN, IT'S GOOD TO SEE YOU TWO. ALEX, HOW'S PATRICIA?
SHE'S GOOD. SHE'S AT HOME WITH THE KIDS TONIGHT.
KIDS?! MAN, THINGS HAVE CHANGED...
TEN FUCKIN' YEARS, NOT A WORD FROM YOU, EXCEPT FOR LETTERS FROM YOUR FUCKIN' ATTORNEY. THAT'S HOW YOU TREAT US?
IT'S COMPLICATED, PRIMO...
WHY THE FUCK DID YOU EVEN COME HERE? YOU COULDA SIGNED THE PAPERS FROM WHERE-THE-FUCK-EVER AND SAVED US SEEIN' YOUR PRICK FACE.
YOU DIDN'T WANT THE LIFE NO MORE BUT YOU'RE HAPPY TO COME CRAWLIN' BACK WHEN THERE'S MONEY ON THE TABLE.
NOT HERE, GUYS...C'MON, LET'S GET OUTTA HERE.

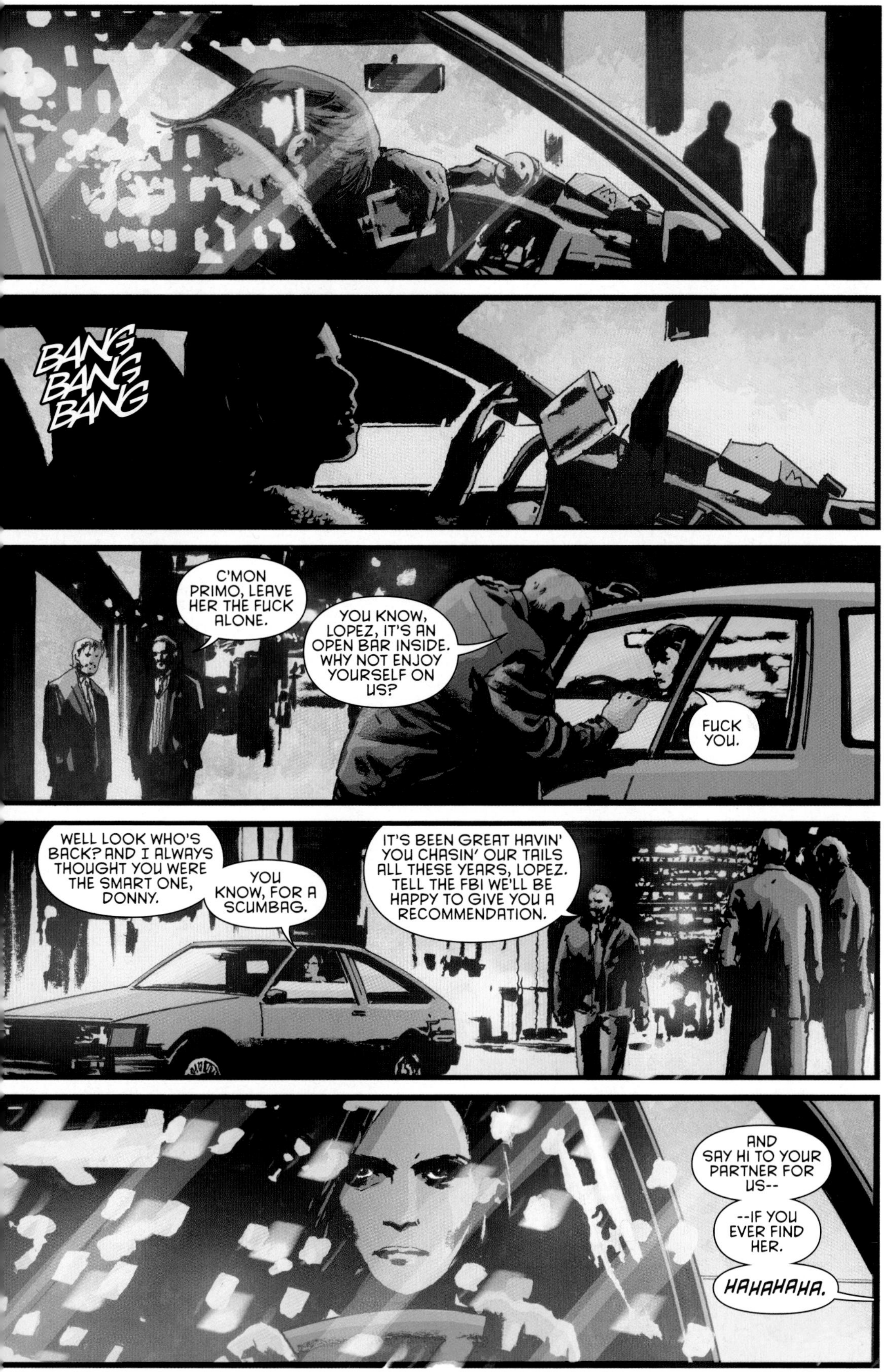

BANG BANG BANG
C'MON PRIMO, LEAVE HER THE FUCK ALONE.
YOU KNOW, LOPEZ, IT'S AN OPEN BAR INSIDE. WHY NOT ENJOY YOURSELF ON US?
FUCK YOU.
WELL LOOK WHO'S BACK? AND I ALWAYS THOUGHT YOU WERE THE SMART ONE, DONNY.
YOU KNOW, FOR A SCUMBAG.
IT'S BEEN GREAT HAVIN' YOU CHASIN' OUR TAILS ALL THESE YEARS, LOPEZ. TELL THE FBI WE'LL BE HAPPY TO GIVE YOU A RECOMMENDATION.
AND SAY HI TO YOUR PARTNER FOR US--
--IF YOU EVER FIND HER.
HAHAHAHA.

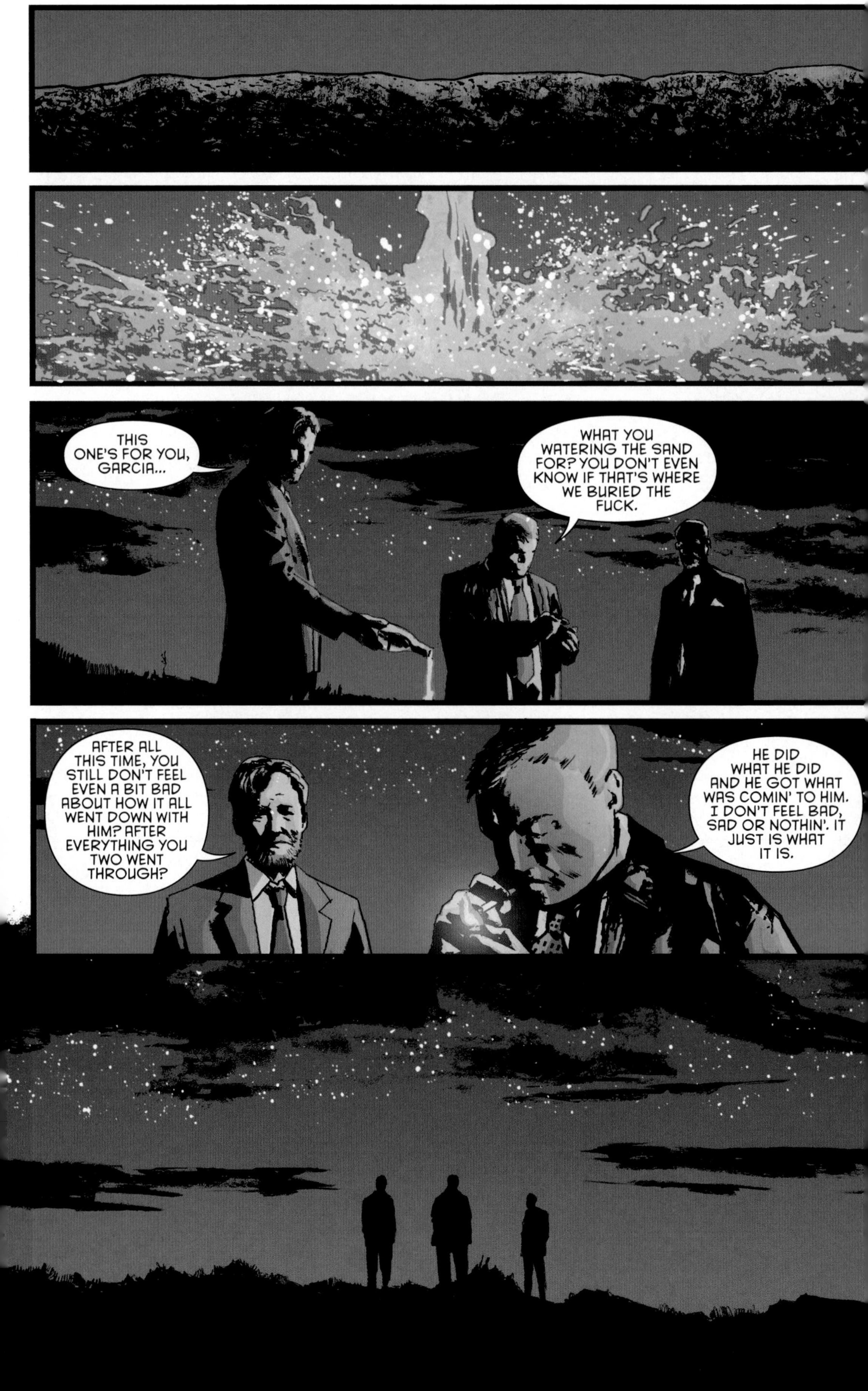
THIS ONE'S FOR YOU, GARCIA...
WHAT YOU WATERING THE SAND FOR? YOU DON'T EVEN KNOW IF THAT'S WHERE WE BURIED THE FUCK.
AFTER ALL THIS TIME, YOU STILL DON'T FEEL EVEN A BIT BAD ABOUT HOW IT ALL WENT DOWN WITH HIM? AFTER EVERYTHING YOU TWO WENT THROUGH?
HE DID WHAT HE DID AND HE GOT WHAT WAS COMIN' TO HIM. I DON'T FEEL BAD, SAD OR NOTHIN'. IT JUST IS WHAT IT IS.

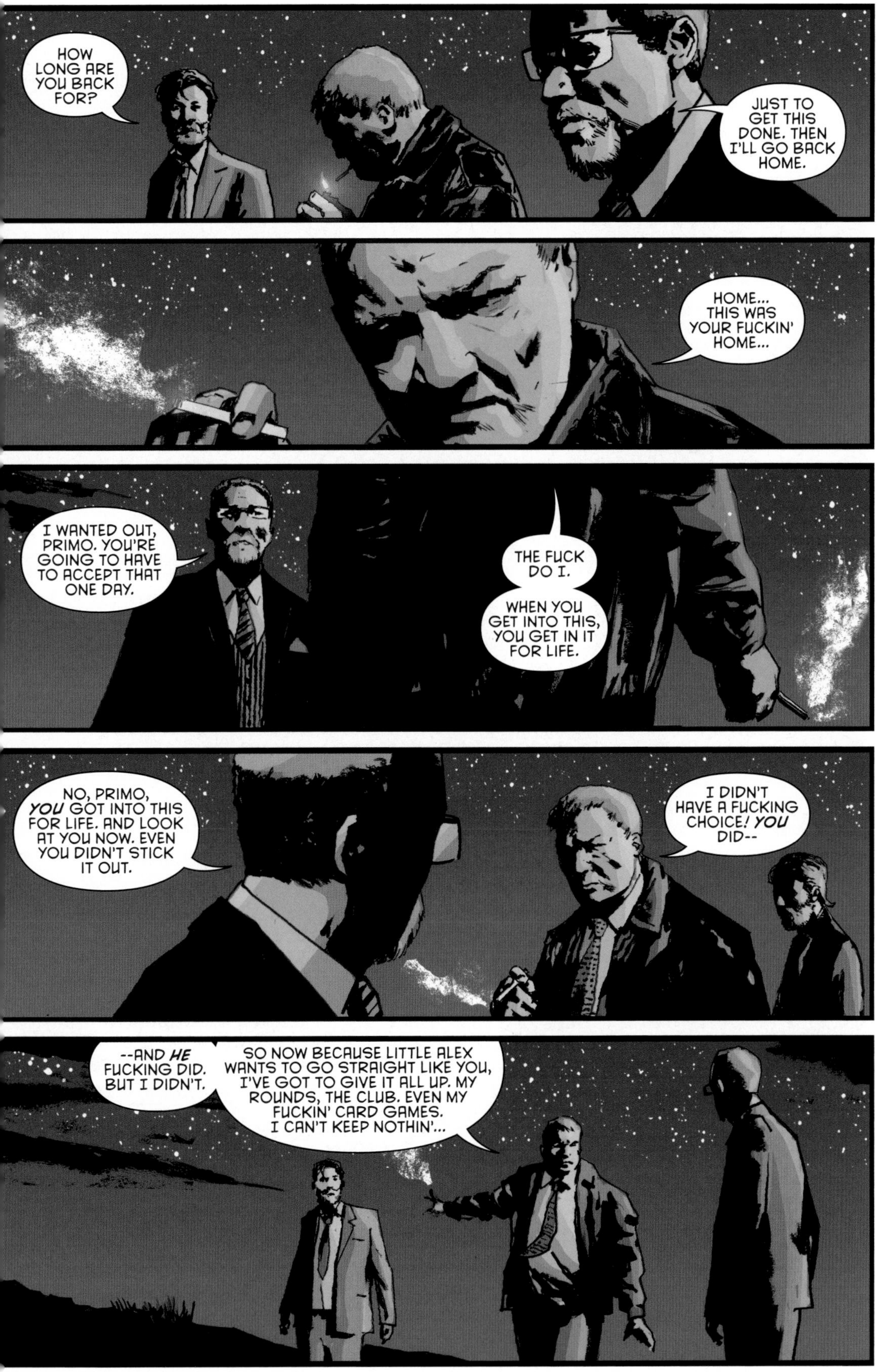
HOW LONG ARE YOU BACK FOR?
JUST TO GET THIS DONE. THEN I'LL GO BACK HOME.
HOME... THIS WAS YOUR FUCKIN' HOME...
I WANTED OUT, PRIMO. YOU'RE GOING TO HAVE TO ACCEPT THAT ONE DAY.
THE FUCK DO I.
WHEN YOU GET INTO THIS, YOU GET IN IT FOR LIFE.
NO, PRIMO, *YOU* GOT INTO THIS FOR LIFE. AND LOOK AT YOU NOW. EVEN YOU DIDN'T STICK IT OUT.
I DIDN'T HAVE A FUCKING CHOICE! *YOU* DID--
--AND *HE* FUCKING DID. BUT I DIDN'T.
SO NOW BECAUSE LITTLE ALEX WANTS TO GO STRAIGHT LIKE YOU, I'VE GOT TO GIVE IT ALL UP. MY ROUNDS, THE CLUB. EVEN MY FUCKIN' CARD GAMES. I CAN'T KEEP NOTHIN'...

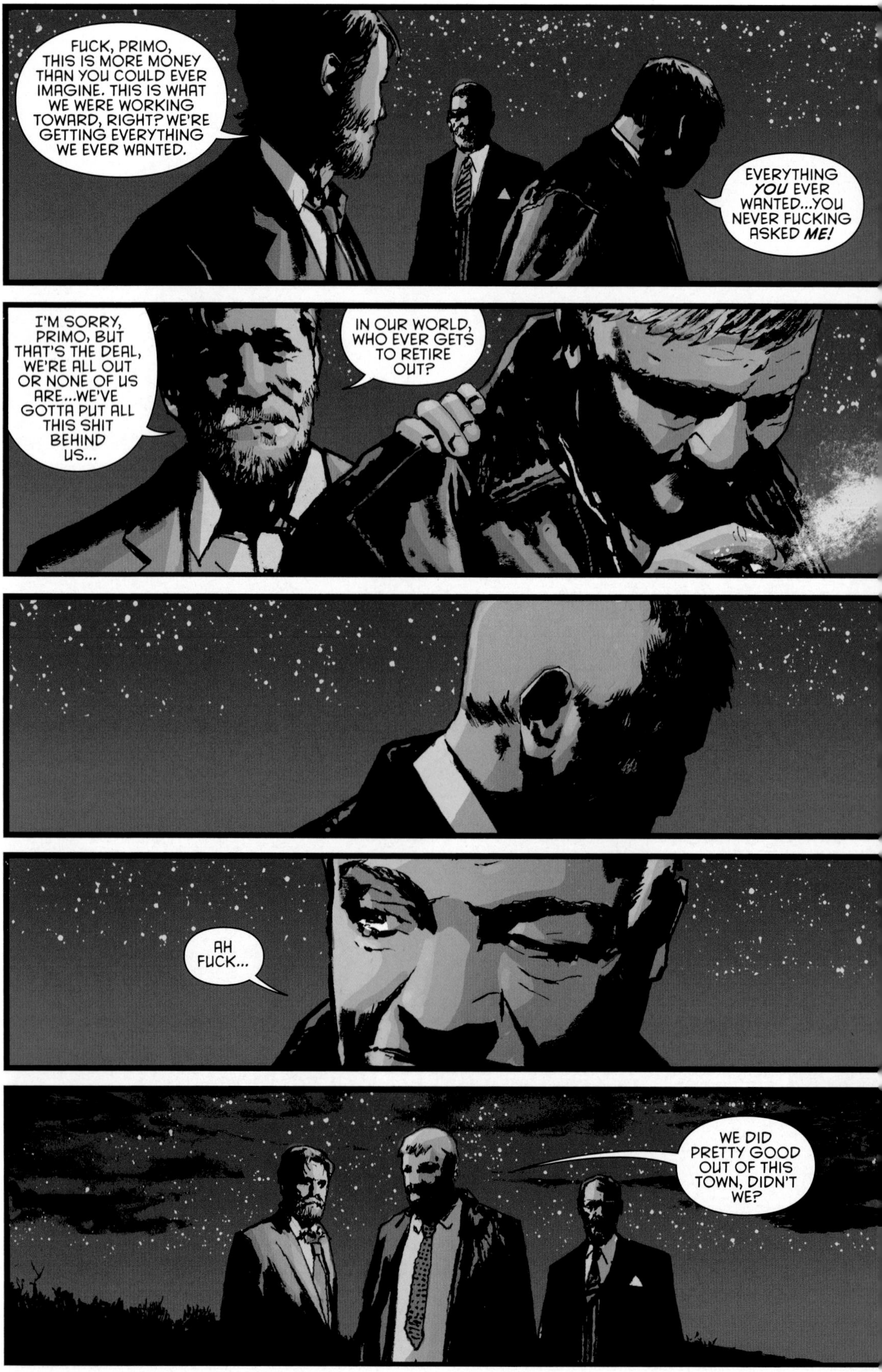

FUCK, PRIMO, THIS IS MORE MONEY THAN YOU COULD EVER IMAGINE. THIS IS WHAT WE WERE WORKING TOWARD, RIGHT? WE'RE GETTING EVERYTHING WE EVER WANTED.
EVERYTHING *YOU* EVER WANTED...YOU NEVER FUCKING ASKED *ME!*
I'M SORRY, PRIMO, BUT THAT'S THE DEAL, WE'RE ALL OUT OR NONE OF US ARE...WE'VE GOTTA PUT ALL THIS SHIT BEHIND US...
IN OUR WORLD, WHO EVER GETS TO RETIRE OUT?
AH FUCK...
WE DID PRETTY GOOD OUT OF THIS TOWN, DIDN'T WE?

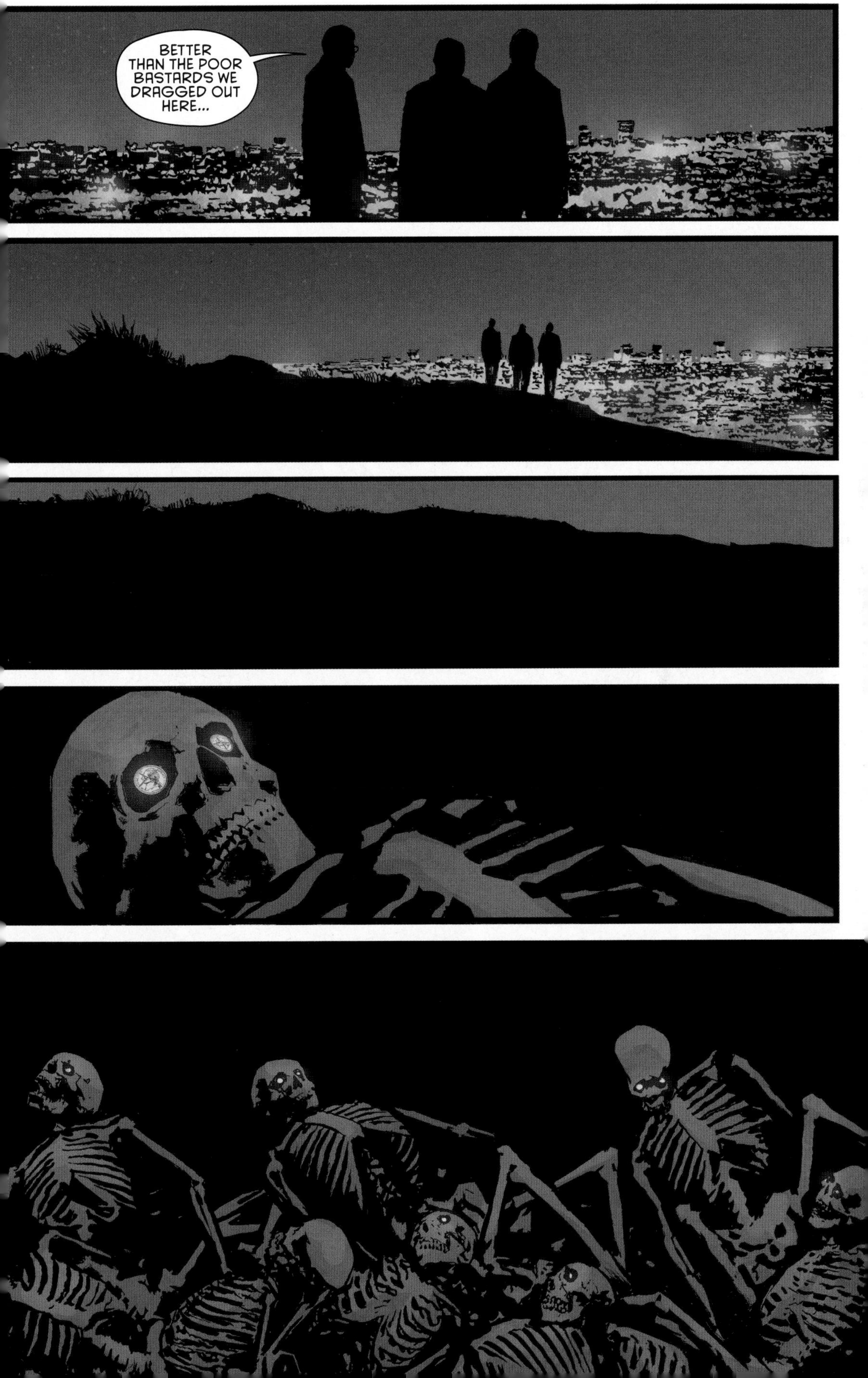
BETTER THAN THE POOR BASTARDS WE DRAGGED OUT HERE...

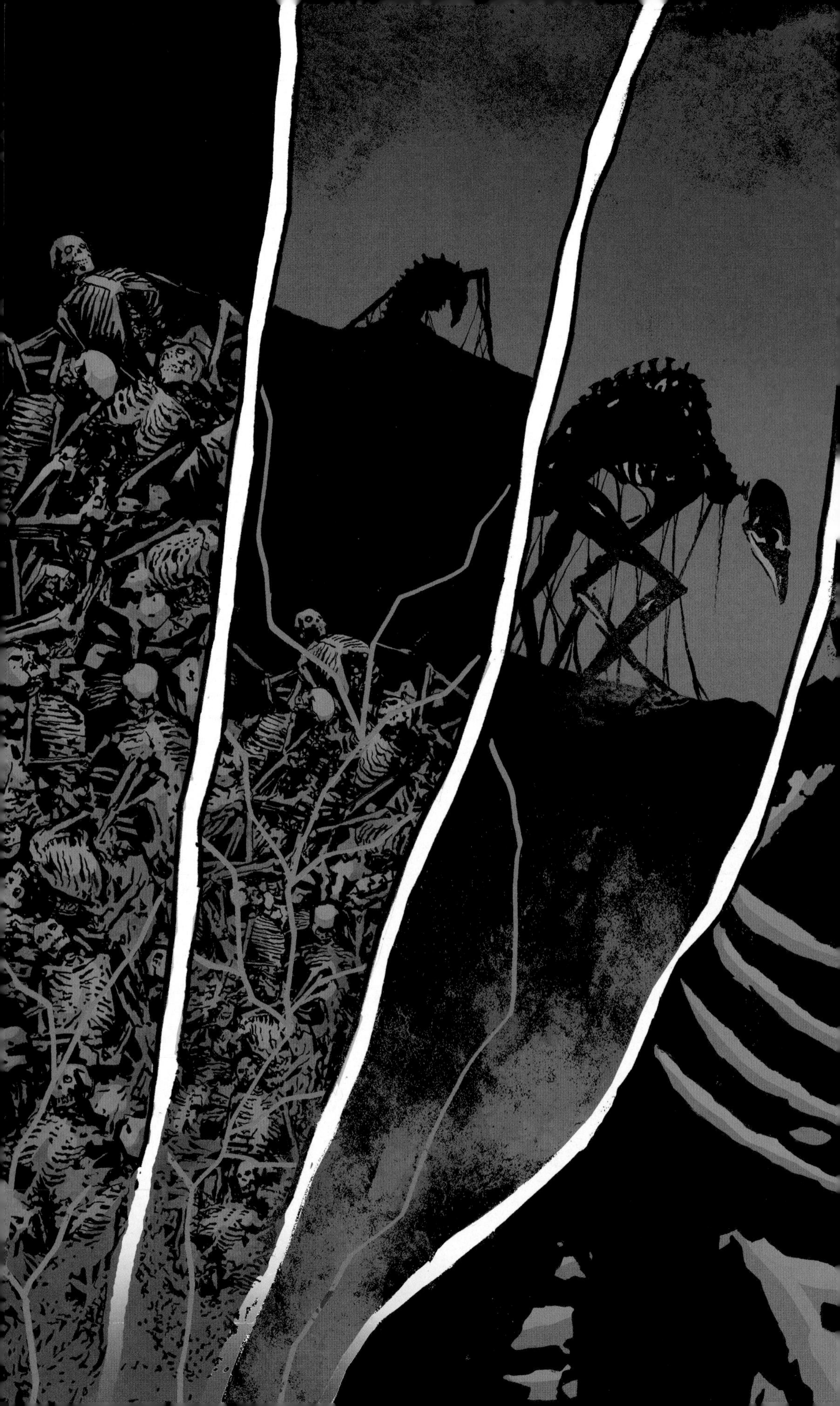

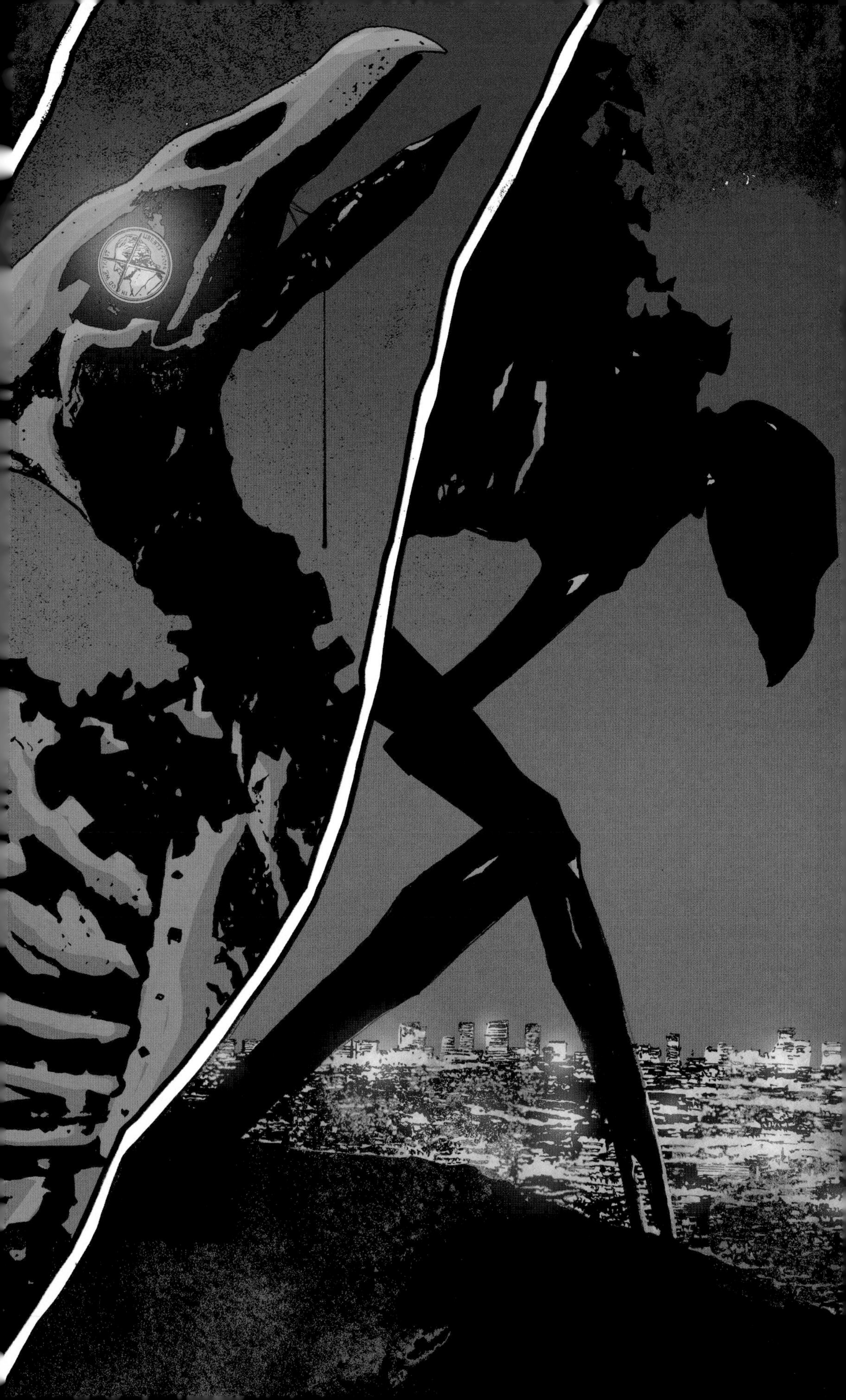

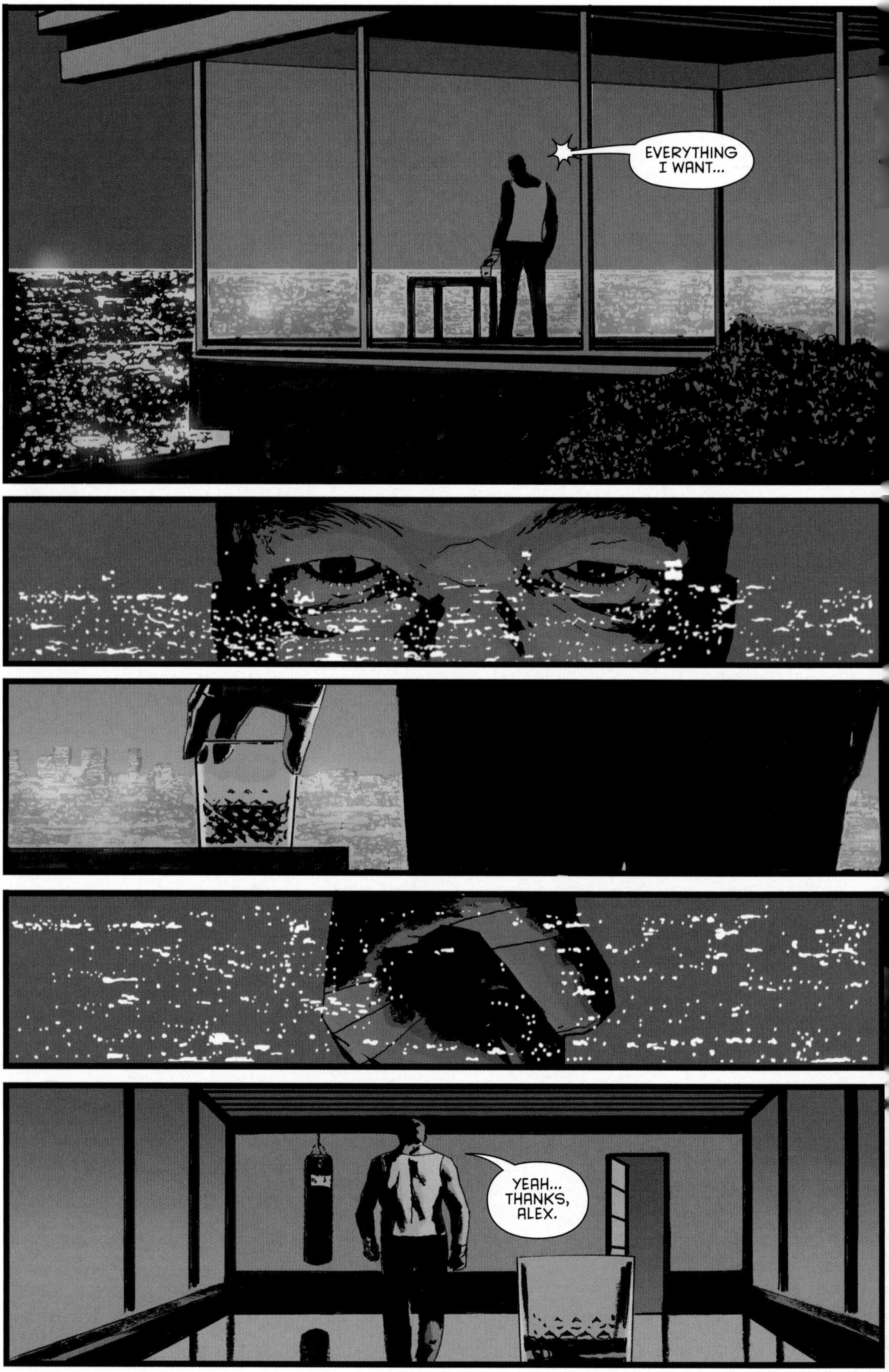
EVERYTHING I WANT...
YEAH... THANKS, ALEX.

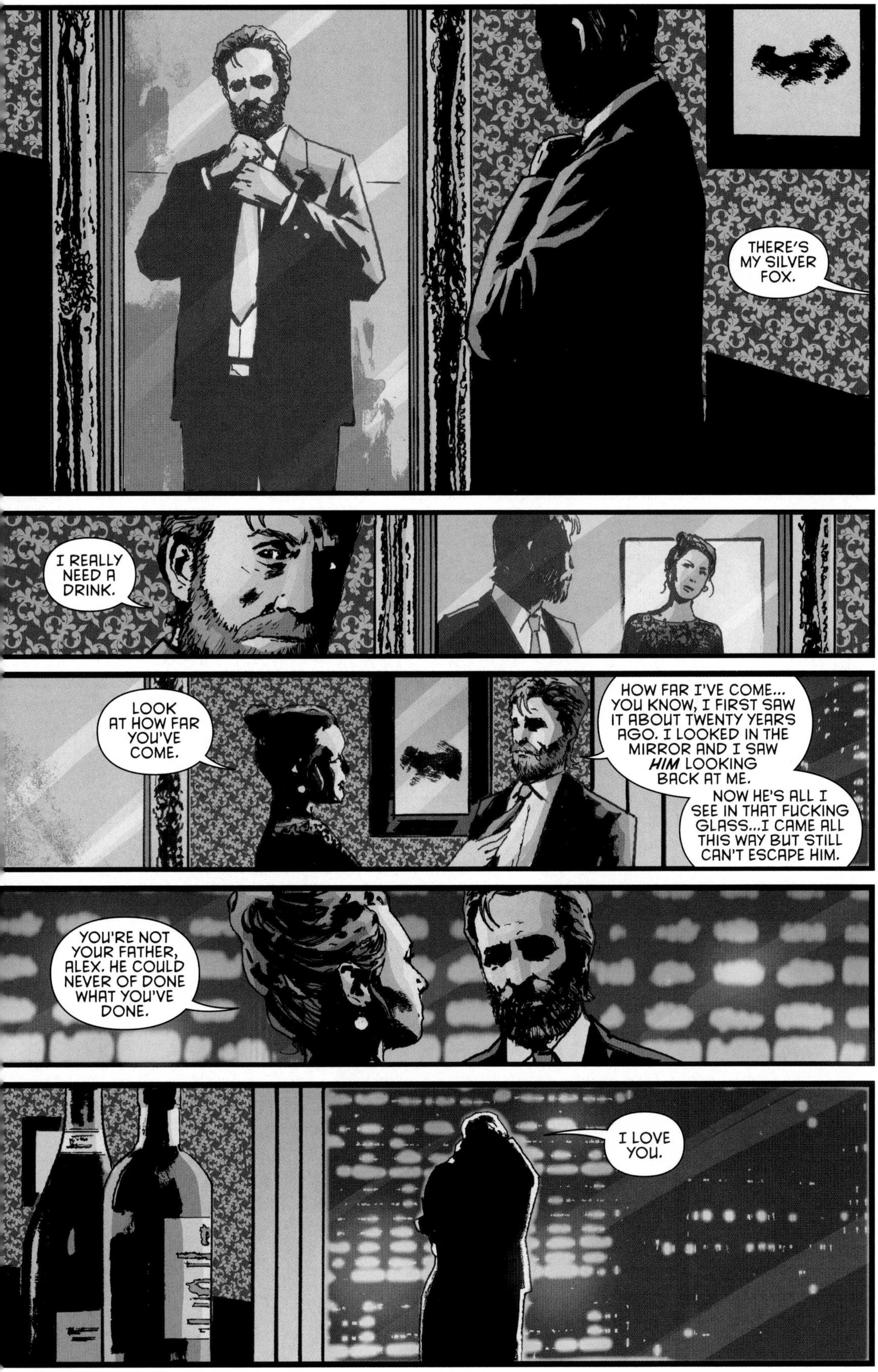
THERE'S MY SILVER FOX.
I REALLY NEED A DRINK.
LOOK AT HOW FAR YOU'VE COME.
HOW FAR I'VE COME... YOU KNOW, I FIRST SAW IT ABOUT TWENTY YEARS AGO. I LOOKED IN THE MIRROR AND I SAW *HIM* LOOKING BACK AT ME.
NOW HE'S ALL I SEE IN THAT FUCKING GLASS...I CAME ALL THIS WAY BUT STILL CAN'T ESCAPE HIM.
YOU'RE NOT YOUR FATHER, ALEX. HE COULD NEVER OF DONE WHAT YOU'VE DONE.
I LOVE YOU.

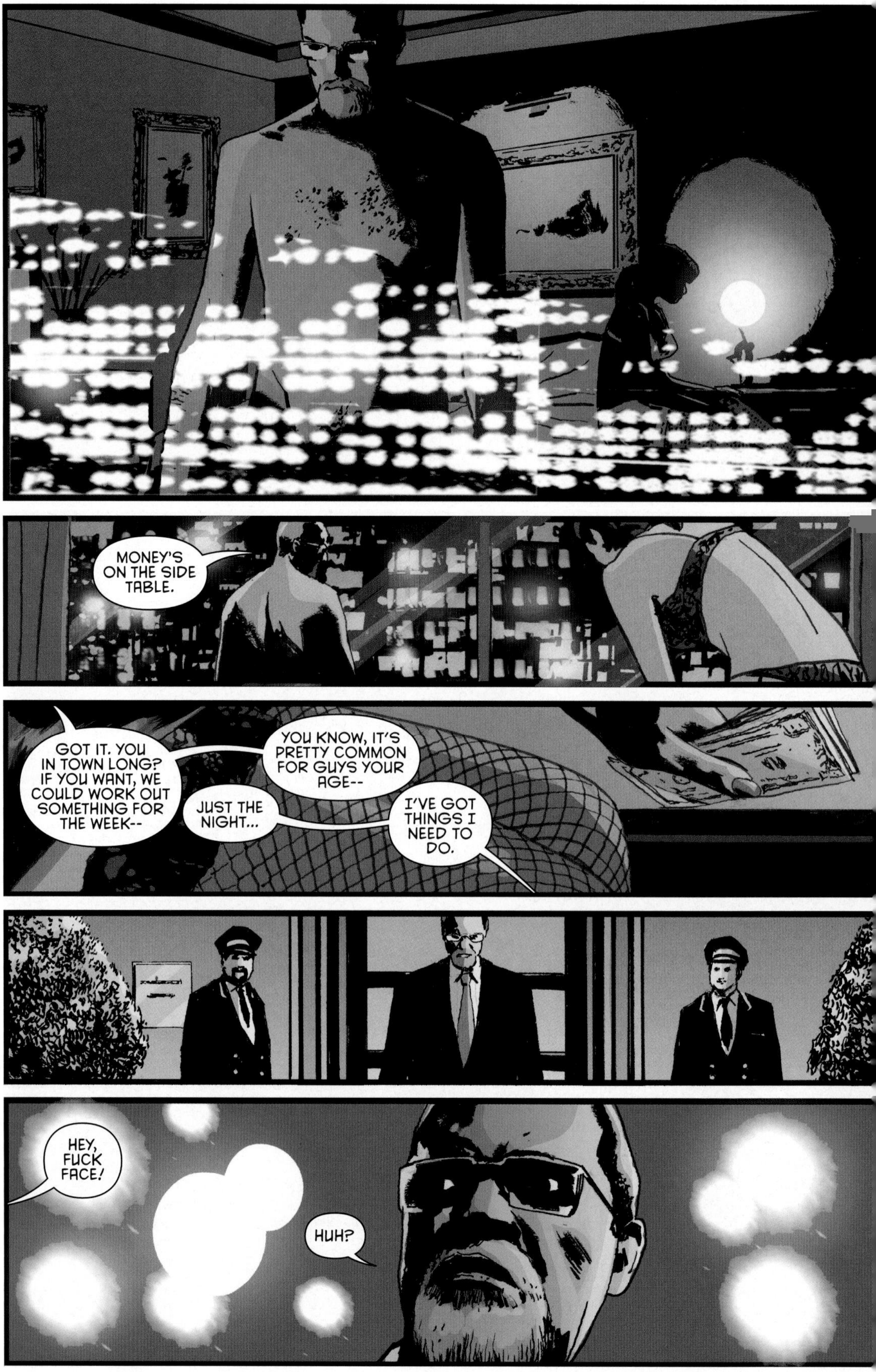
MONEY'S ON THE SIDE TABLE.
GOT IT. YOU IN TOWN LONG? IF YOU WANT, WE COULD WORK OUT SOMETHING FOR THE WEEK--
JUST THE NIGHT...
YOU KNOW, IT'S PRETTY COMMON FOR GUYS YOUR AGE--
I'VE GOT THINGS I NEED TO DO.
HEY, FUCK FACE!
HUH?

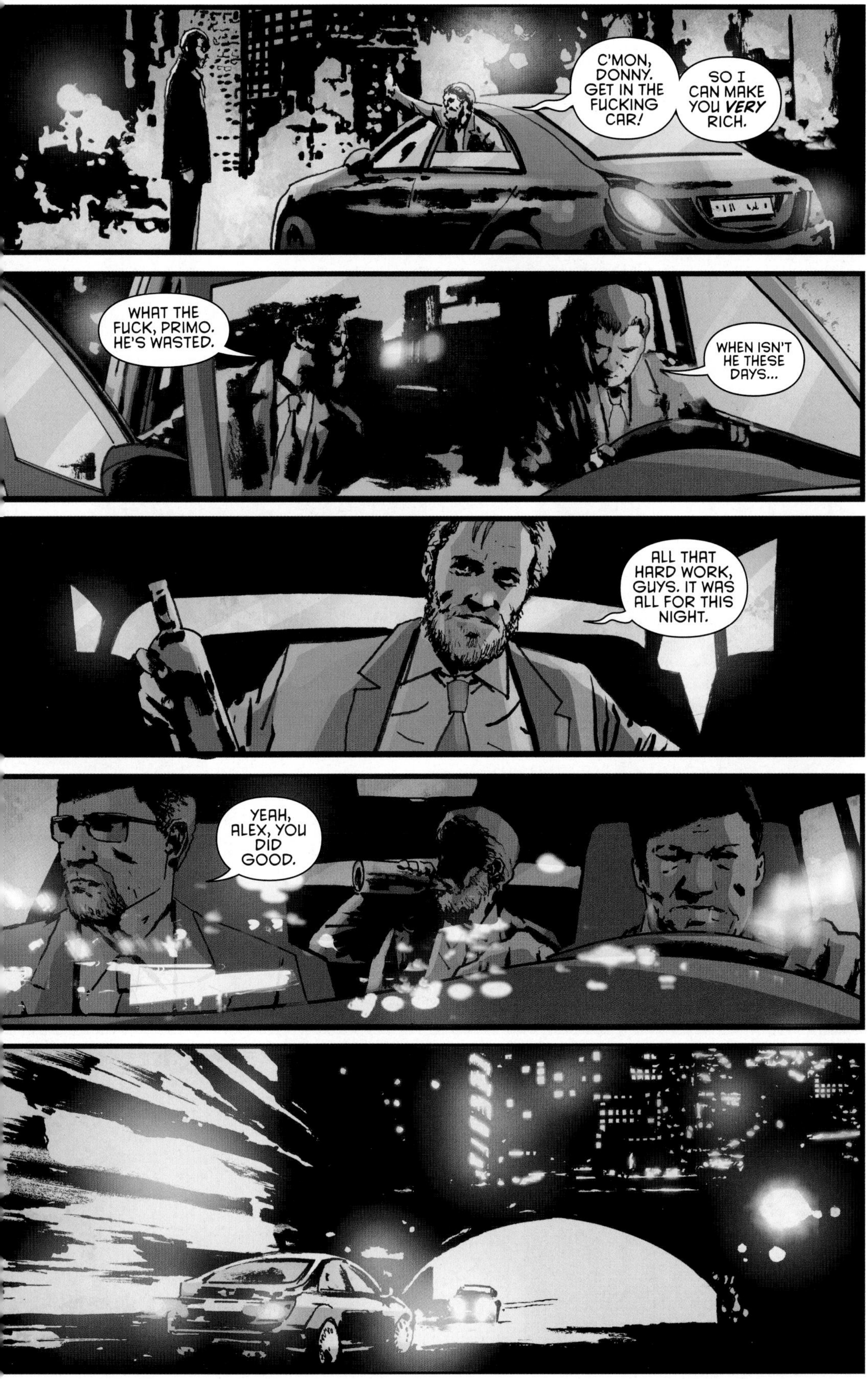
C'MON, DONNY. GET IN THE FUCKING CAR!
SO I CAN MAKE YOU VERY RICH.
WHAT THE FUCK, PRIMO. HE'S WASTED.
WHEN ISN'T HE THESE DAYS...
ALL THAT HARD WORK, GUYS. IT WAS ALL FOR THIS NIGHT.
YEAH, ALEX, YOU DID GOOD.

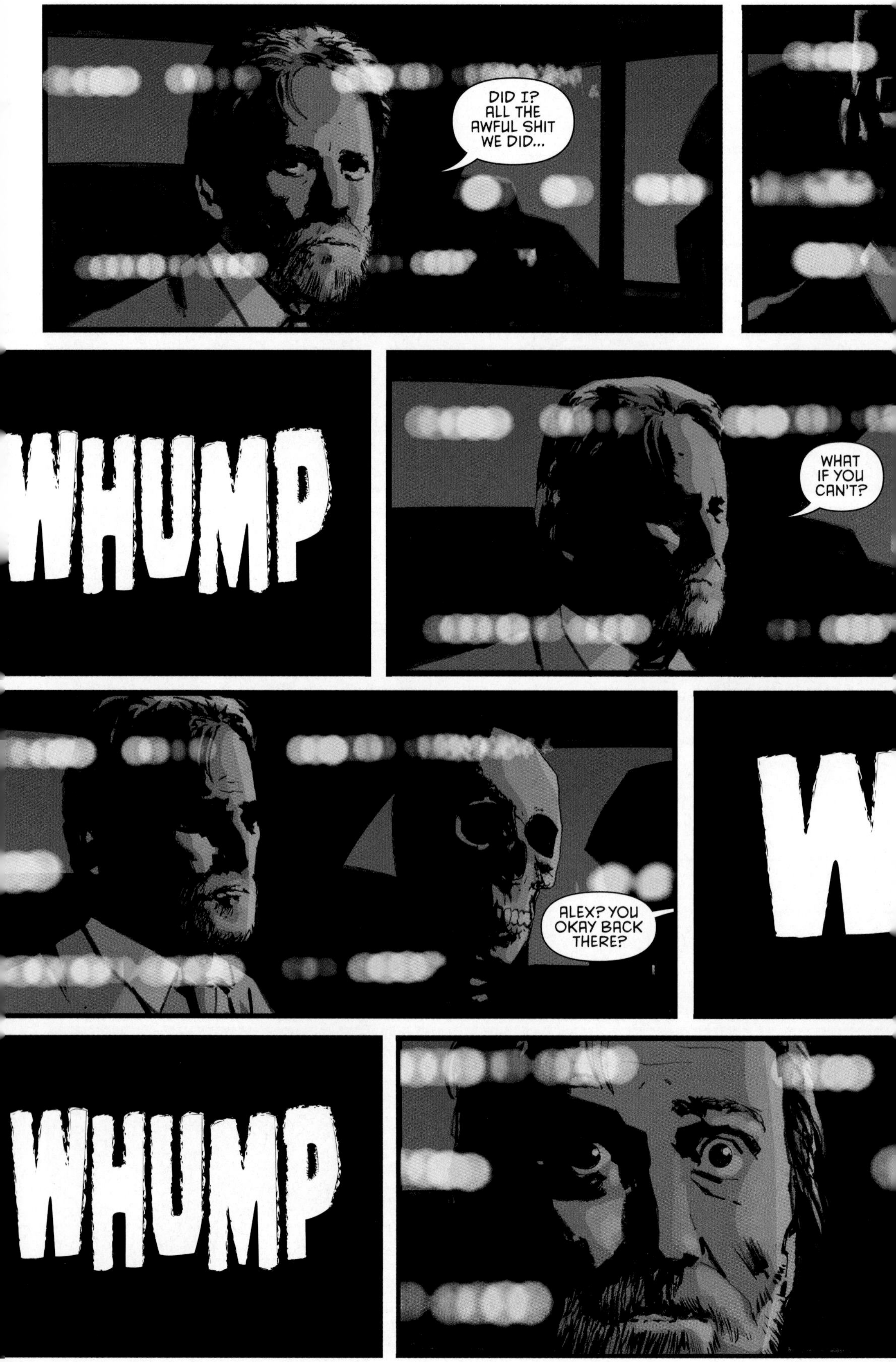
DID I? ALL THE AWFUL SHIT WE DID...
WHUMP
WHAT IF YOU CAN'T?
ALEX? YOU OKAY BACK THERE?
WHUMP

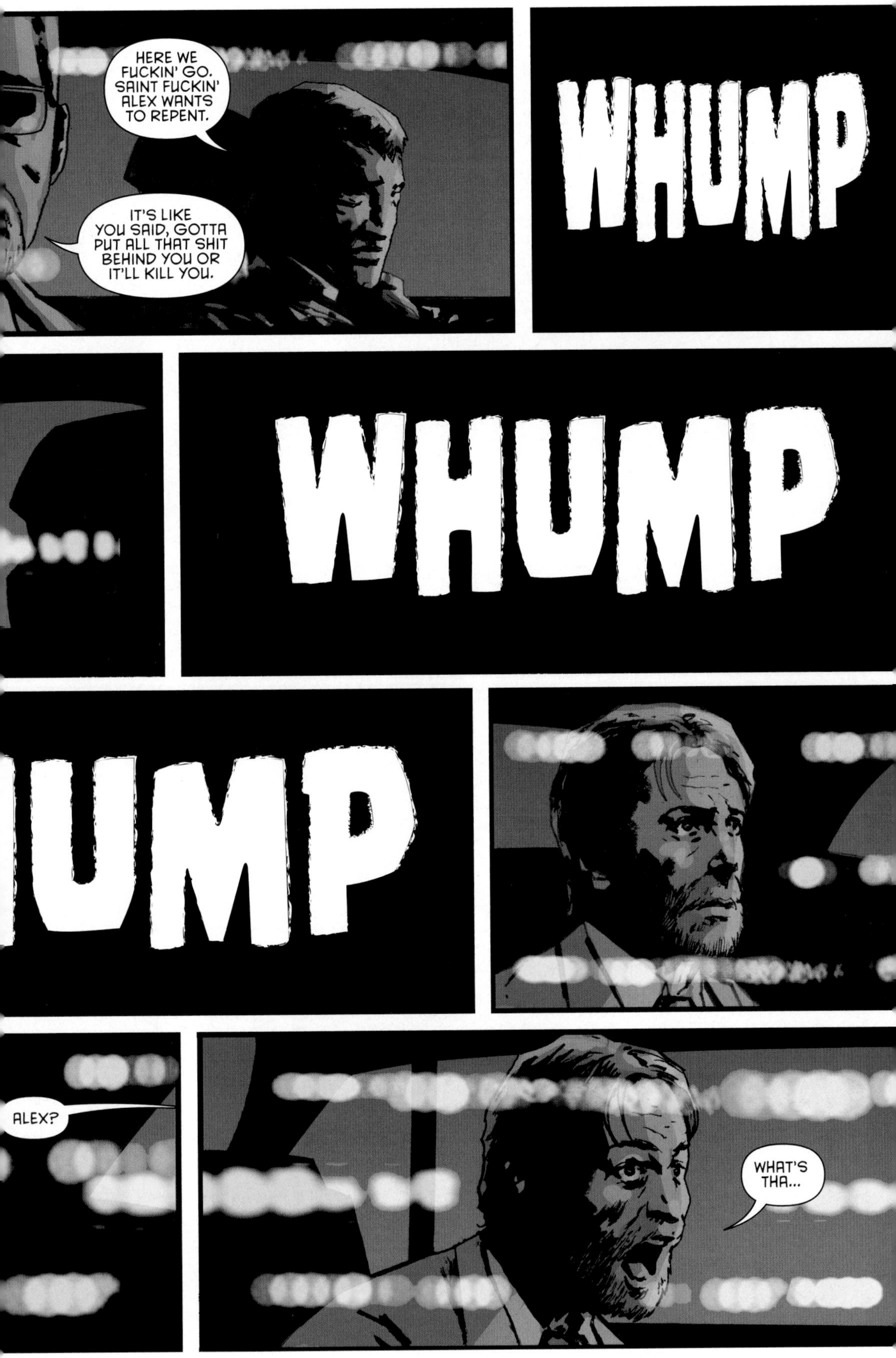
HERE WE FUCKIN' GO. SAINT FUCKIN' ALEX WANTS TO REPENT.
IT'S LIKE YOU SAID, GOTTA PUT ALL THAT SHIT BEHIND YOU OR IT'LL KILL YOU.
WHUMP
WHUMP
UMP
ALEX?
WHAT'S THA...

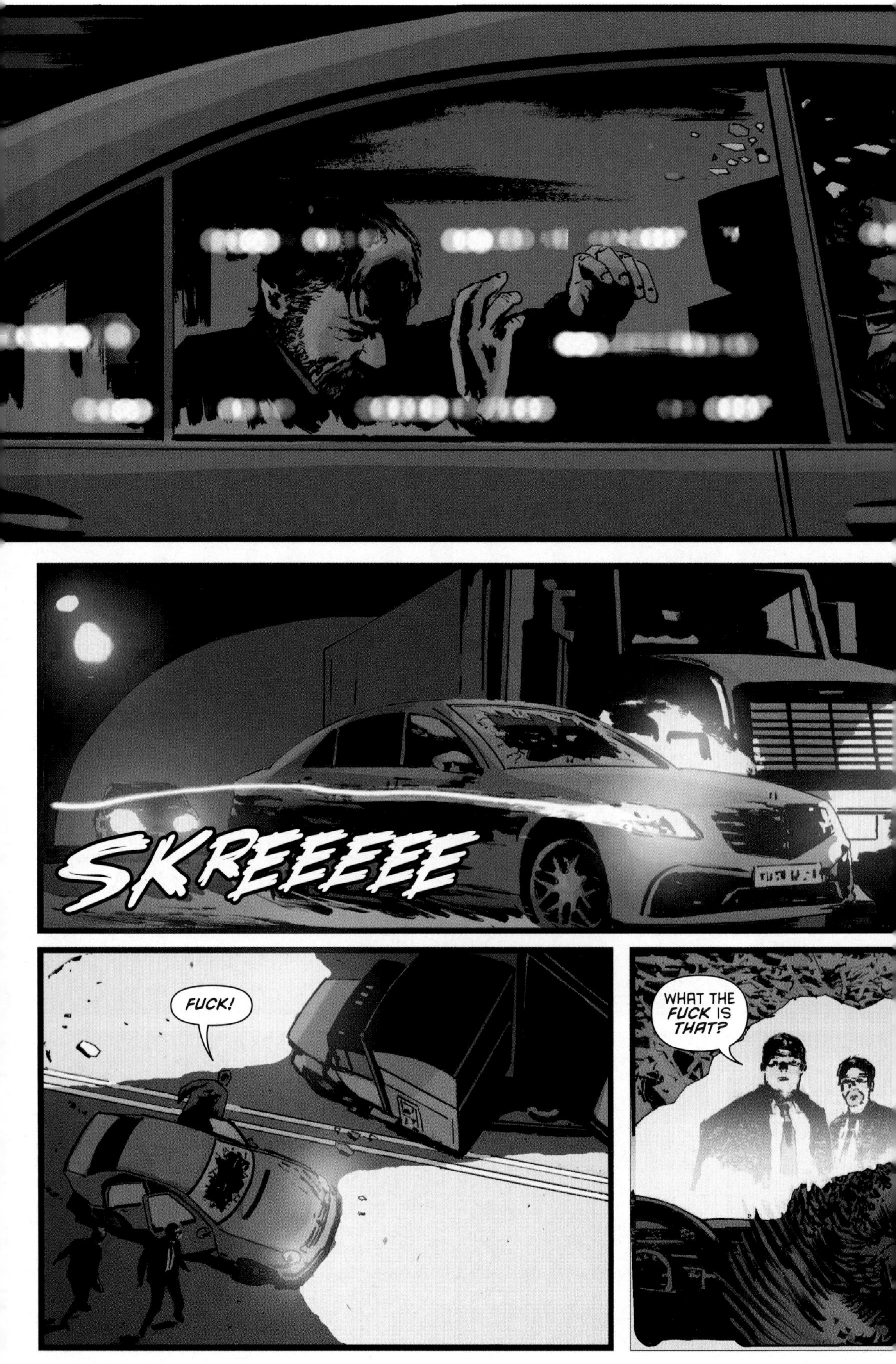
SKREEEEEE
FUCK!
WHAT THE FUCK IS THAT?

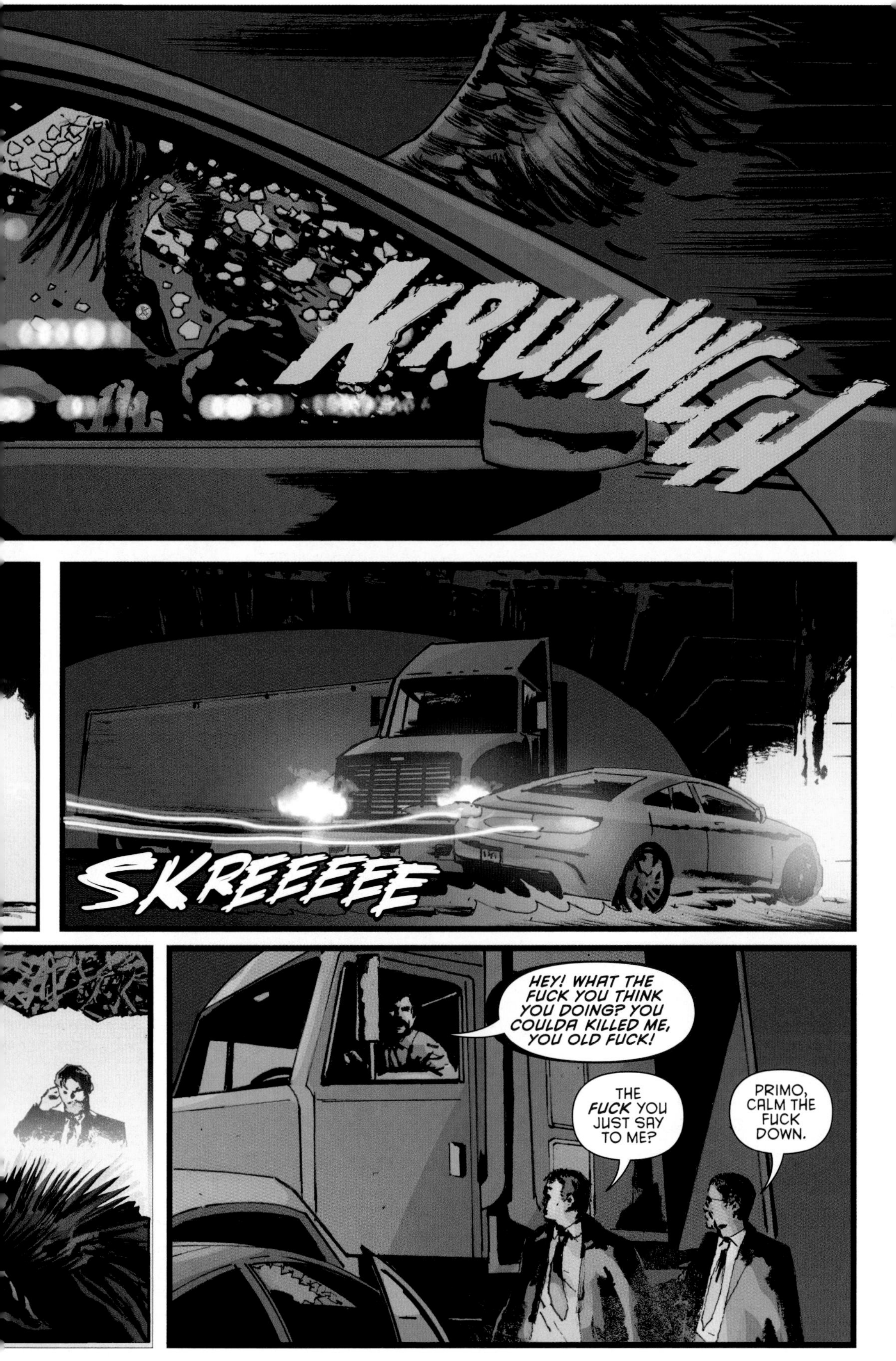
KRUNNCH
SKREEEEEE
HEY! WHAT THE FUCK YOU THINK YOU DOING? YOU COULDA KILLED ME, YOU OLD FUCK!
THE FUCK YOU JUST SAY TO ME?
PRIMO, CALM THE FUCK DOWN.

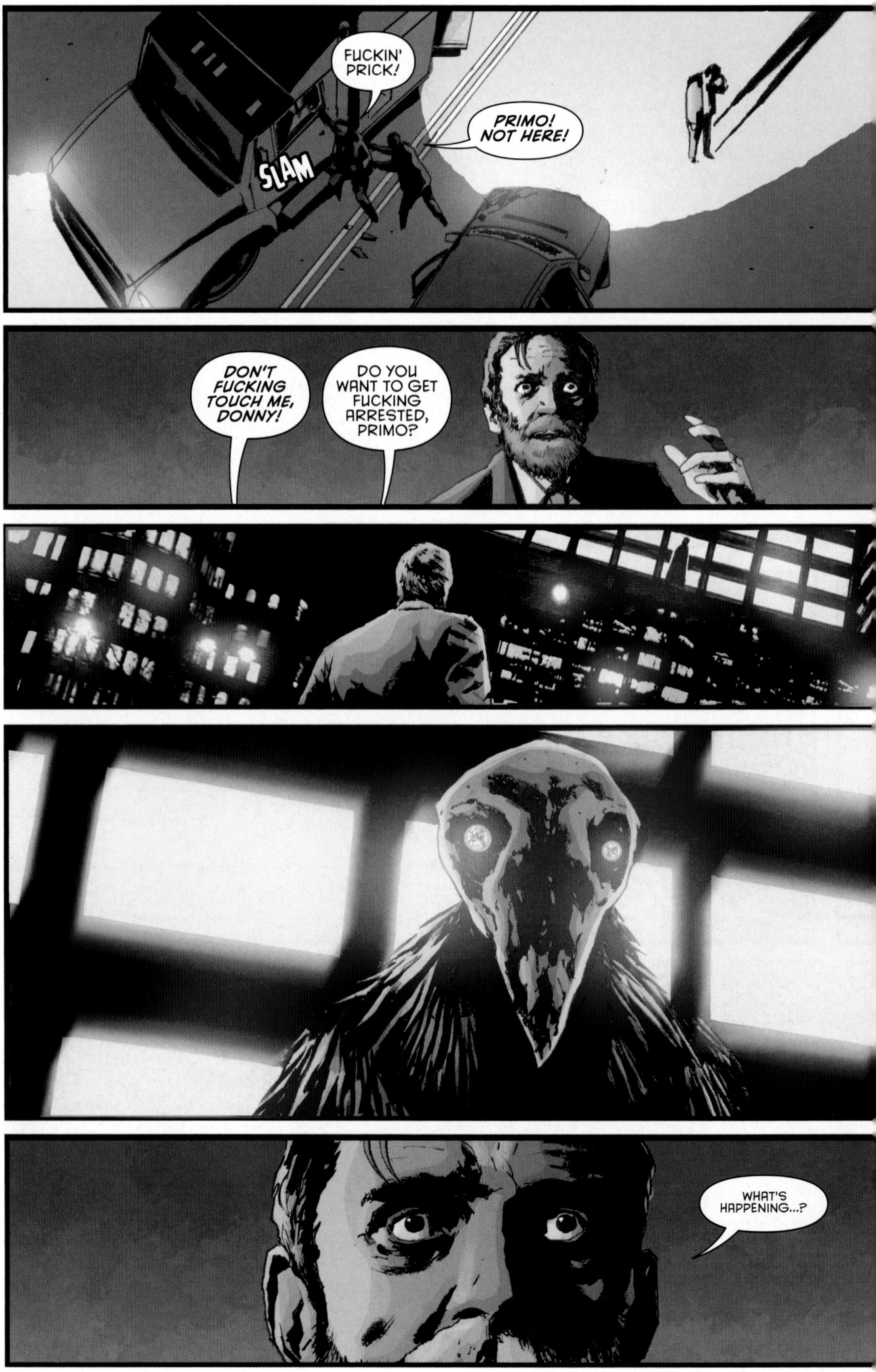
FUCKIN' PRICK!
PRIMO! NOT HERE!
SLAM
DON'T FUCKING TOUCH ME, DONNY!
DO YOU WANT TO GET FUCKING ARRESTED, PRIMO?
WHAT'S HAPPENING...?

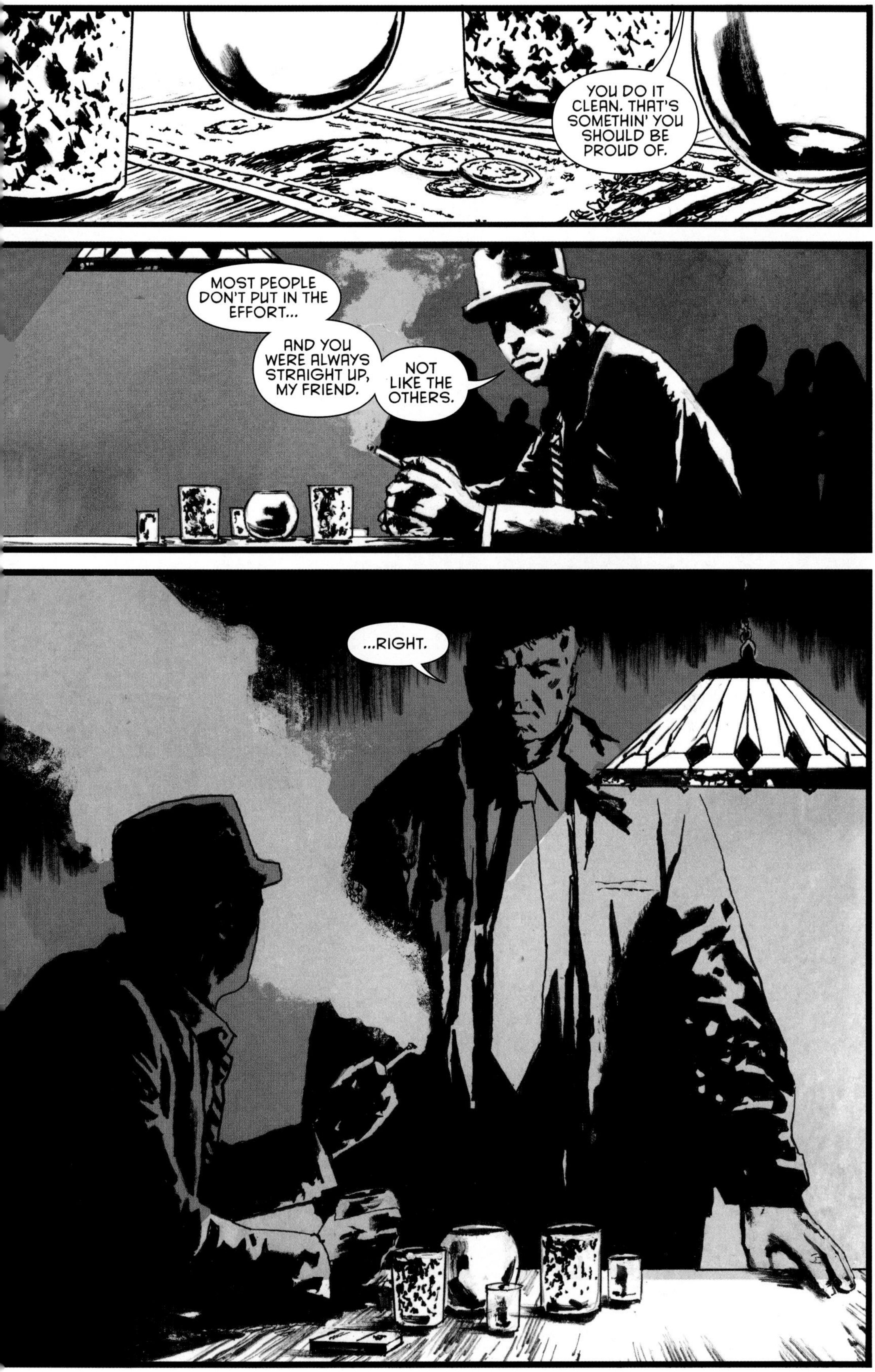
YOU DO IT CLEAN. THAT'S SOMETHIN' YOU SHOULD BE PROUD OF.
MOST PEOPLE DON'T PUT IN THE EFFORT...
AND YOU WERE ALWAYS STRAIGHT UP, MY FRIEND.
NOT LIKE THE OTHERS.
...RIGHT.

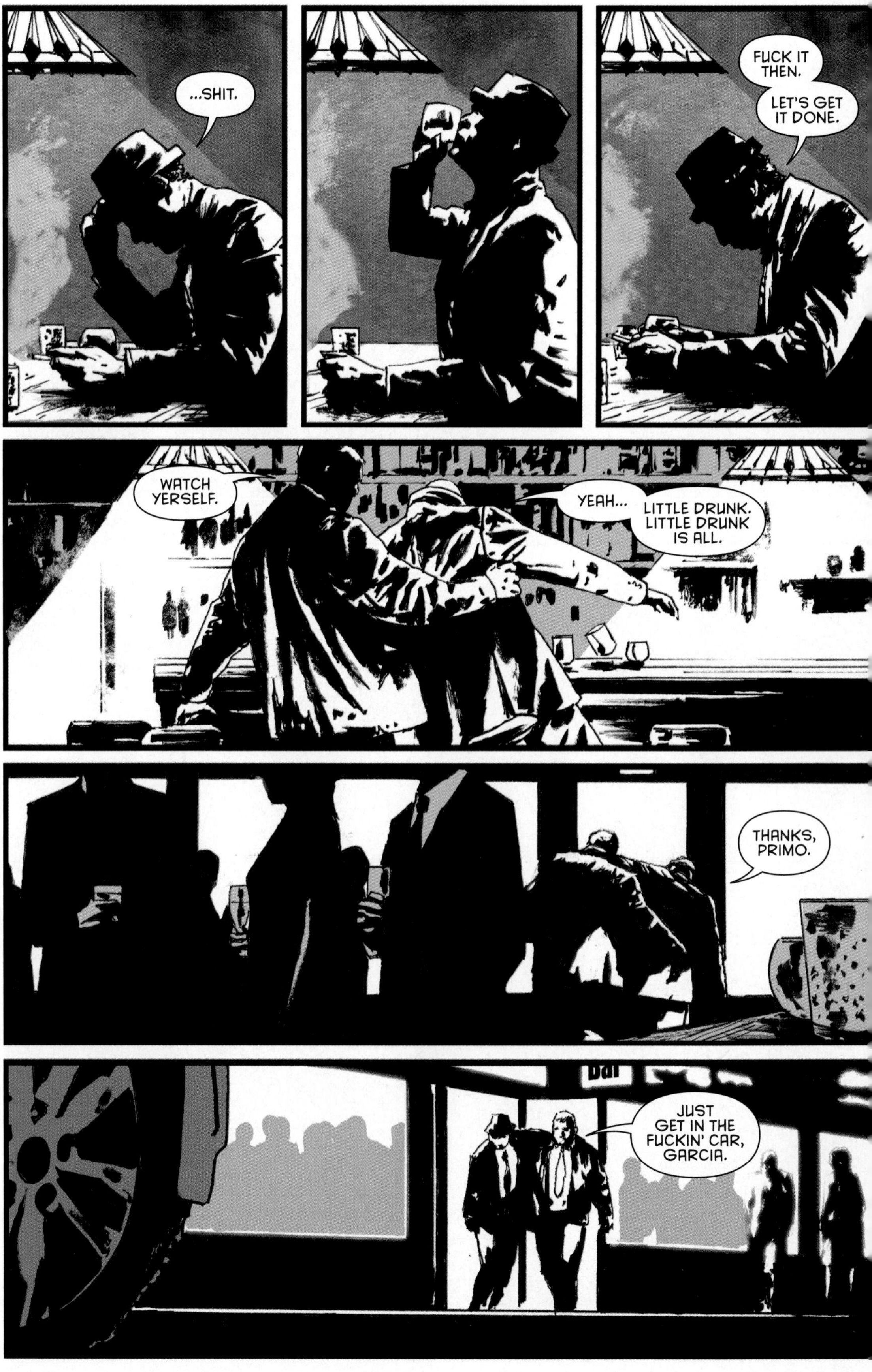
...SHIT.
FUCK IT THEN.
LET'S GET IT DONE.
WATCH YERSELF.
YEAH...
LITTLE DRUNK. LITTLE DRUNK IS ALL.
THANKS, PRIMO.
JUST GET IN THE FUCKIN' CAR, GARCIA.

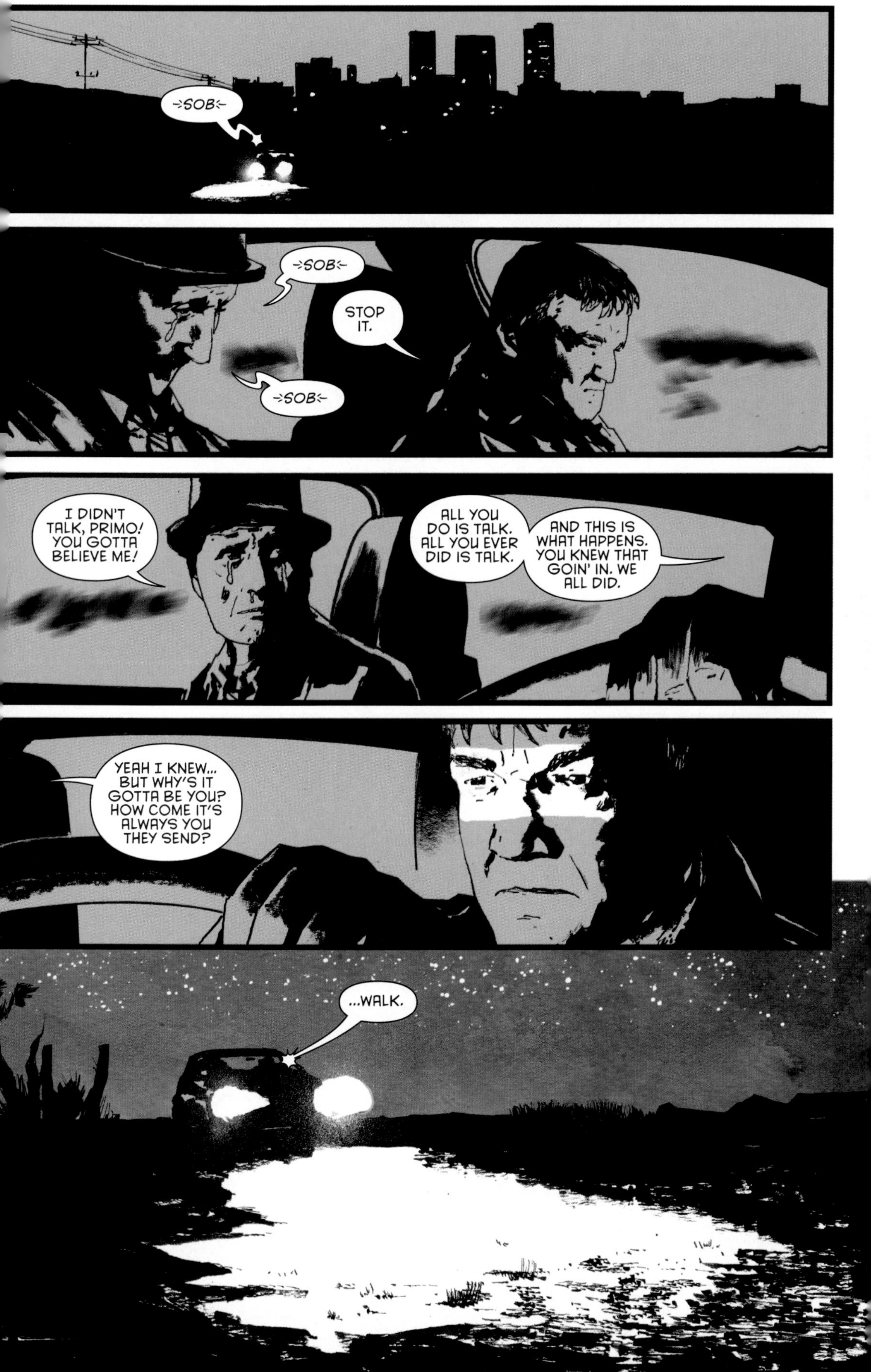

SOB
SOB
STOP IT.
SOB
I DIDN'T TALK, PRIMO! YOU GOTTA BELIEVE ME!
ALL YOU DO IS TALK. ALL YOU EVER DID IS TALK.
AND THIS IS WHAT HAPPENS. YOU KNEW THAT GOIN' IN. WE ALL DID.
YEAH I KNEW... BUT WHY'S IT GOTTA BE YOU? HOW COME IT'S ALWAYS YOU THEY SEND?
...WALK.

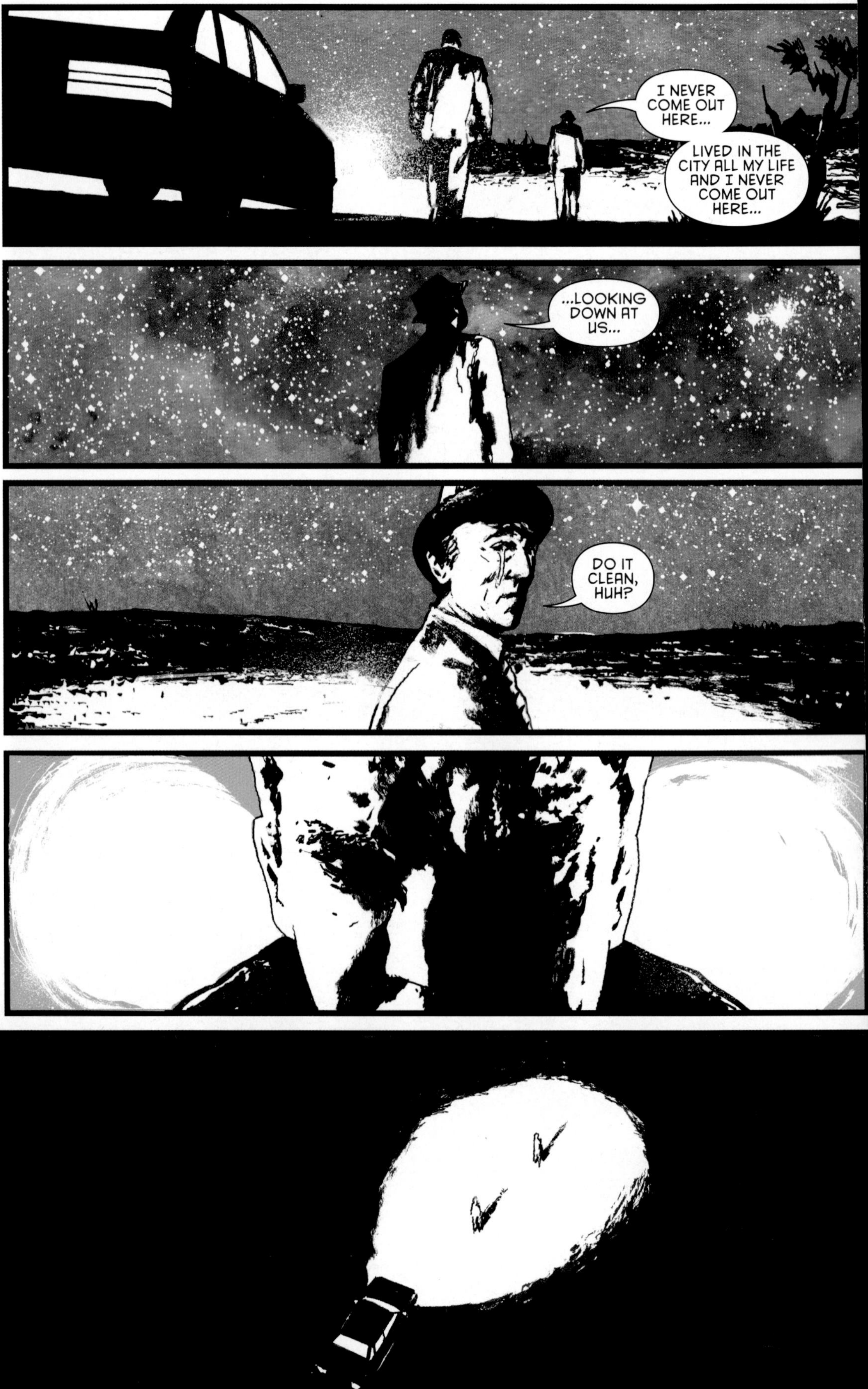
I NEVER COME OUT HERE...
LIVED IN THE CITY ALL MY LIFE AND I NEVER COME OUT HERE...
...LOOKING DOWN AT US...
DO IT CLEAN, HUH?

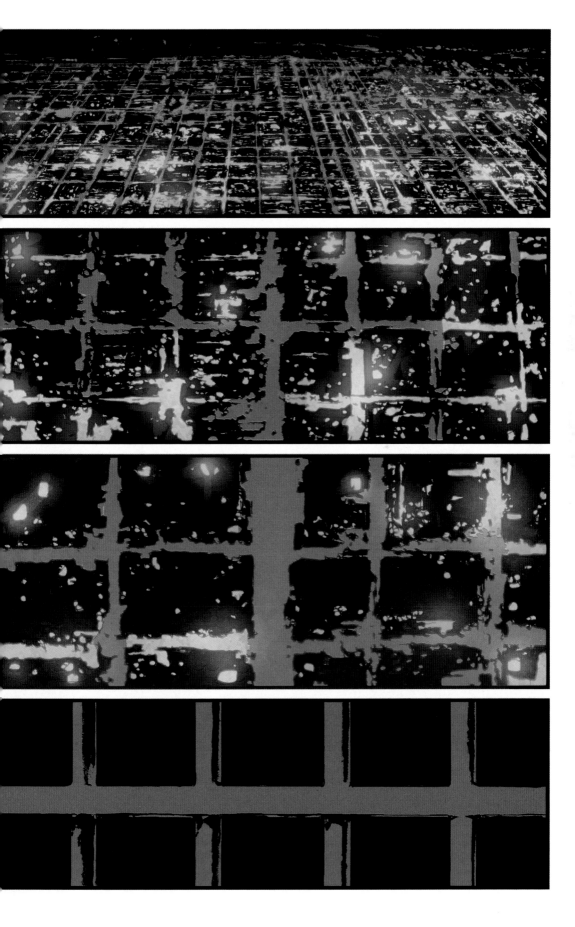

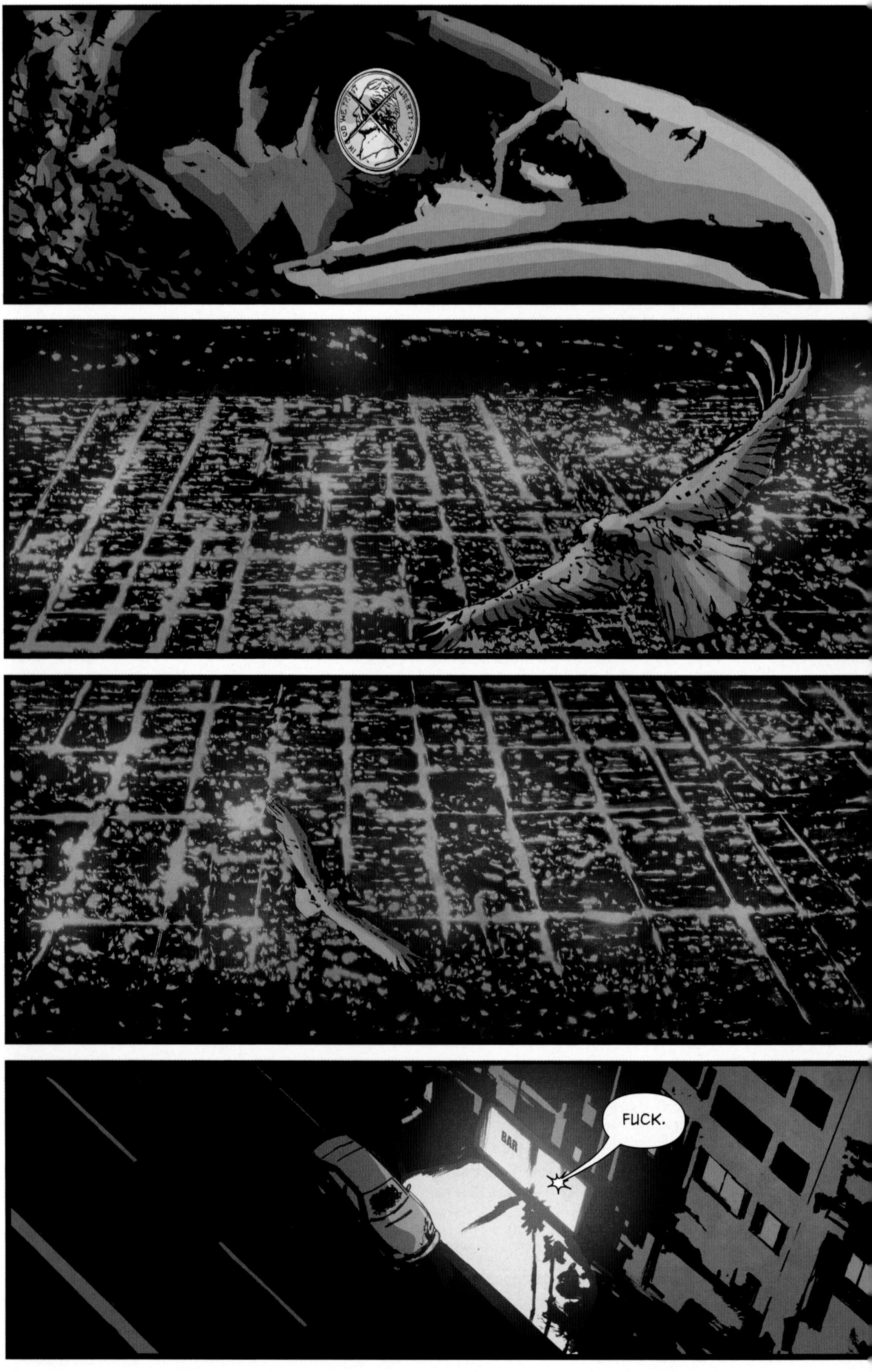
BAR
FUCK.

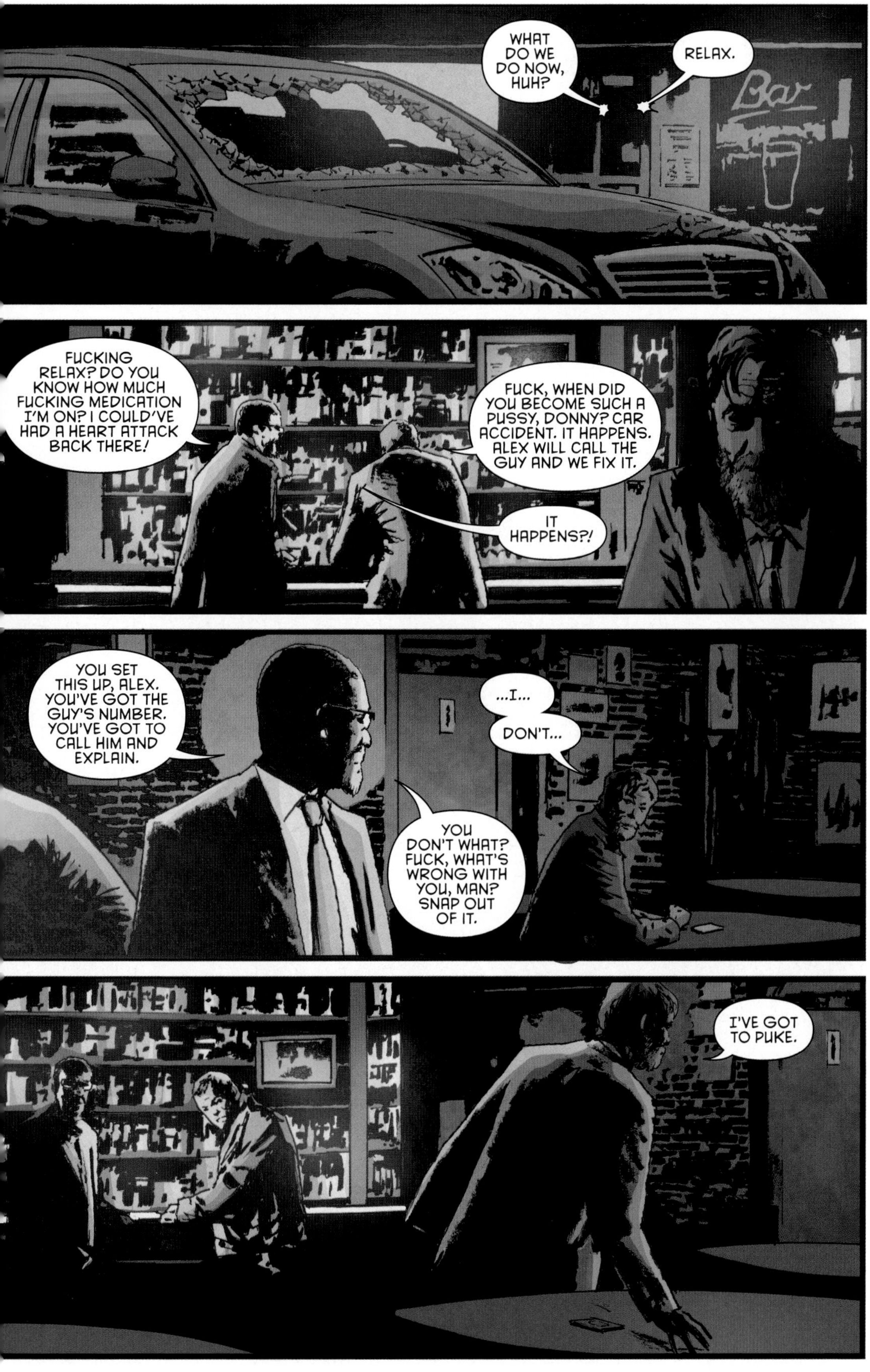
WHAT DO WE DO NOW, HUH?
RELAX.
Bar
FUCKING RELAX? DO YOU KNOW HOW MUCH FUCKING MEDICATION I'M ON? I COULD'VE HAD A HEART ATTACK BACK THERE!
FUCK, WHEN DID YOU BECOME SUCH A PUSSY, DONNY? CAR ACCIDENT. IT HAPPENS. ALEX WILL CALL THE GUY AND WE FIX IT.
IT HAPPENS?!
YOU SET THIS UP, ALEX. YOU'VE GOT THE GUY'S NUMBER. YOU'VE GOT TO CALL HIM AND EXPLAIN.
...I...
DON'T...
YOU DON'T WHAT? FUCK, WHAT'S WRONG WITH YOU, MAN? SNAP OUT OF IT.
I'VE GOT TO PUKE.

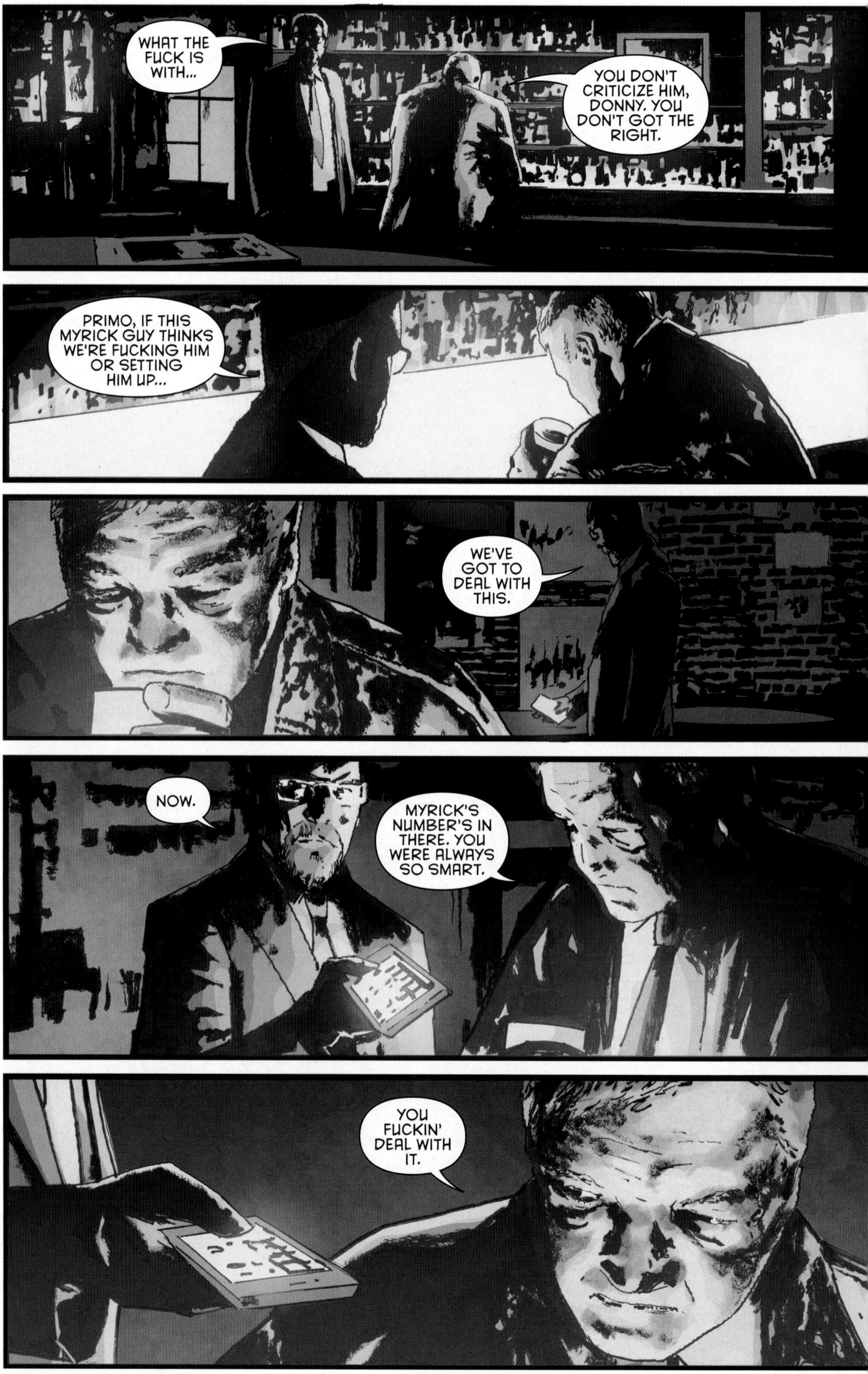
WHAT THE FUCK IS WITH...
YOU DON'T CRITICIZE HIM, DONNY. YOU DON'T GOT THE RIGHT.
PRIMO, IF THIS MYRICK GUY THINKS WE'RE FUCKING HIM OR SETTING HIM UP...
WE'VE GOT TO DEAL WITH THIS.
NOW.
MYRICK'S NUMBER'S IN THERE. YOU WERE ALWAYS SO SMART.
YOU FUCKIN' DEAL WITH IT.

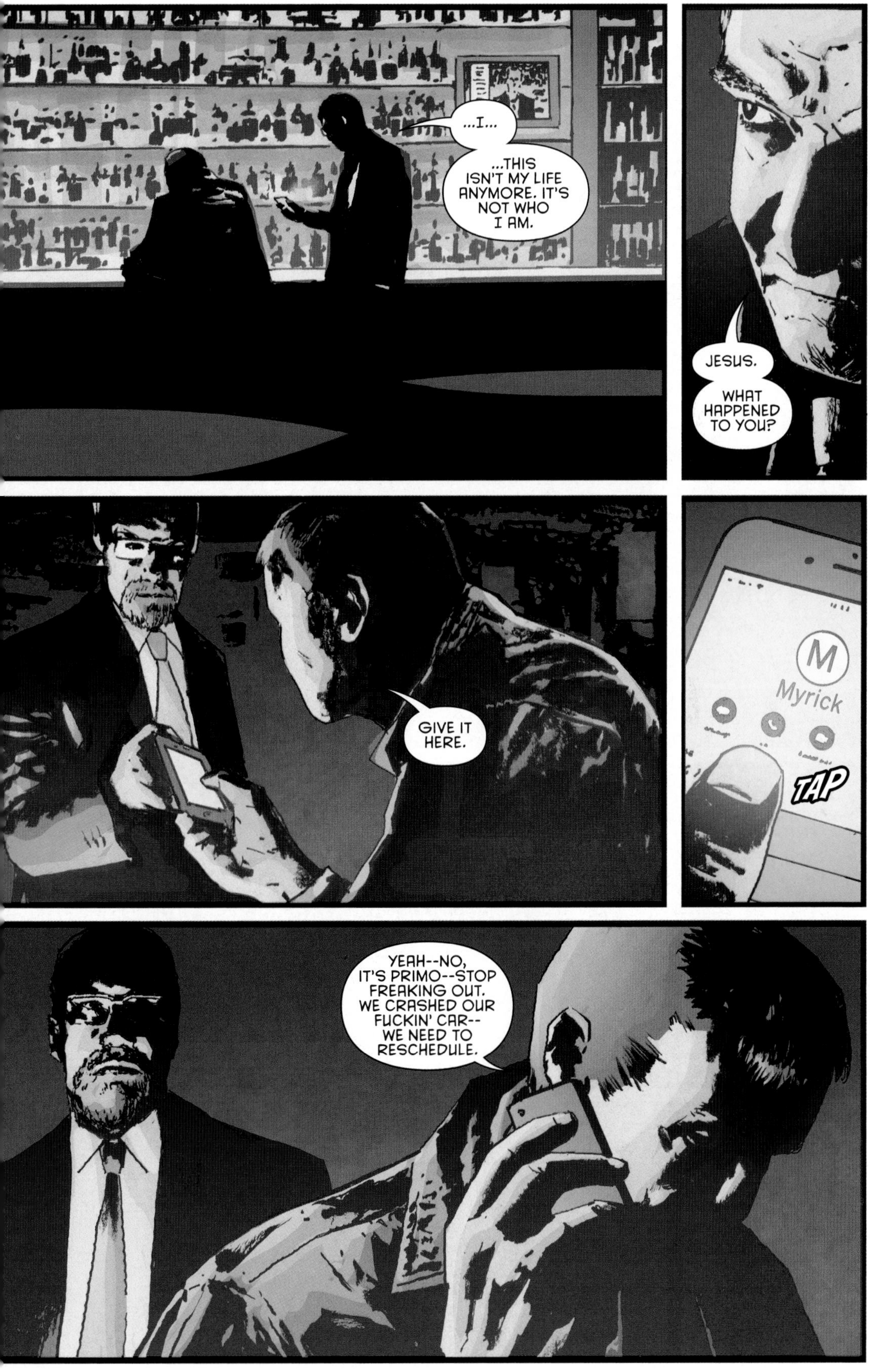
...I...
...THIS ISN'T MY LIFE ANYMORE. IT'S NOT WHO I AM.
JESUS.
WHAT HAPPENED TO YOU?
GIVE IT HERE.
Myrick
TAP
YEAH--NO, IT'S PRIMO--STOP FREAKING OUT. WE CRASHED OUR FUCKIN' CAR-- WE NEED TO RESCHEDULE.

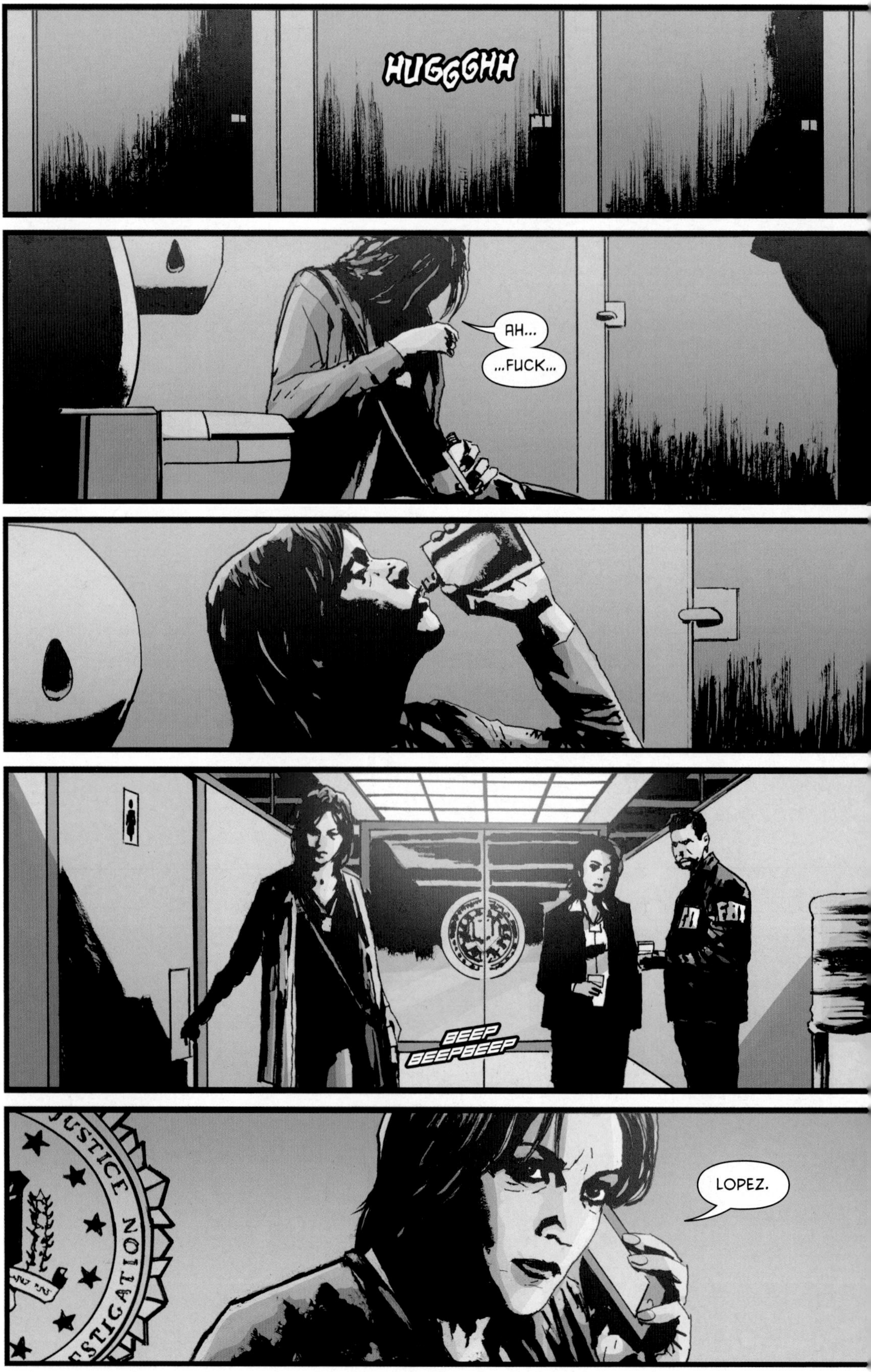
HUGGGHH
AH...
...FUCK...
BEEP
BEEPBEEP
LOPEZ.

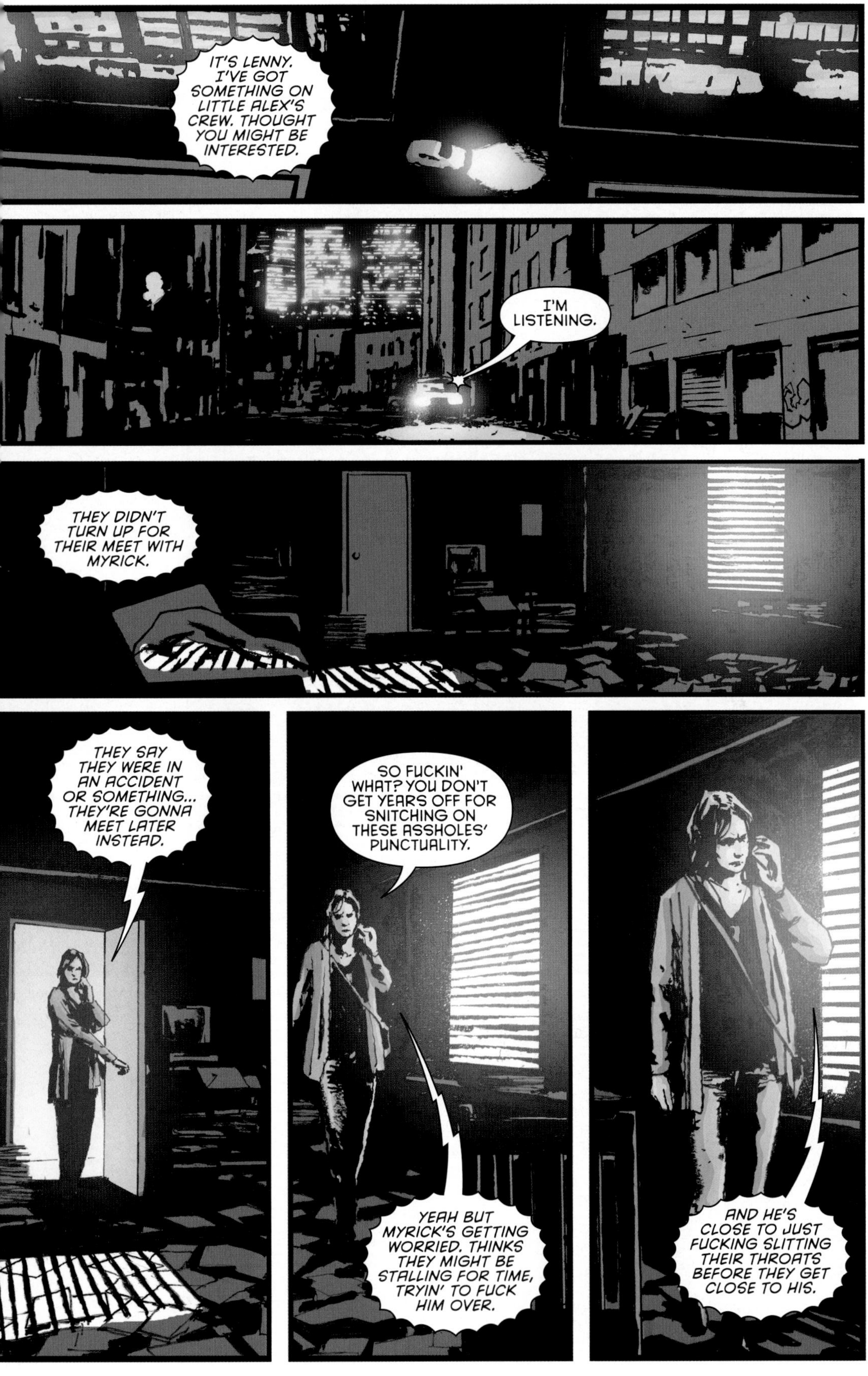

IT'S LENNY. I'VE GOT SOMETHING ON LITTLE ALEX'S CREW. THOUGHT YOU MIGHT BE INTERESTED.
I'M LISTENING.
THEY DIDN'T TURN UP FOR THEIR MEET WITH MYRICK.
THEY SAY THEY WERE IN AN ACCIDENT OR SOMETHING... THEY'RE GONNA MEET LATER INSTEAD.
SO FUCKIN' WHAT? YOU DON'T GET YEARS OFF FOR SNITCHING ON THESE ASSHOLES' PUNCTUALITY.
YEAH BUT MYRICK'S GETTING WORRIED. THINKS THEY MIGHT BE STALLING FOR TIME, TRYIN' TO FUCK HIM OVER.
AND HE'S CLOSE TO JUST FUCKING SLITTING THEIR THROATS BEFORE THEY GET CLOSE TO HIS.

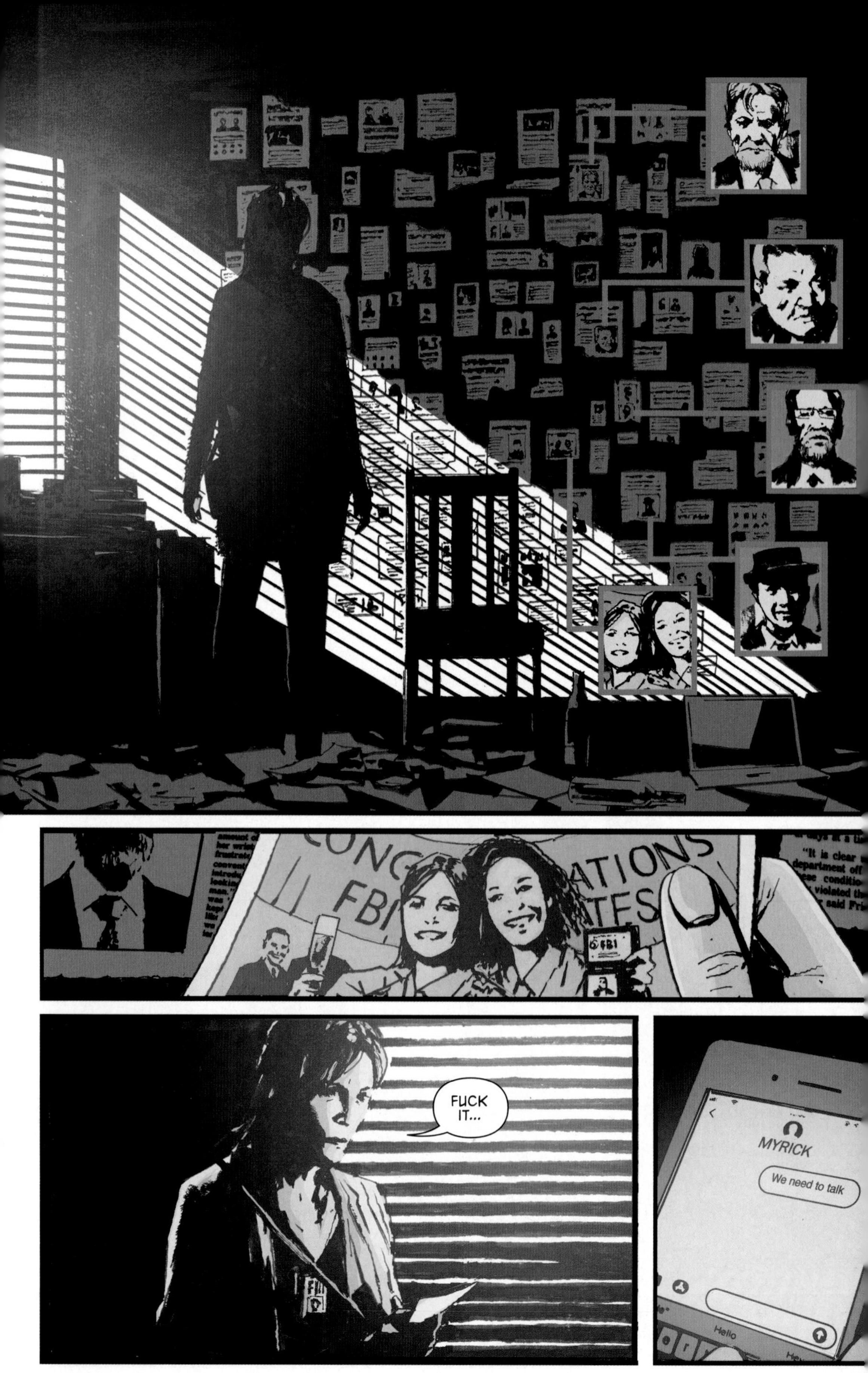
FUCK IT...
MYRICK
We need to talk

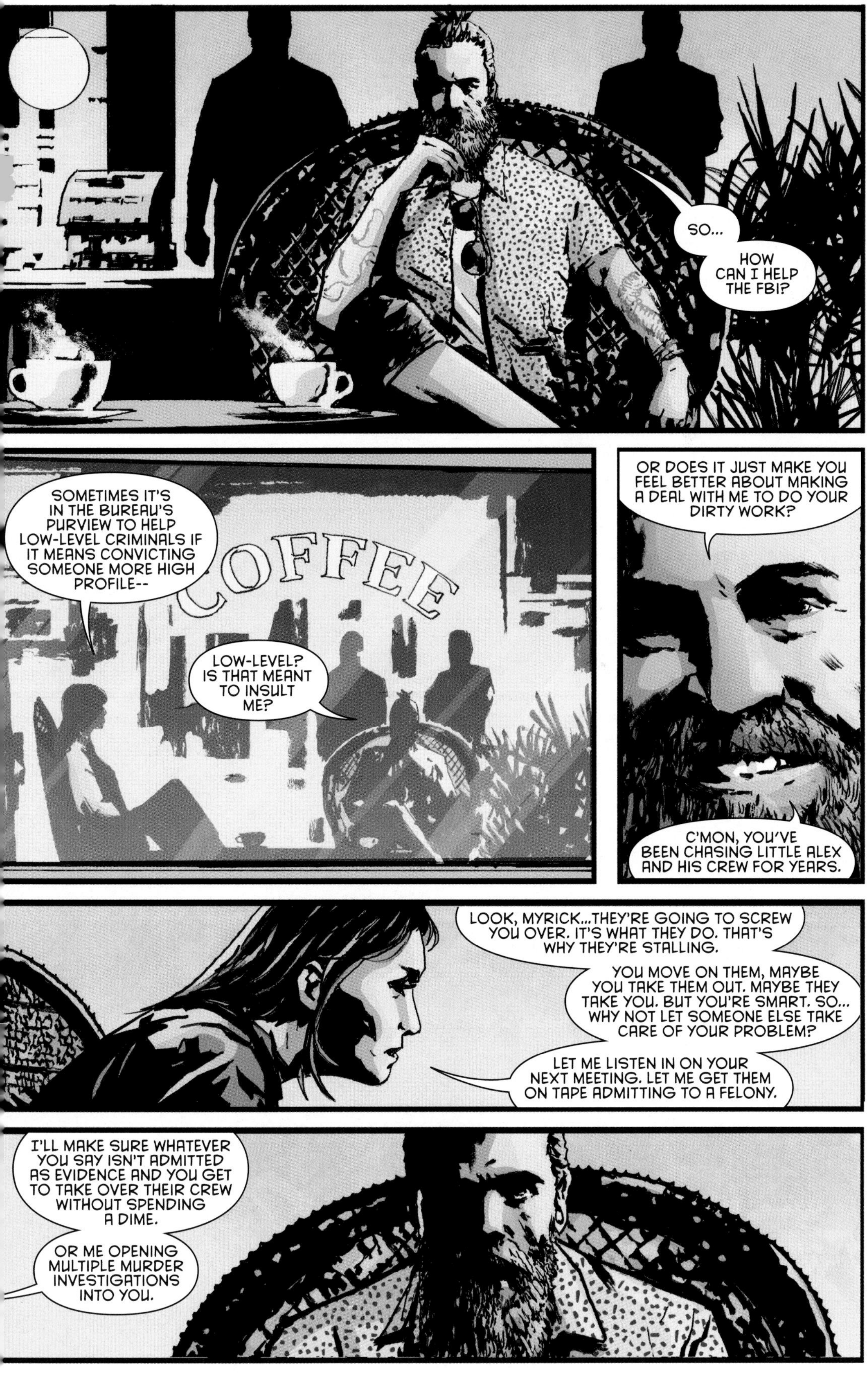
SO...
HOW CAN I HELP THE FBI?
SOMETIMES IT'S IN THE BUREAU'S PURVIEW TO HELP LOW-LEVEL CRIMINALS IF IT MEANS CONVICTING SOMEONE MORE HIGH PROFILE--
COFFEE
LOW-LEVEL? IS THAT MEANT TO INSULT ME?
OR DOES IT JUST MAKE YOU FEEL BETTER ABOUT MAKING A DEAL WITH ME TO DO YOUR DIRTY WORK?
C'MON, YOU'VE BEEN CHASING LITTLE ALEX AND HIS CREW FOR YEARS.
LOOK, MYRICK...THEY'RE GOING TO SCREW YOU OVER. IT'S WHAT THEY DO. THAT'S WHY THEY'RE STALLING.
YOU MOVE ON THEM, MAYBE YOU TAKE THEM OUT. MAYBE THEY TAKE YOU. BUT YOU'RE SMART. SO... WHY NOT LET SOMEONE ELSE TAKE CARE OF YOUR PROBLEM?
LET ME LISTEN IN ON YOUR NEXT MEETING. LET ME GET THEM ON TAPE ADMITTING TO A FELONY.
I'LL MAKE SURE WHATEVER YOU SAY ISN'T ADMITTED AS EVIDENCE AND YOU GET TO TAKE OVER THEIR CREW WITHOUT SPENDING A DIME.
OR ME OPENING MULTIPLE MURDER INVESTIGATIONS INTO YOU.

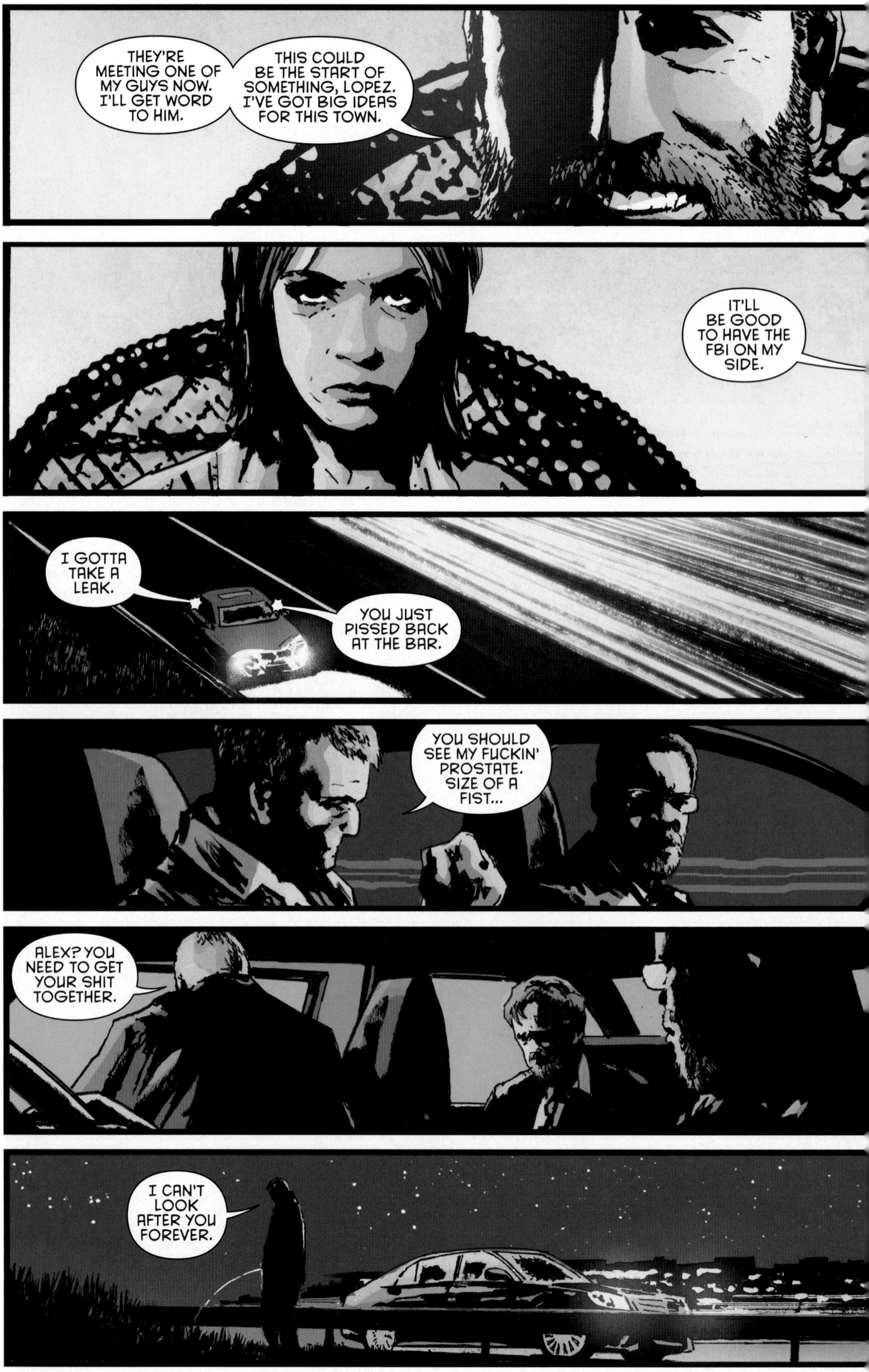
THEY'RE MEETING ONE OF MY GUYS NOW. I'LL GET WORD TO HIM.
THIS COULD BE THE START OF SOMETHING, LOPEZ. I'VE GOT BIG IDEAS FOR THIS TOWN.
IT'LL BE GOOD TO HAVE THE FBI ON MY SIDE.
I GOTTA TAKE A LEAK.
YOU JUST PISSED BACK AT THE BAR.
YOU SHOULD SEE MY FUCKIN' PROSTATE. SIZE OF A FIST...
ALEX? YOU NEED TO GET YOUR SHIT TOGETHER.
I CAN'T LOOK AFTER YOU FOREVER.

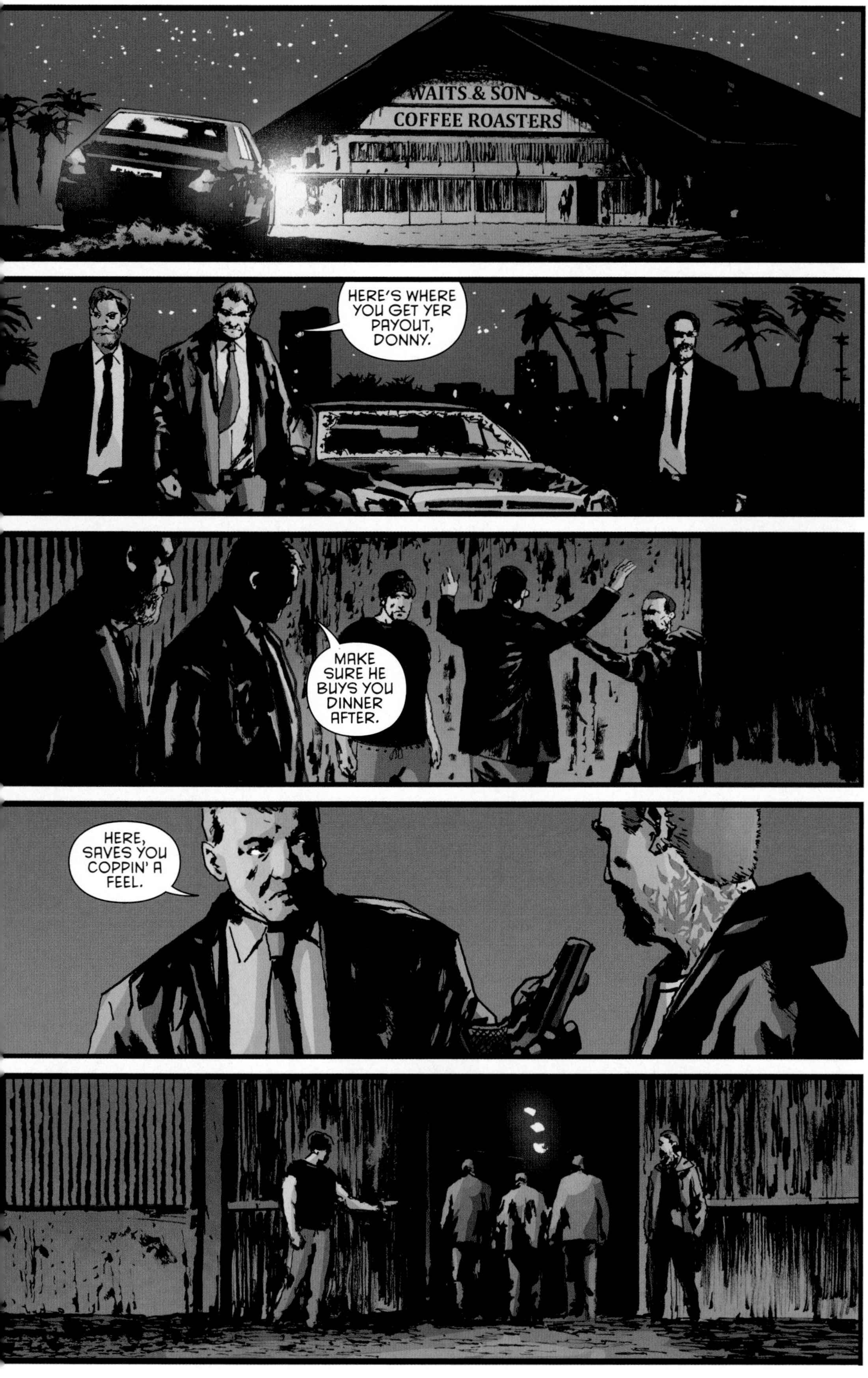
WAITS & SONS
COFFEE ROASTERS
HERE'S WHERE YOU GET YER PAYOUT, DONNY.
MAKE SURE HE BUYS YOU DINNER AFTER.
HERE, SAVES YOU COPPIN' A FEEL.

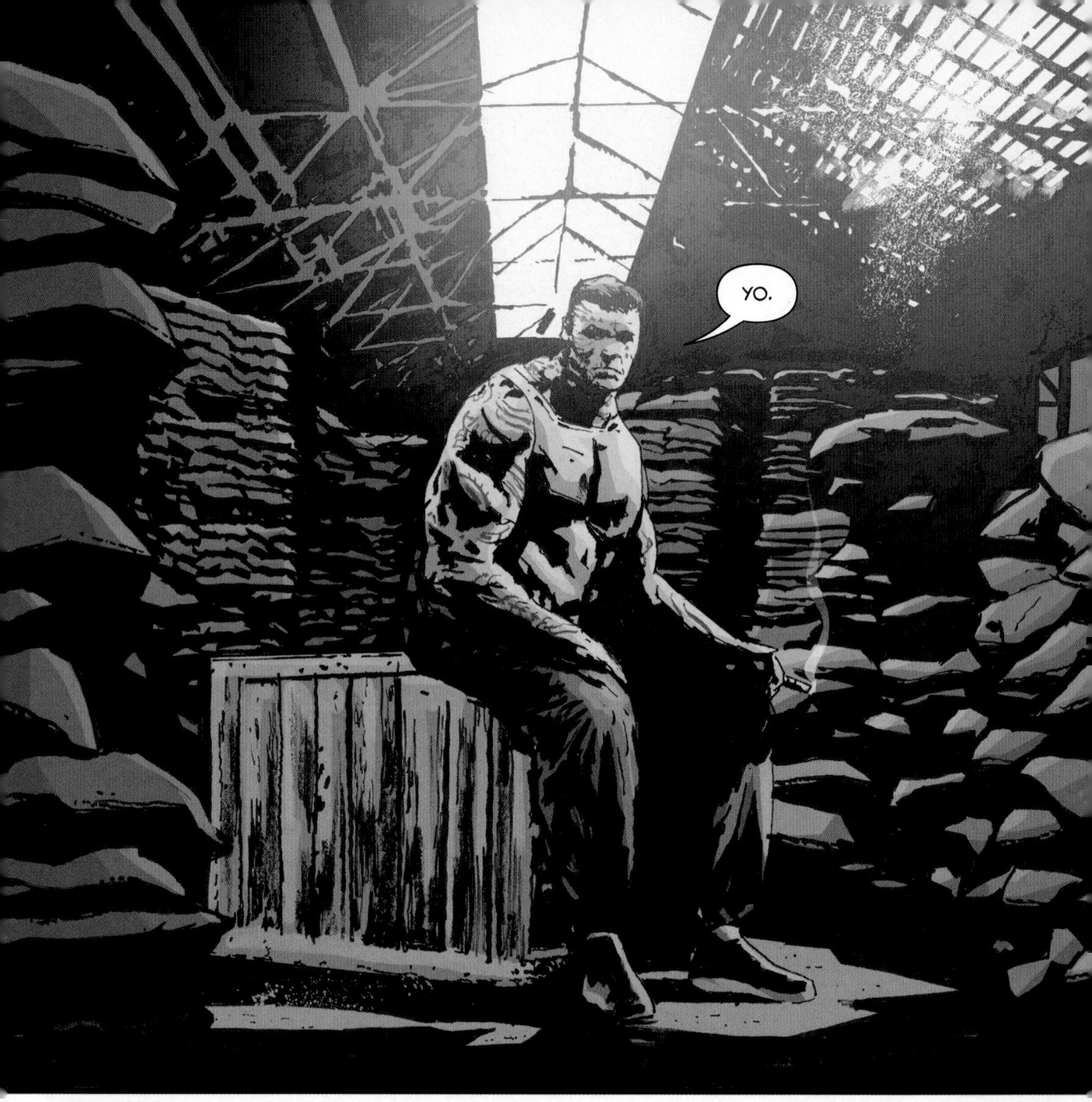
YO.

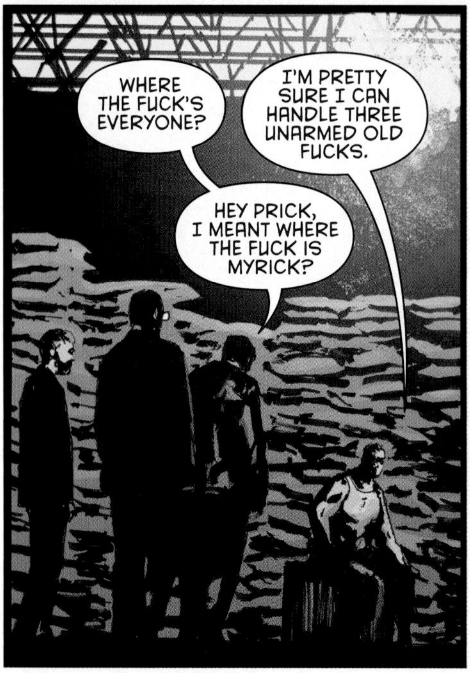
WHERE THE FUCK'S EVERYONE?
I'M PRETTY SURE I CAN HANDLE THREE UNARMED OLD FUCKS.
HEY PRICK, I MEANT WHERE THE FUCK IS MYRICK?

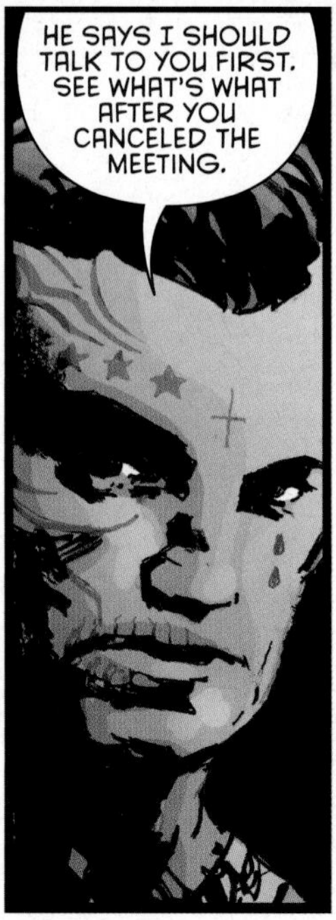
HE SAYS I SHOULD TALK TO YOU FIRST. SEE WHAT'S WHAT AFTER YOU CANCELED THE MEETING.

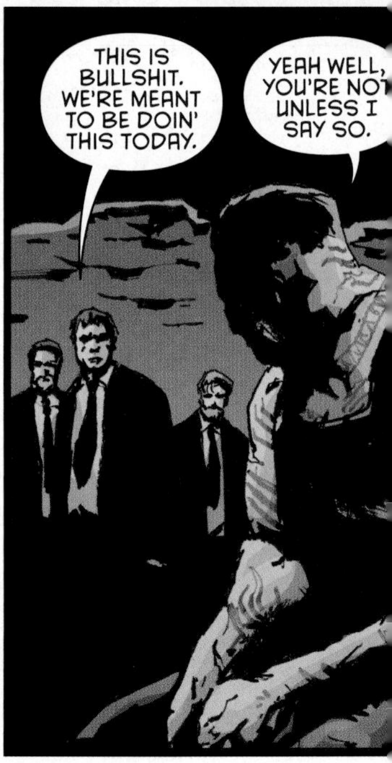
THIS IS BULLSHIT. WE'RE MEANT TO BE DOIN' THIS TODAY.
YEAH WELL, YOU'RE NOT UNLESS I SAY SO.

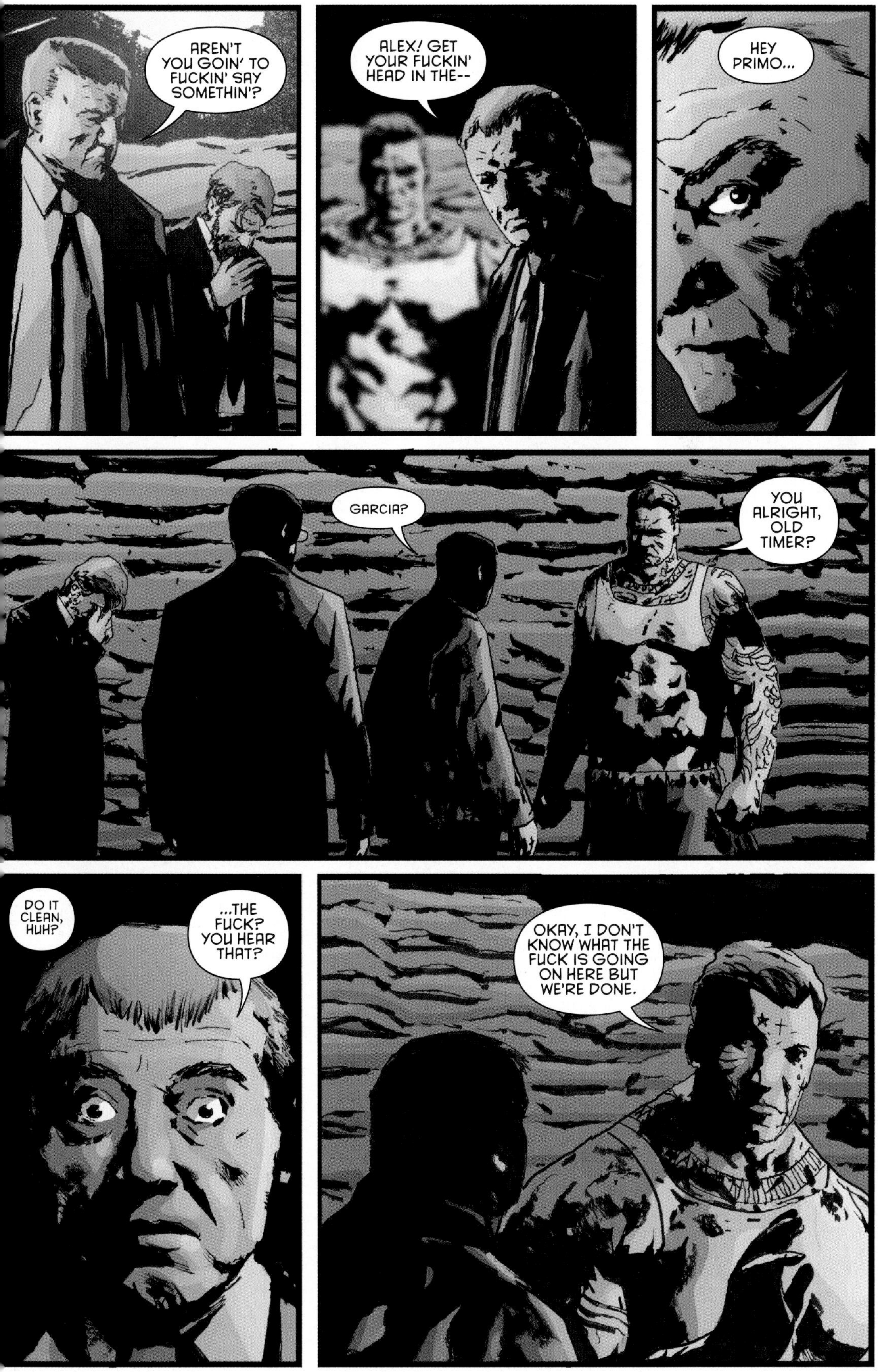
AREN'T YOU GOIN' TO FUCKIN' SAY SOMETHIN'?
ALEX! GET YOUR FUCKIN' HEAD IN THE--
HEY PRIMO...
GARCIA?
YOU ALRIGHT, OLD TIMER?
DO IT CLEAN, HUH?
...THE FUCK? YOU HEAR THAT?
OKAY, I DON'T KNOW WHAT THE FUCK IS GOING ON HERE BUT WE'RE DONE.

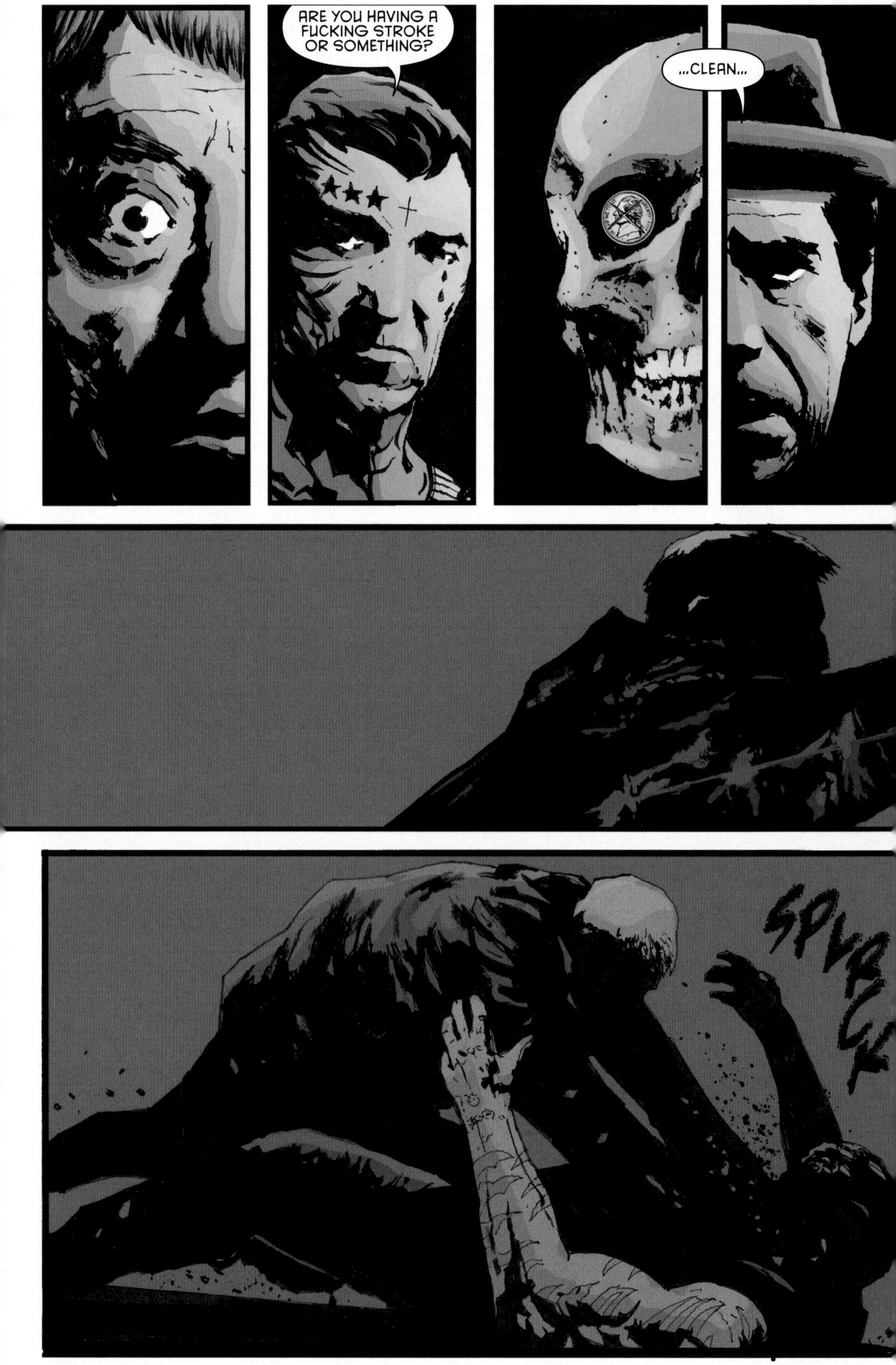
ARE YOU HAVING A FUCKING STROKE OR SOMETHING?
...CLEAN...
SPVRCK

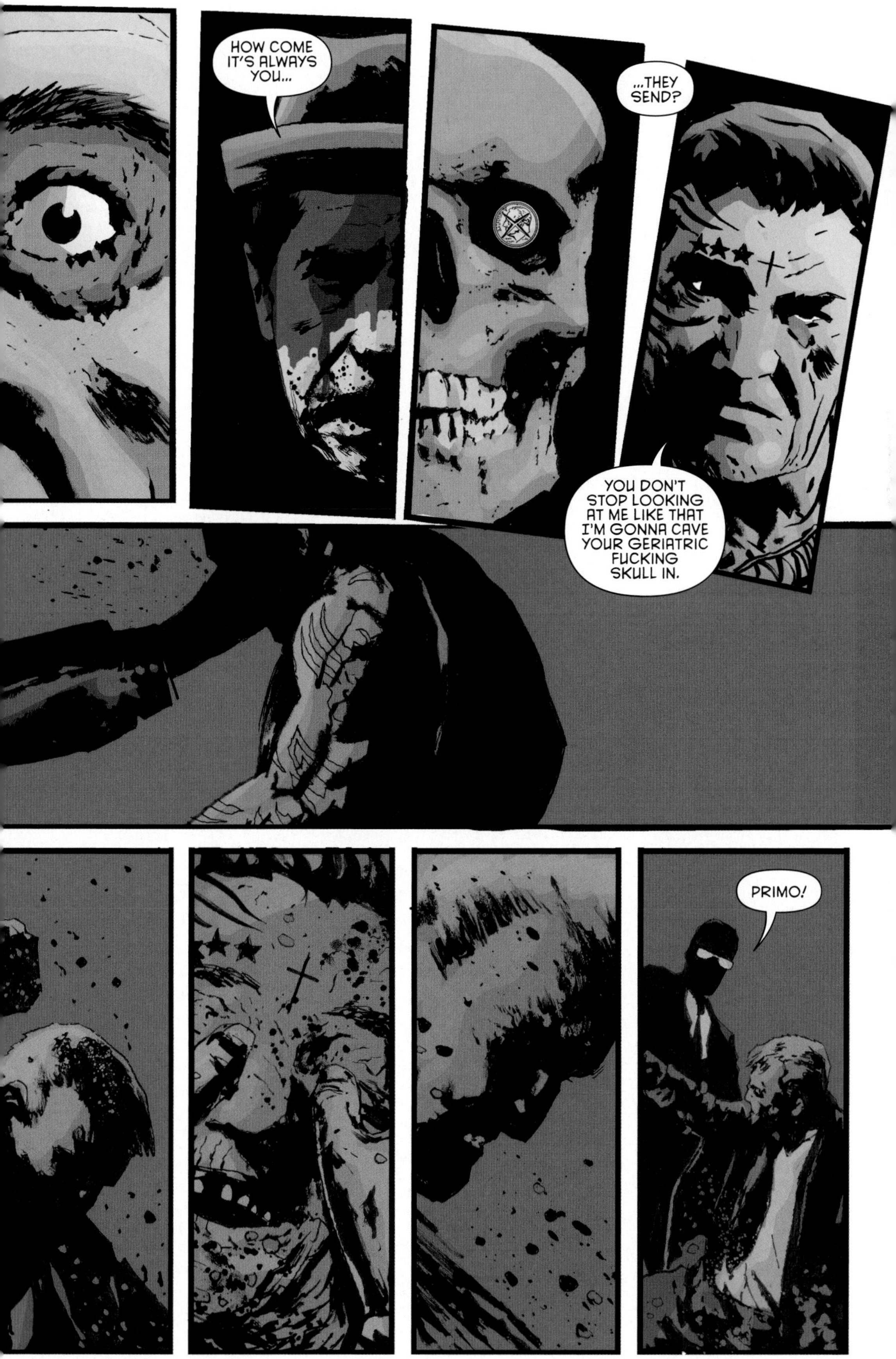
HOW COME IT'S ALWAYS YOU...
...THEY SEND?
YOU DON'T STOP LOOKING AT ME LIKE THAT I'M GONNA CAVE YOUR GERIATRIC FUCKING SKULL IN.
PRIMO!

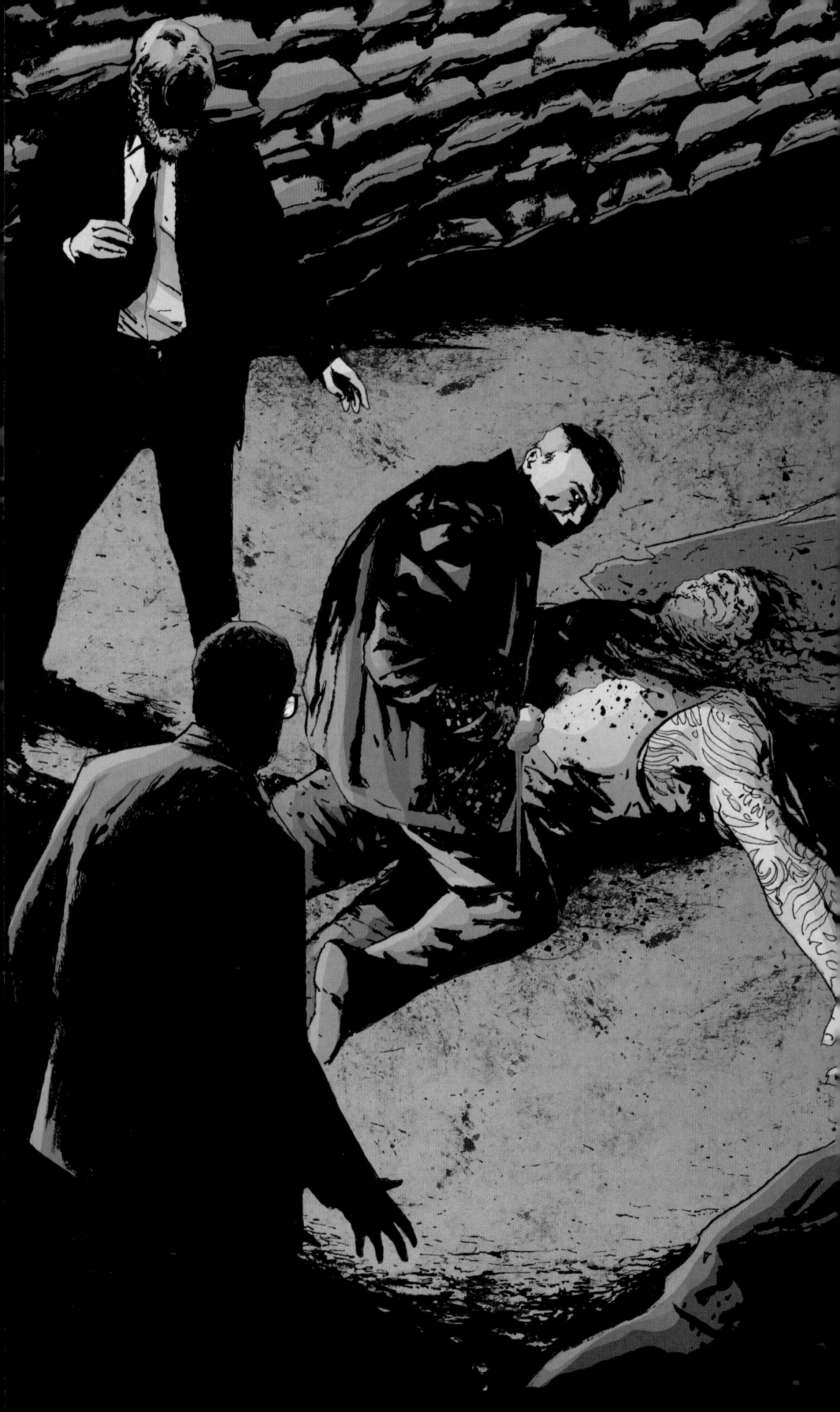

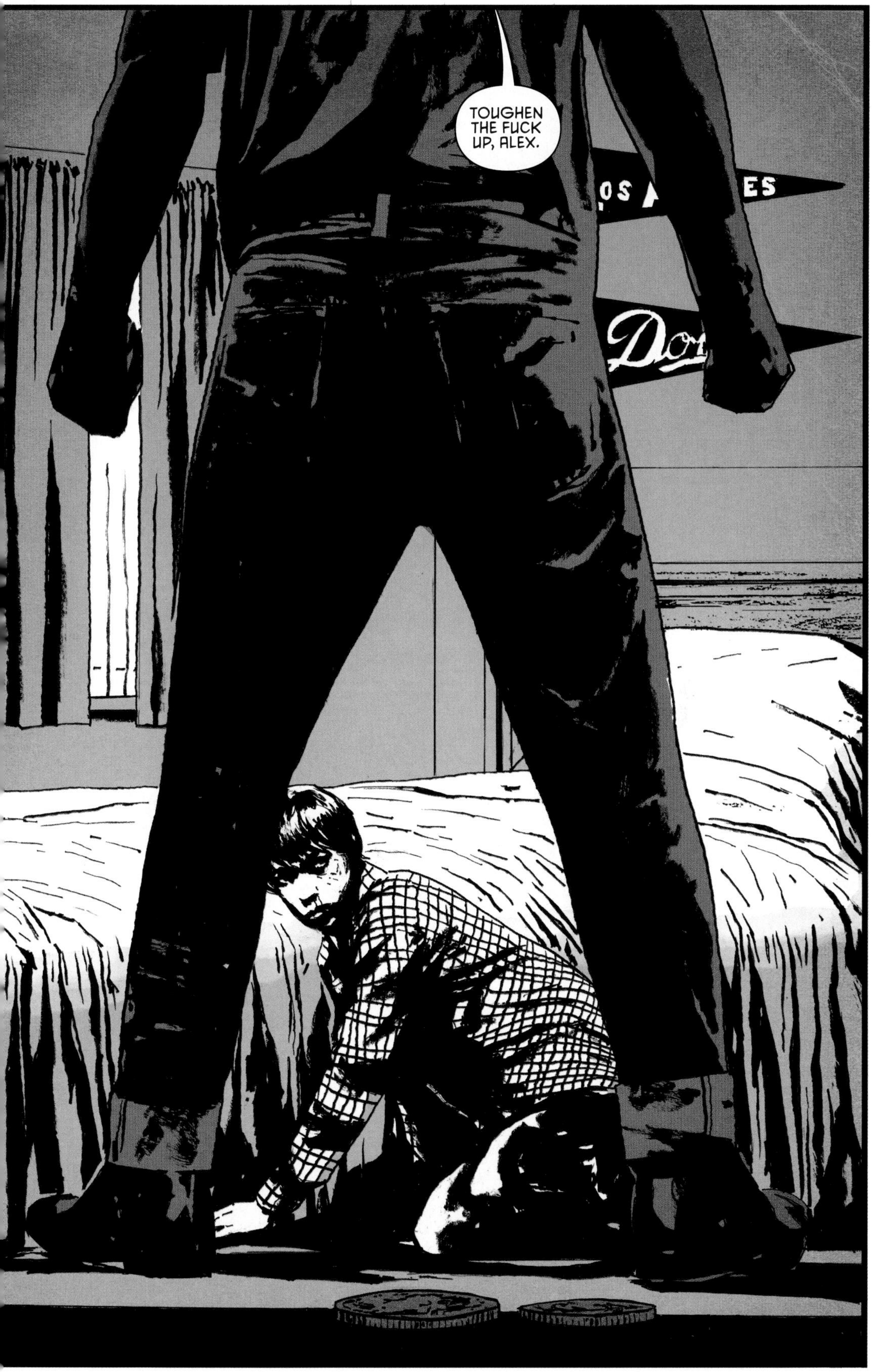
TOUGHEN THE FUCK UP, ALEX.

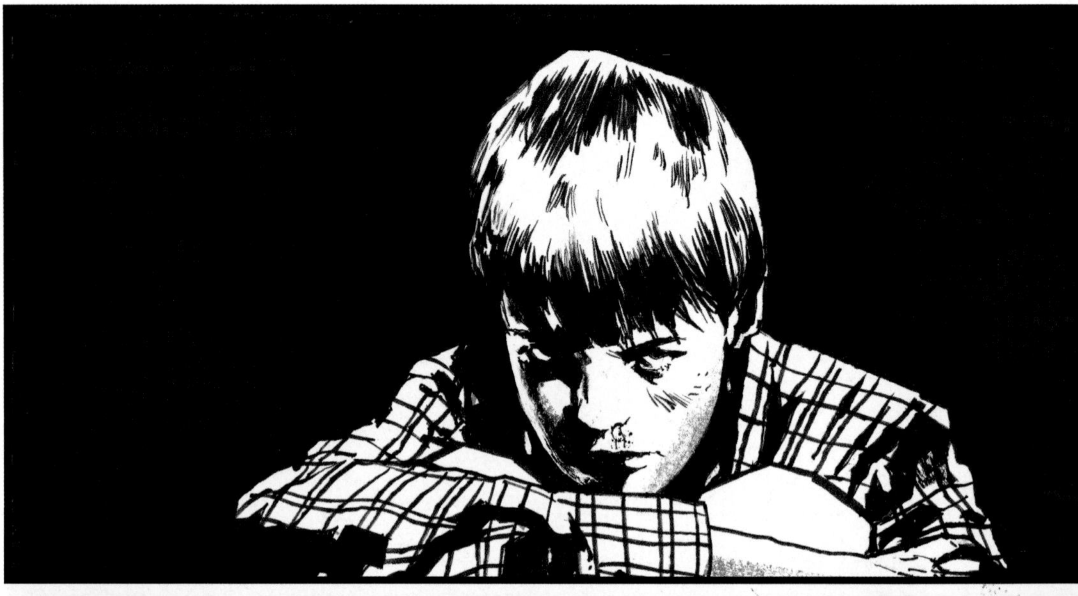

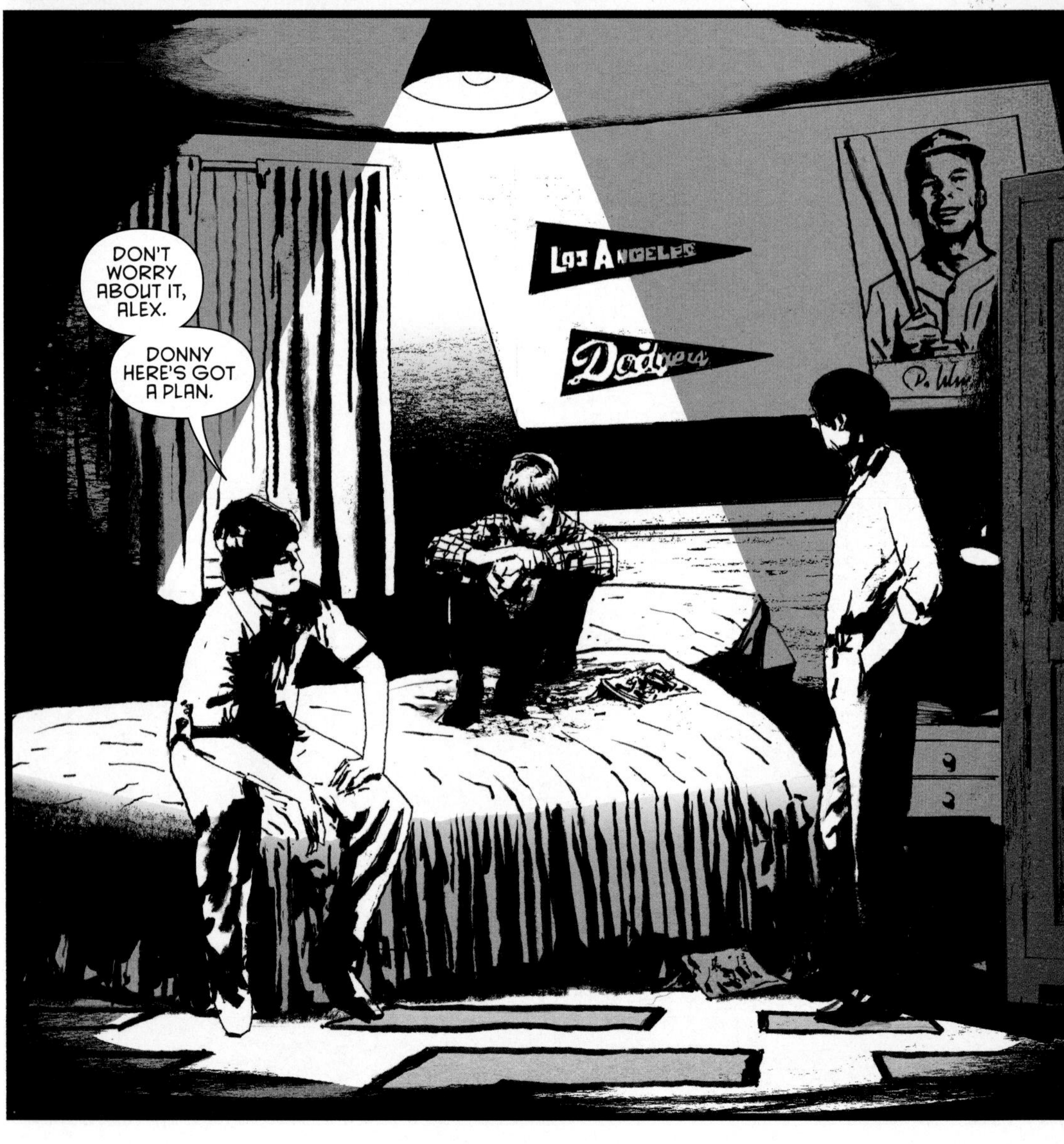
DON'T WORRY ABOUT IT, ALEX.
DONNY HERE'S GOT A PLAN.
LOS ANGELES
Dodgers

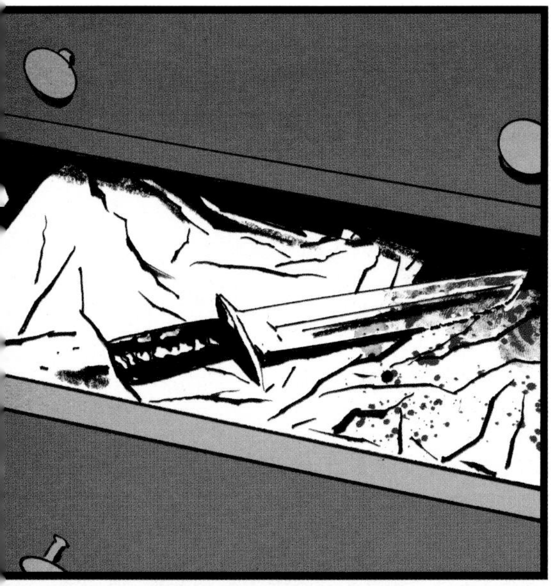

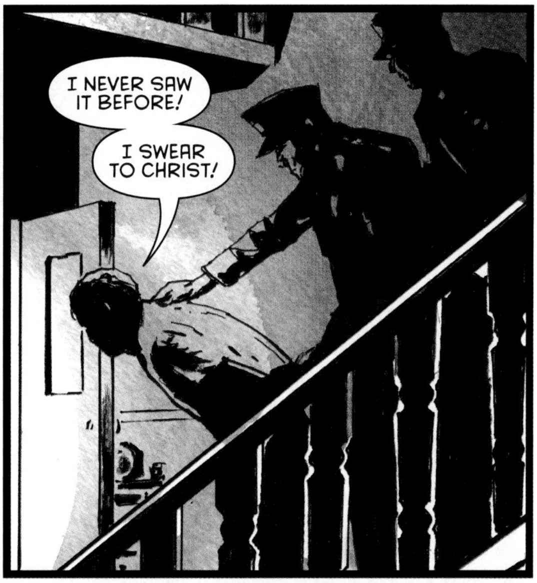
I NEVER SAW IT BEFORE!
I SWEAR TO CHRIST!

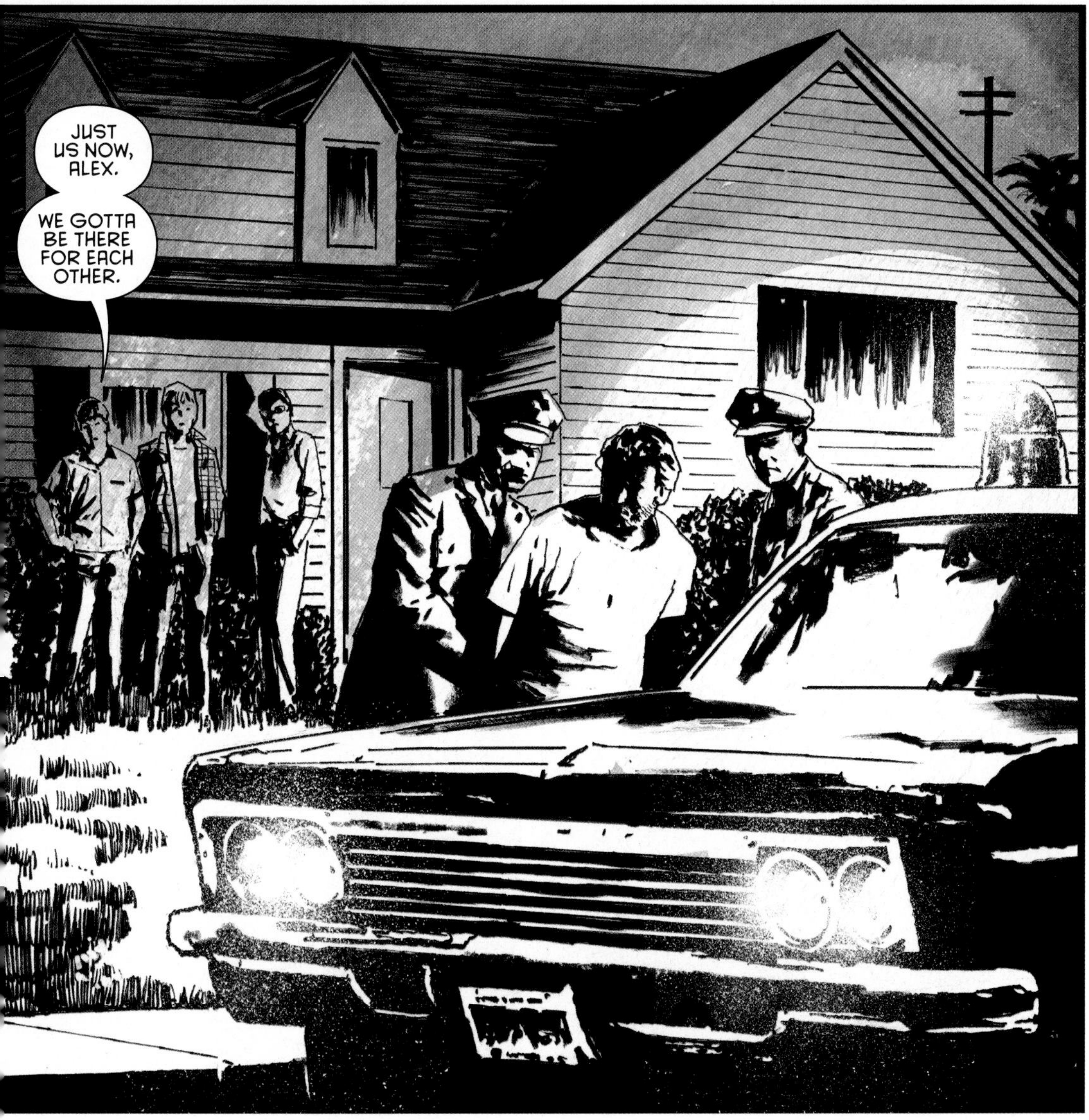
JUST US NOW, ALEX.
WE GOTTA BE THERE FOR EACH OTHER.

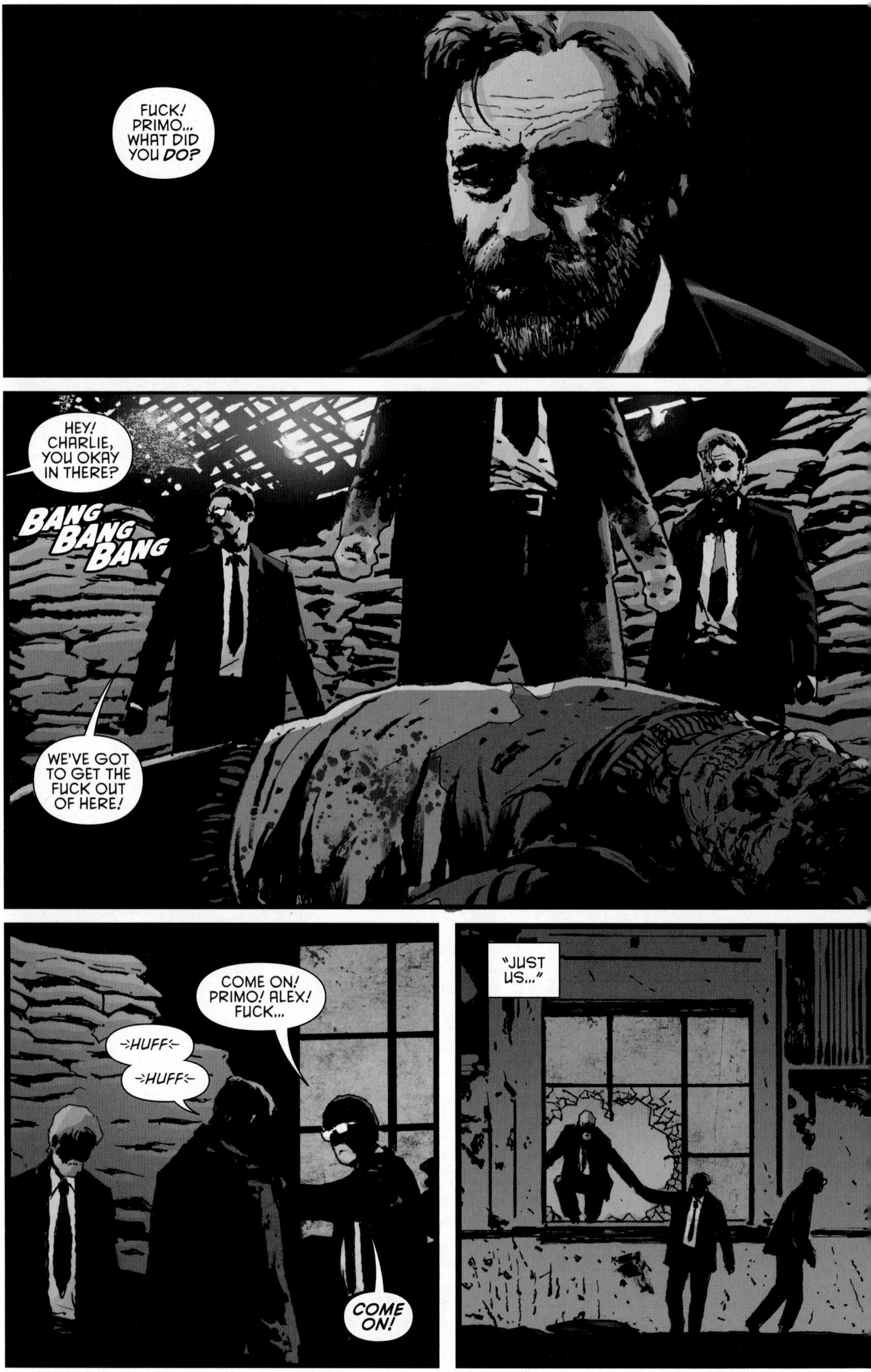
FUCK! PRIMO... WHAT DID YOU *DO?*
HEY! CHARLIE, YOU OKAY IN THERE?
BANG BANG BANG
WE'VE GOT TO GET THE FUCK OUT OF HERE!
COME ON! PRIMO! ALEX! FUCK...
-HUFF-
-HUFF-
COME ON!
"JUST US..."

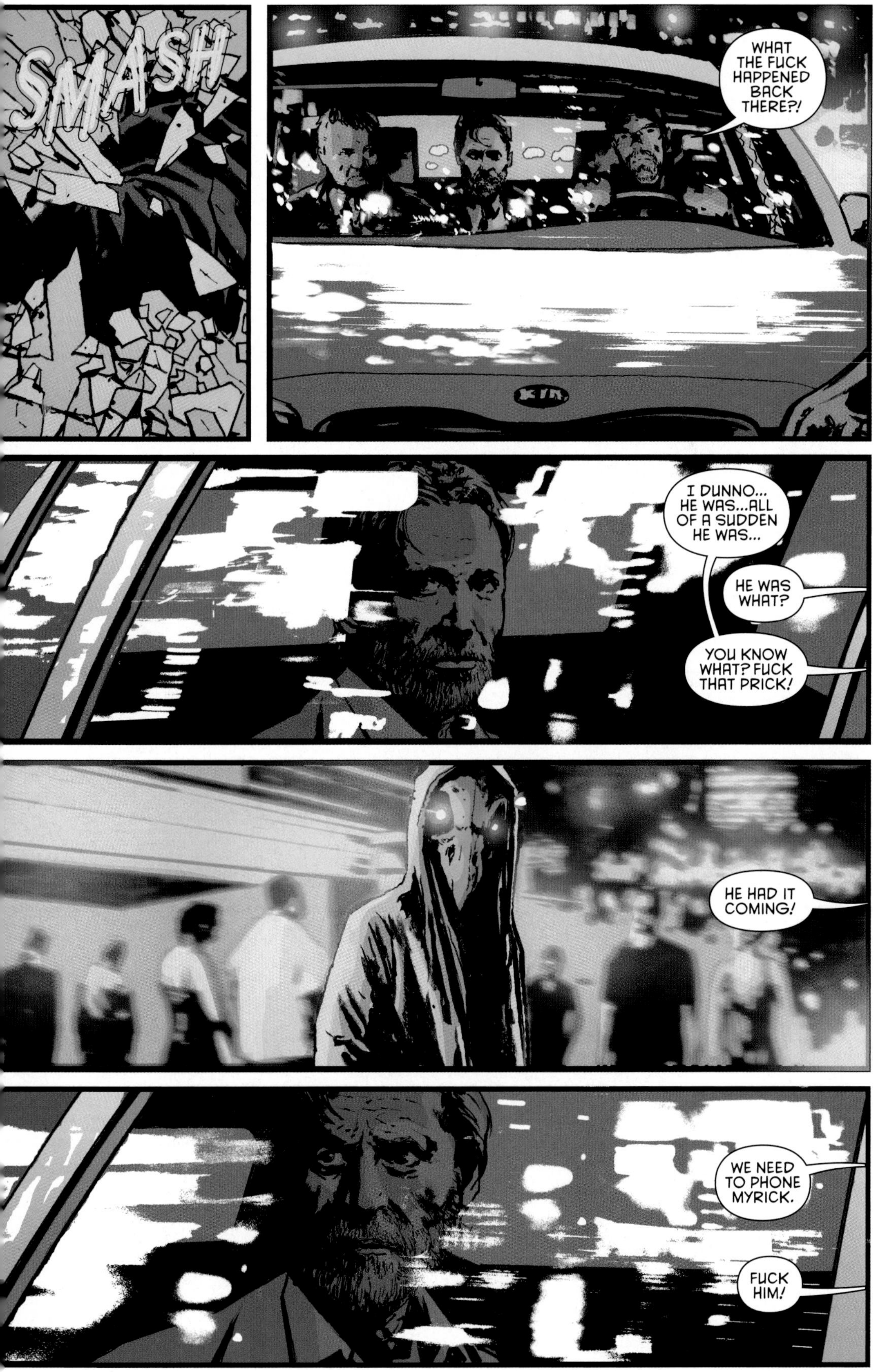
SMASH
WHAT THE FUCK HAPPENED BACK THERE?!
I DUNNO... HE WAS...ALL OF A SUDDEN HE WAS...
HE WAS WHAT?
YOU KNOW WHAT? FUCK THAT PRICK!
HE HAD IT COMING!
WE NEED TO PHONE MYRICK.
FUCK HIM!

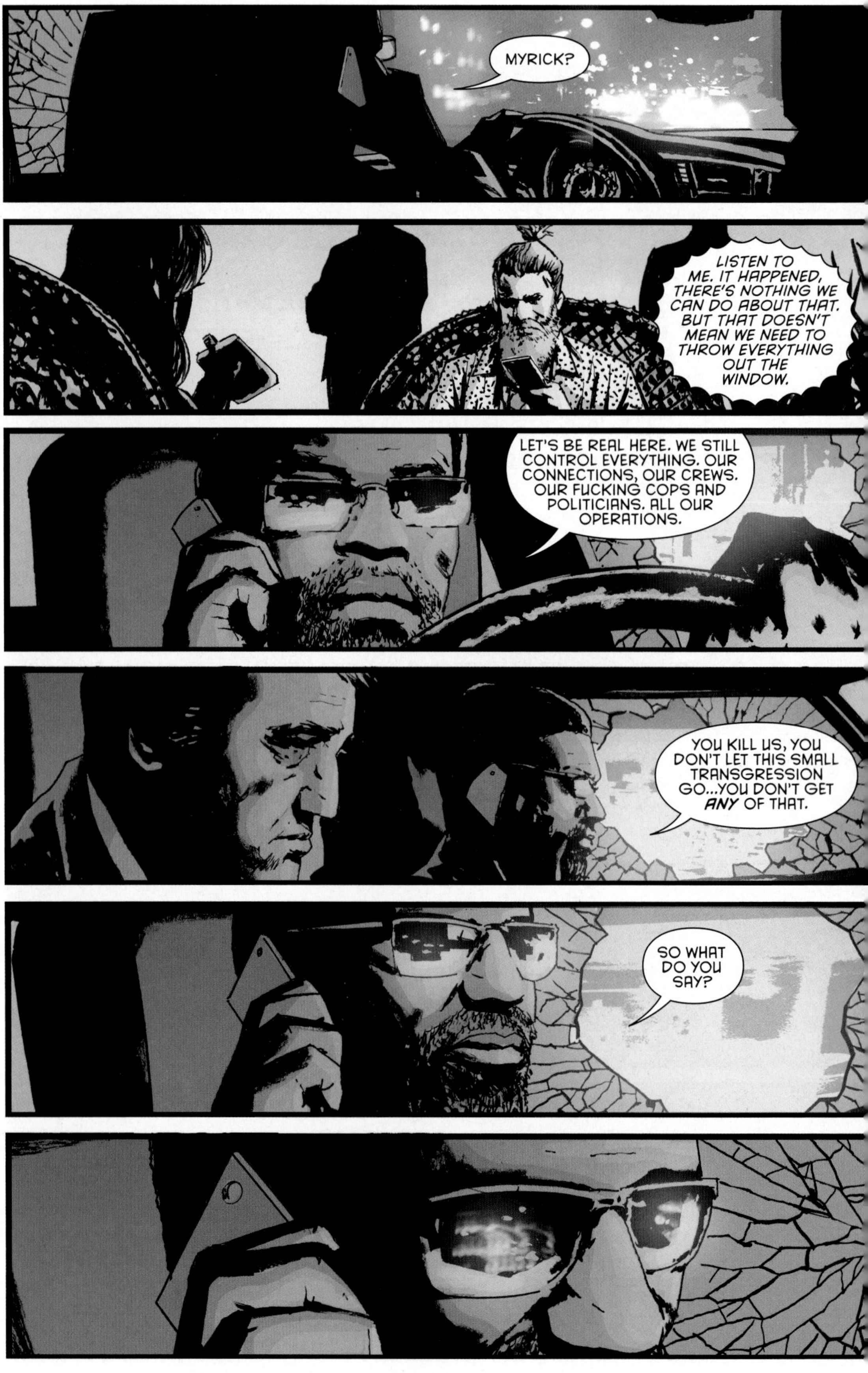
MYRICK?
LISTEN TO ME. IT HAPPENED, THERE'S NOTHING WE CAN DO ABOUT THAT. BUT THAT DOESN'T MEAN WE NEED TO THROW EVERYTHING OUT THE WINDOW.
LET'S BE REAL HERE. WE STILL CONTROL EVERYTHING. OUR CONNECTIONS, OUR CREWS. OUR FUCKING COPS AND POLITICIANS. ALL OUR OPERATIONS.
YOU KILL US, YOU DON'T LET THIS SMALL TRANSGRESSION GO...YOU DON'T GET *ANY* OF THAT.
SO WHAT DO YOU SAY?

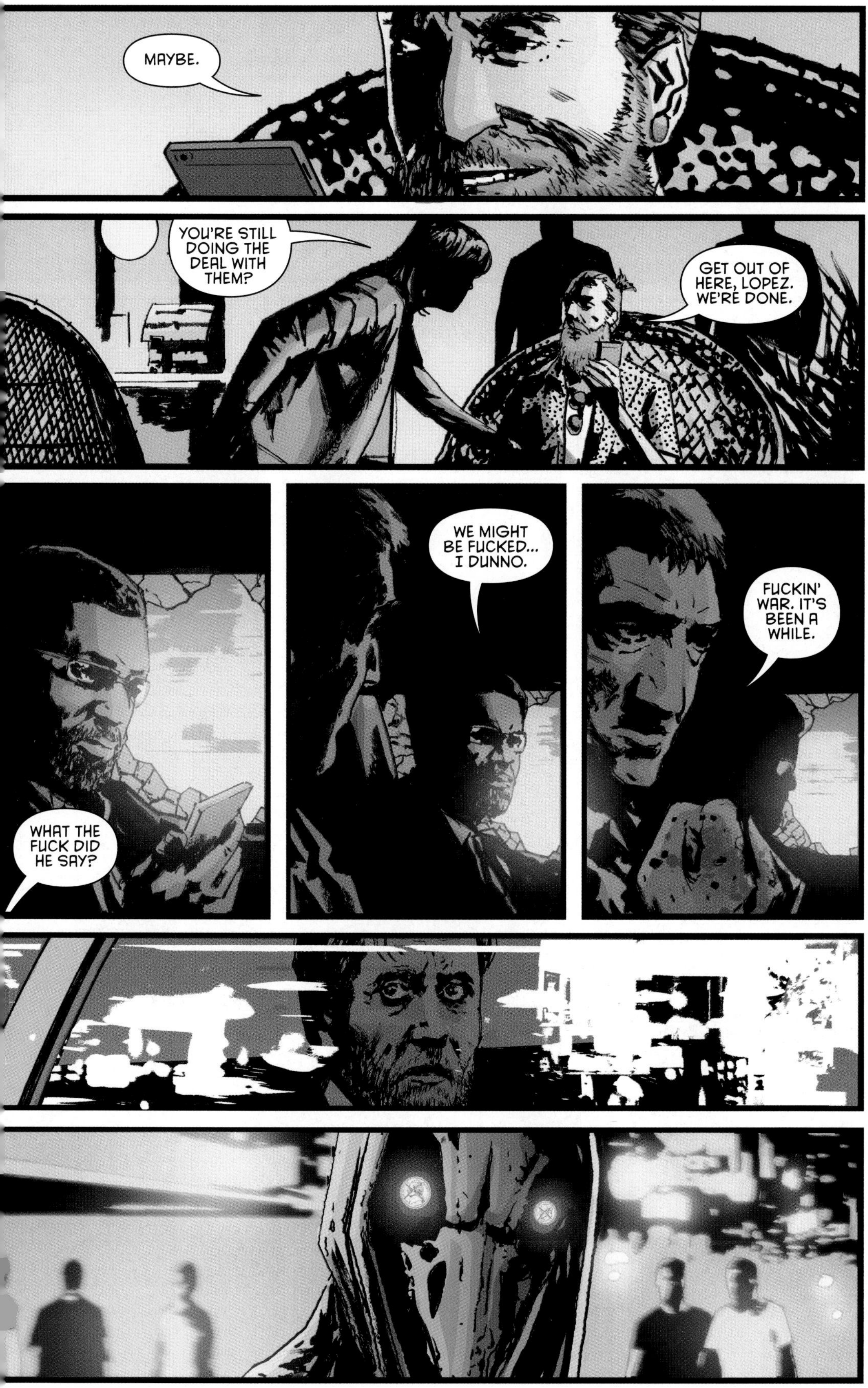
MAYBE.
YOU'RE STILL DOING THE DEAL WITH THEM?
GET OUT OF HERE, LOPEZ. WE'RE DONE.
WHAT THE FUCK DID HE SAY?
WE MIGHT BE FUCKED... I DUNNO.
FUCKIN' WAR. IT'S BEEN A WHILE.

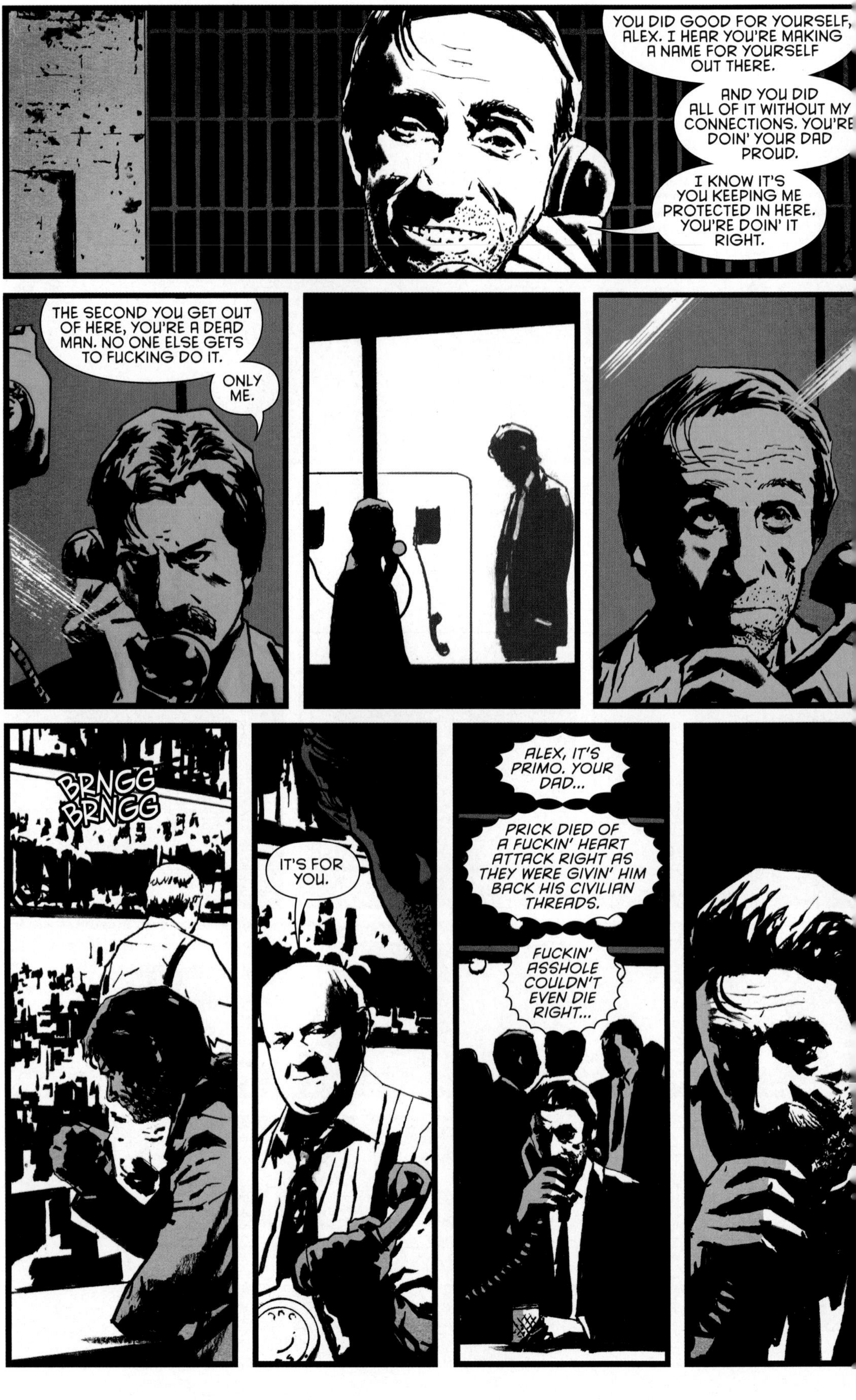

YOU DID GOOD FOR YOURSELF, ALEX. I HEAR YOU'RE MAKING A NAME FOR YOURSELF OUT THERE.
AND YOU DID ALL OF IT WITHOUT MY CONNECTIONS. YOU'RE DOIN' YOUR DAD PROUD.
I KNOW IT'S YOU KEEPING ME PROTECTED IN HERE. YOU'RE DOIN' IT RIGHT.
THE SECOND YOU GET OUT OF HERE, YOU'RE A DEAD MAN. NO ONE ELSE GETS TO FUCKING DO IT.
ONLY ME.
BRNGG BRNGG
IT'S FOR YOU.
ALEX, IT'S PRIMO. YOUR DAD...
PRICK DIED OF A FUCKIN' HEART ATTACK RIGHT AS THEY WERE GIVIN' HIM BACK HIS CIVILIAN THREADS.
FUCKIN' ASSHOLE COULDN'T EVEN DIE RIGHT...

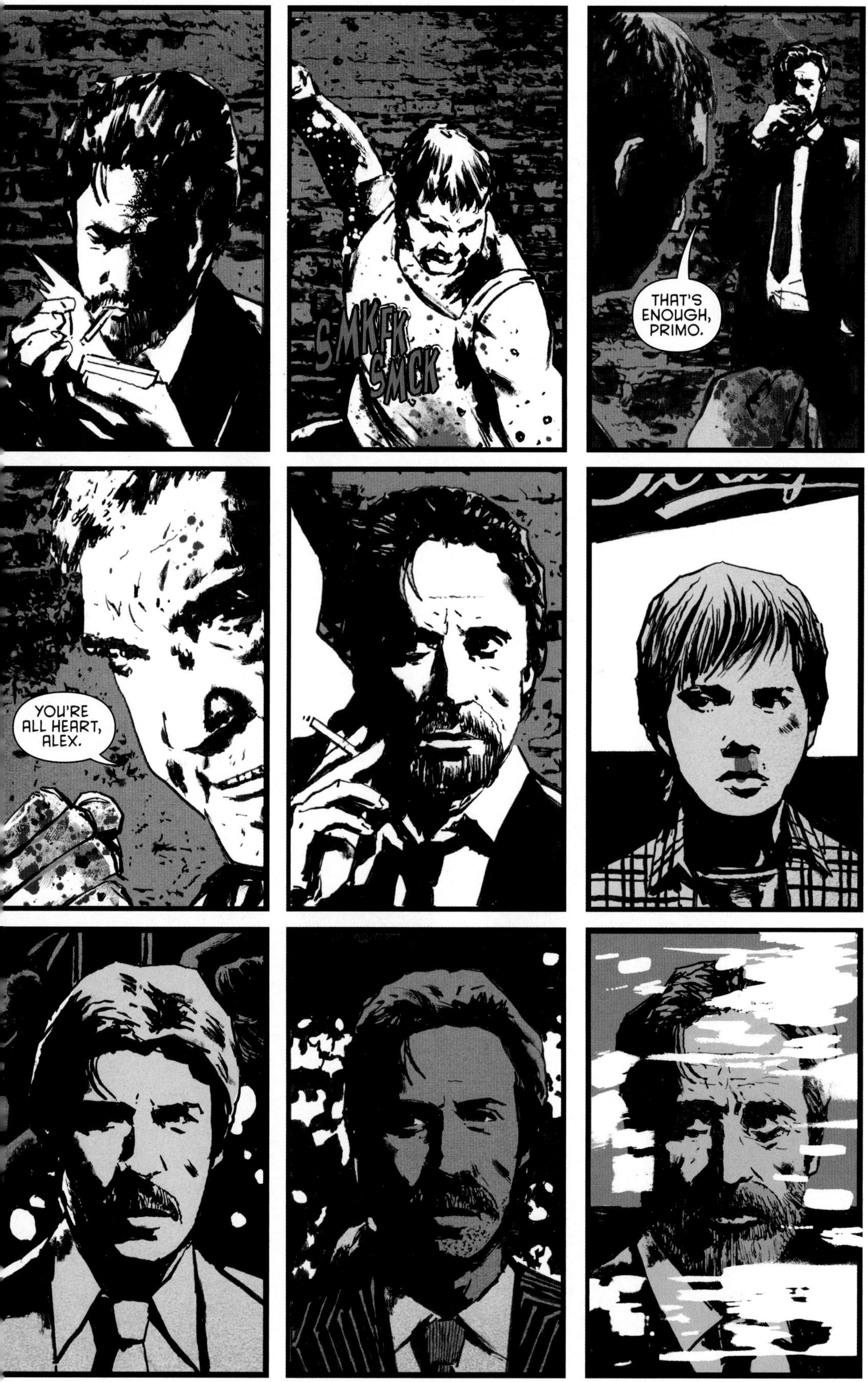
SMKFK
SMCK
THAT'S ENOUGH, PRIMO.
YOU'RE ALL HEART, ALEX.

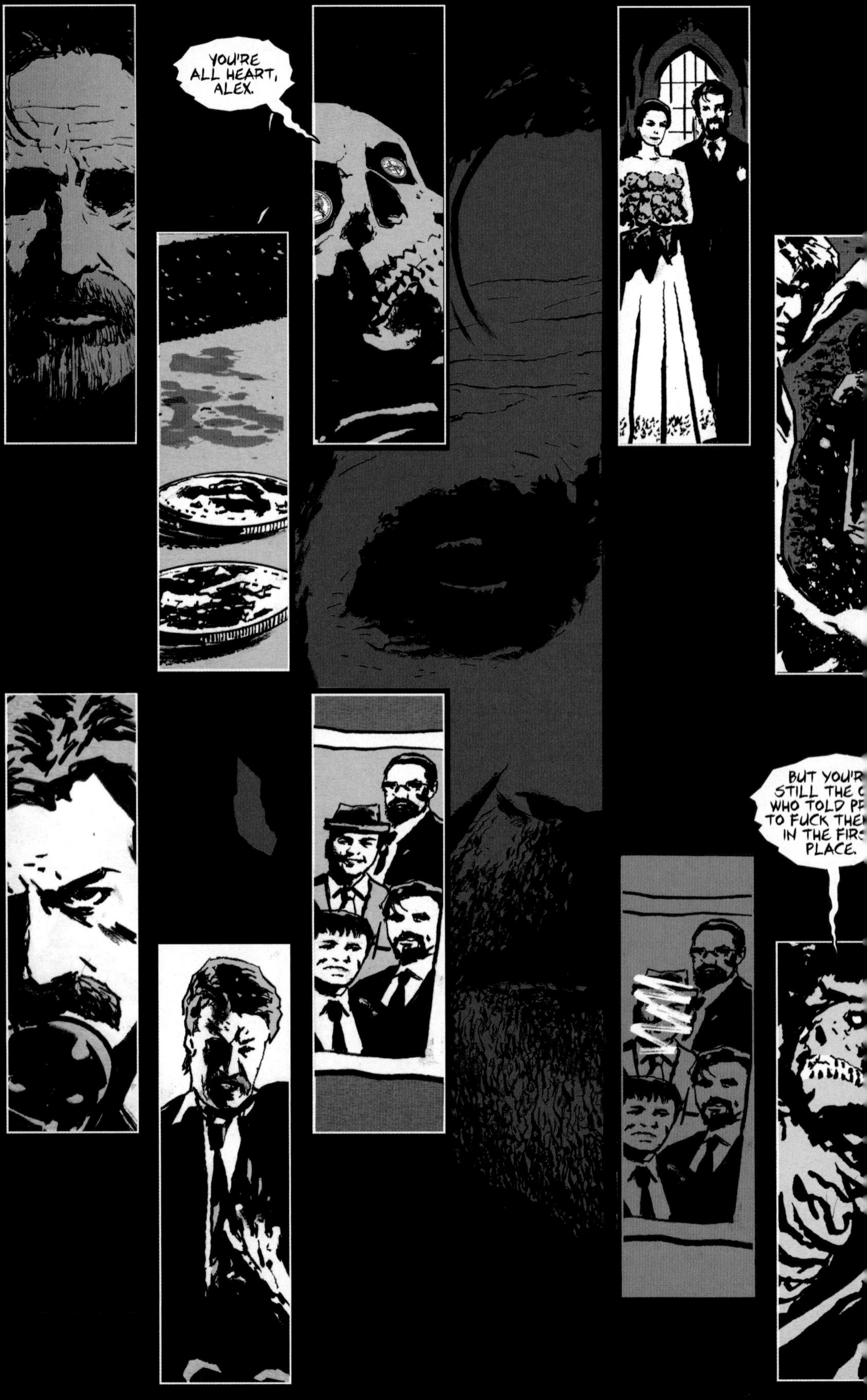
YOU'RE ALL HEART, ALEX.
BUT YOU'R STILL THE WHO TOLD P TO FUCK THE IN THE FIRS PLACE.

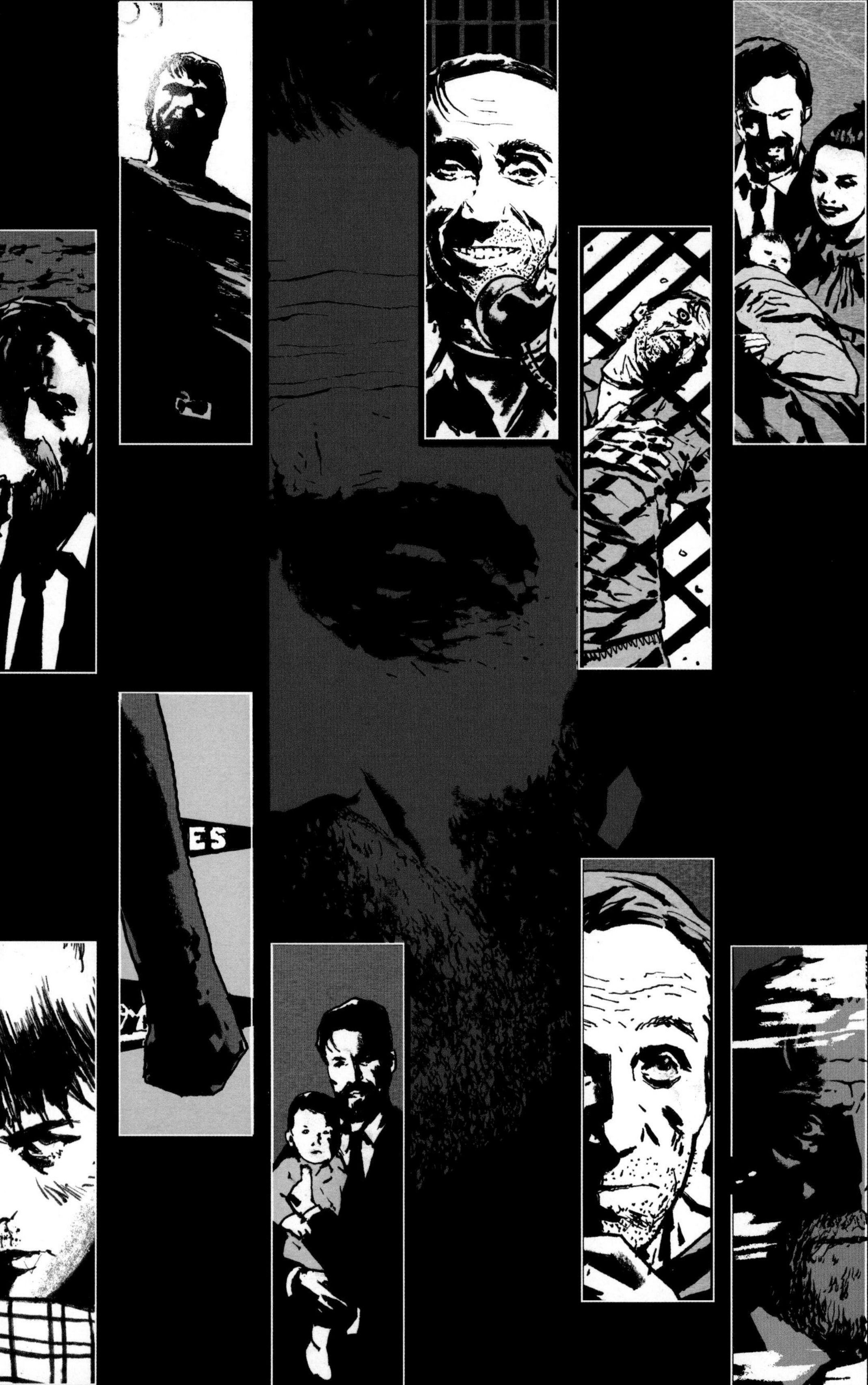

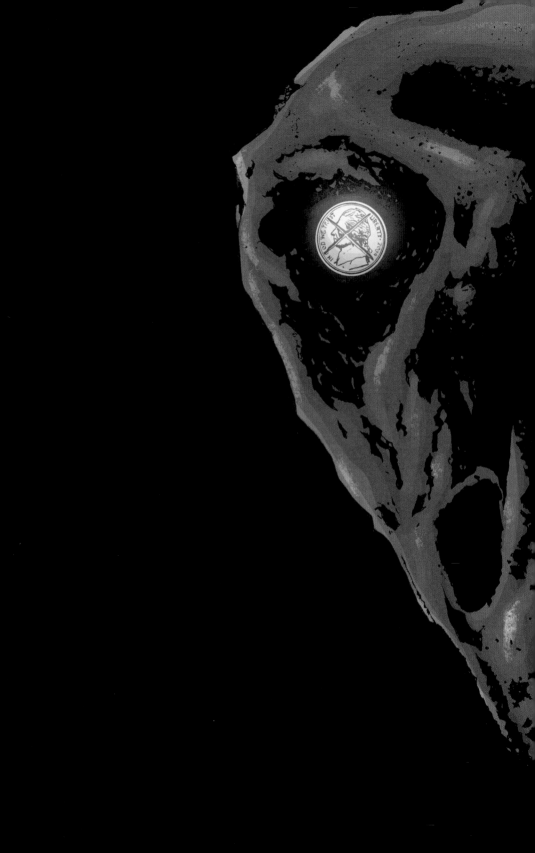

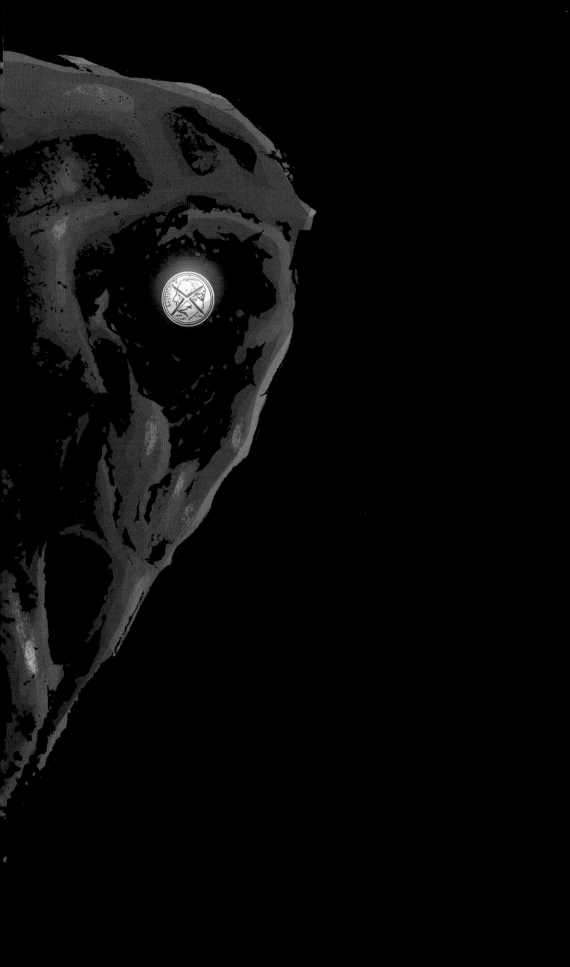

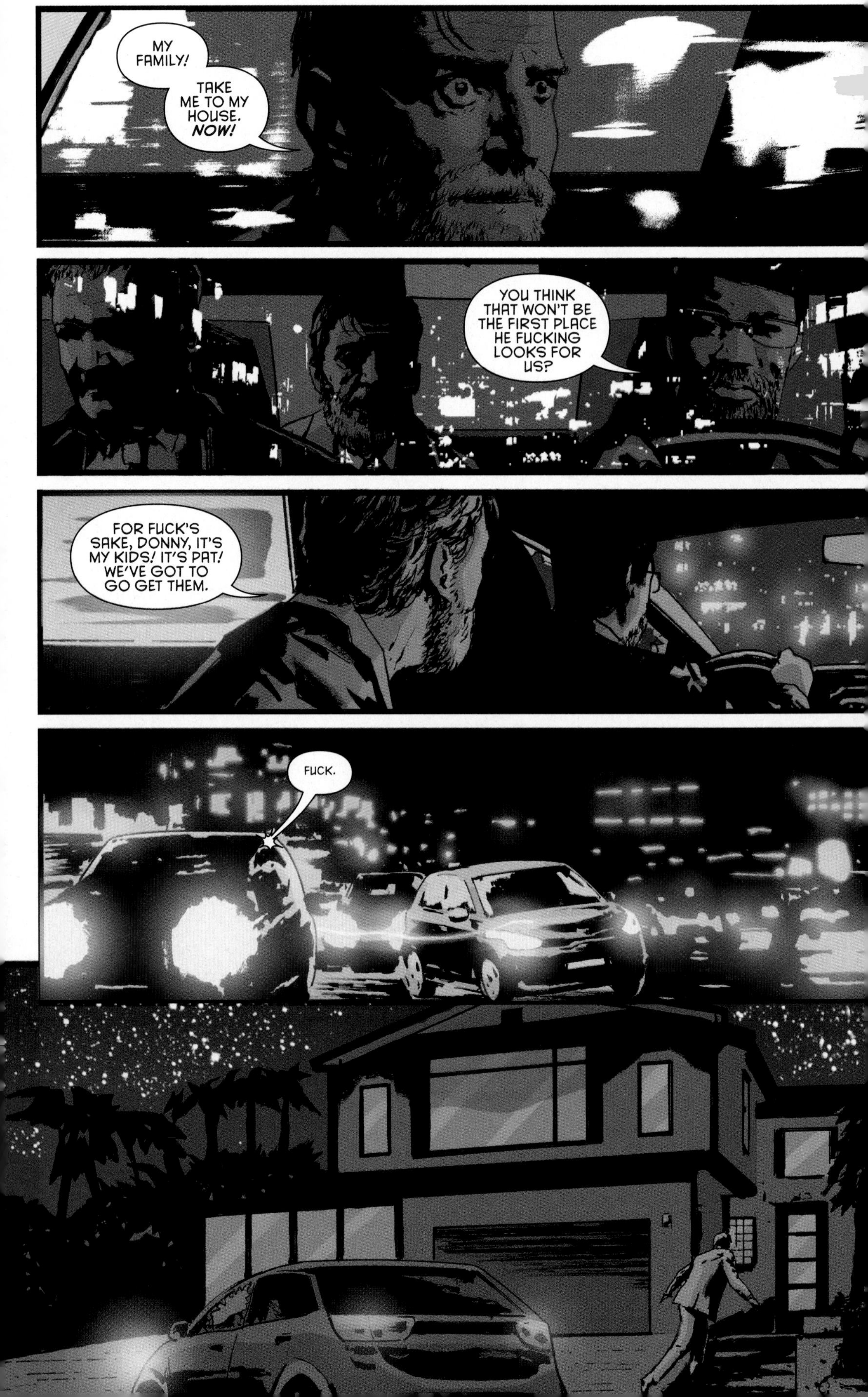
MY FAMILY!
TAKE ME TO MY HOUSE. *NOW!*
YOU THINK THAT WON'T BE THE FIRST PLACE HE FUCKING LOOKS FOR US?
FOR FUCK'S SAKE, DONNY, IT'S MY KIDS! IT'S PAT! WE'VE GOT TO GO GET THEM.
FUCK.

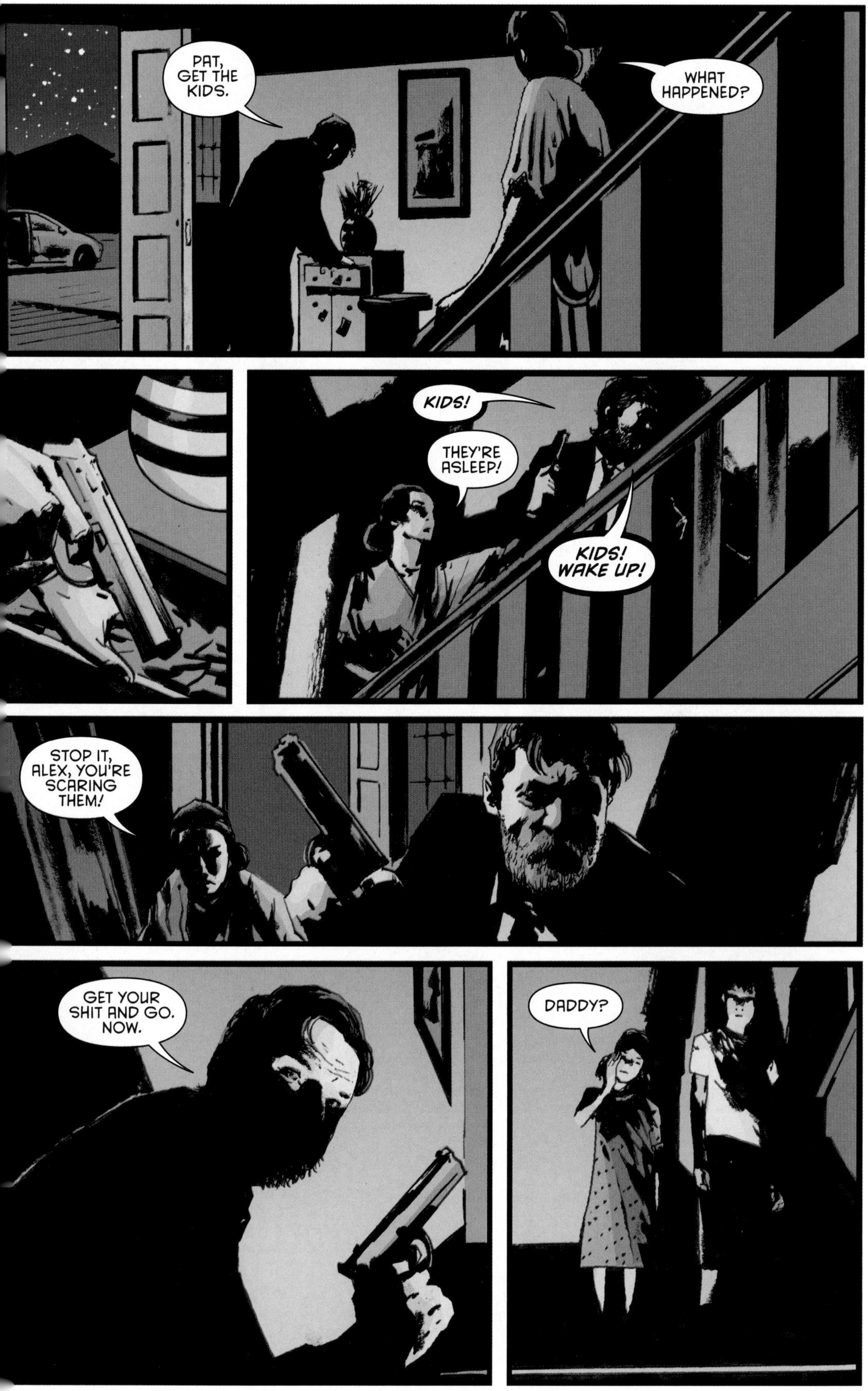
PAT, GET THE KIDS.
WHAT HAPPENED?
KIDS!
THEY'RE ASLEEP!
KIDS! WAKE UP!
STOP IT, ALEX, YOU'RE SCARING THEM!
GET YOUR SHIT AND GO. NOW.
DADDY?

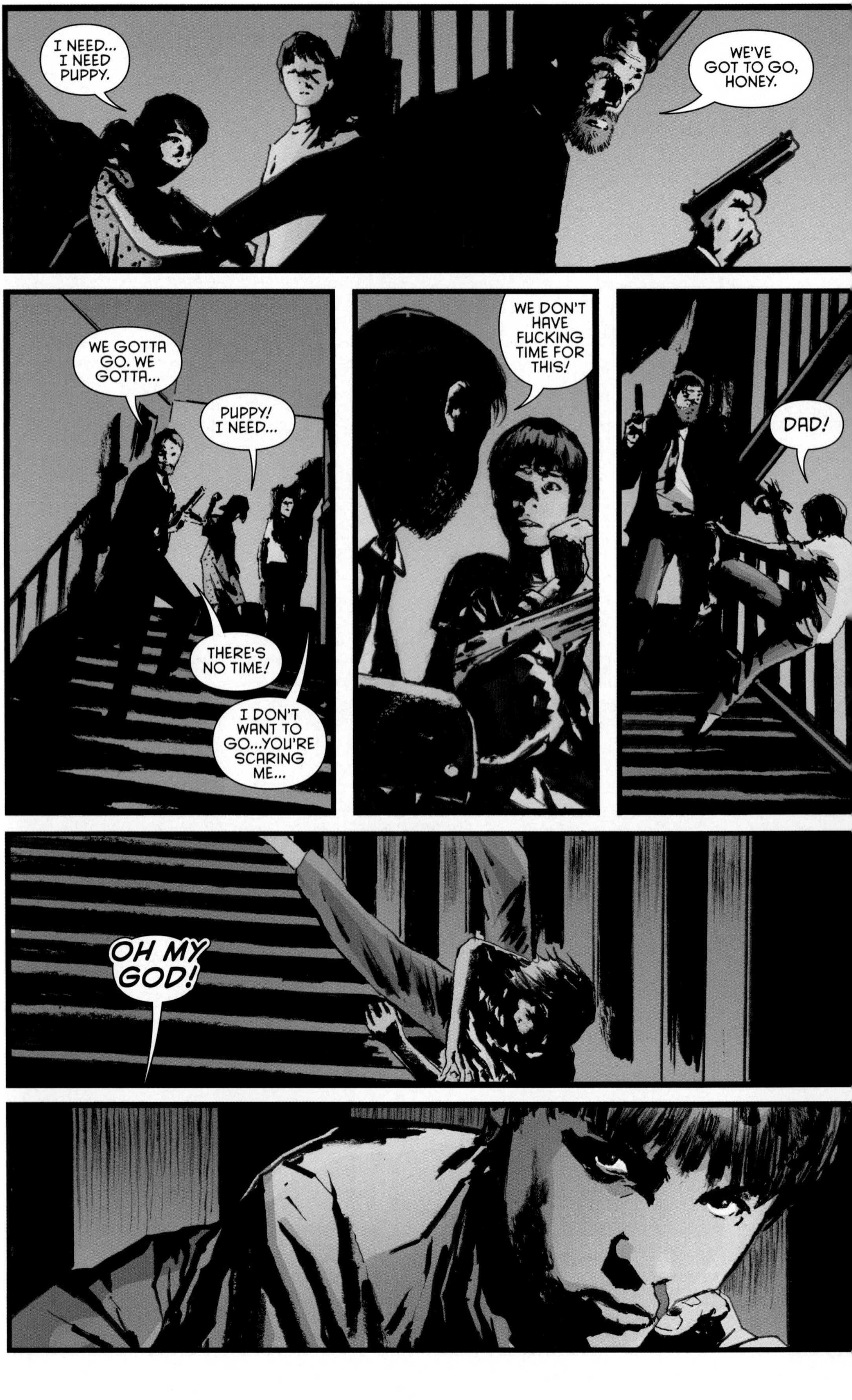
I NEED... I NEED PUPPY.
WE'VE GOT TO GO, HONEY.
WE GOTTA GO. WE GOTTA...
PUPPY! I NEED...
THERE'S NO TIME!
I DON'T WANT TO GO...YOU'RE SCARING ME...
WE DON'T HAVE FUCKING TIME FOR THIS!
DAD!
OH MY GOD!

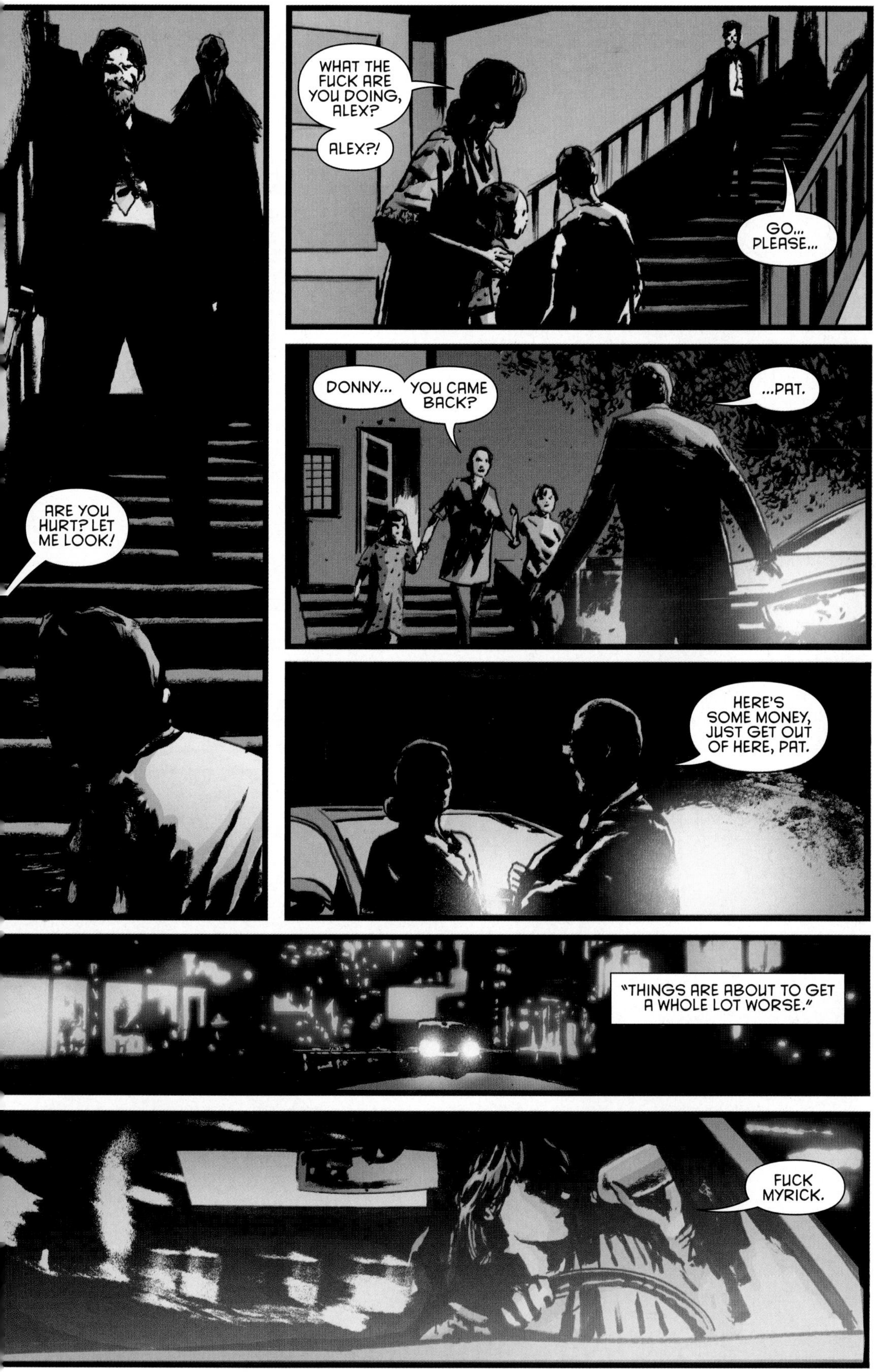
WHAT THE FUCK ARE YOU DOING, ALEX?
ALEX?!
GO... PLEASE...
ARE YOU HURT? LET ME LOOK!
DONNY...
YOU CAME BACK?
...PAT.
HERE'S SOME MONEY, JUST GET OUT OF HERE, PAT.
"THINGS ARE ABOUT TO GET A WHOLE LOT WORSE."
FUCK MYRICK.

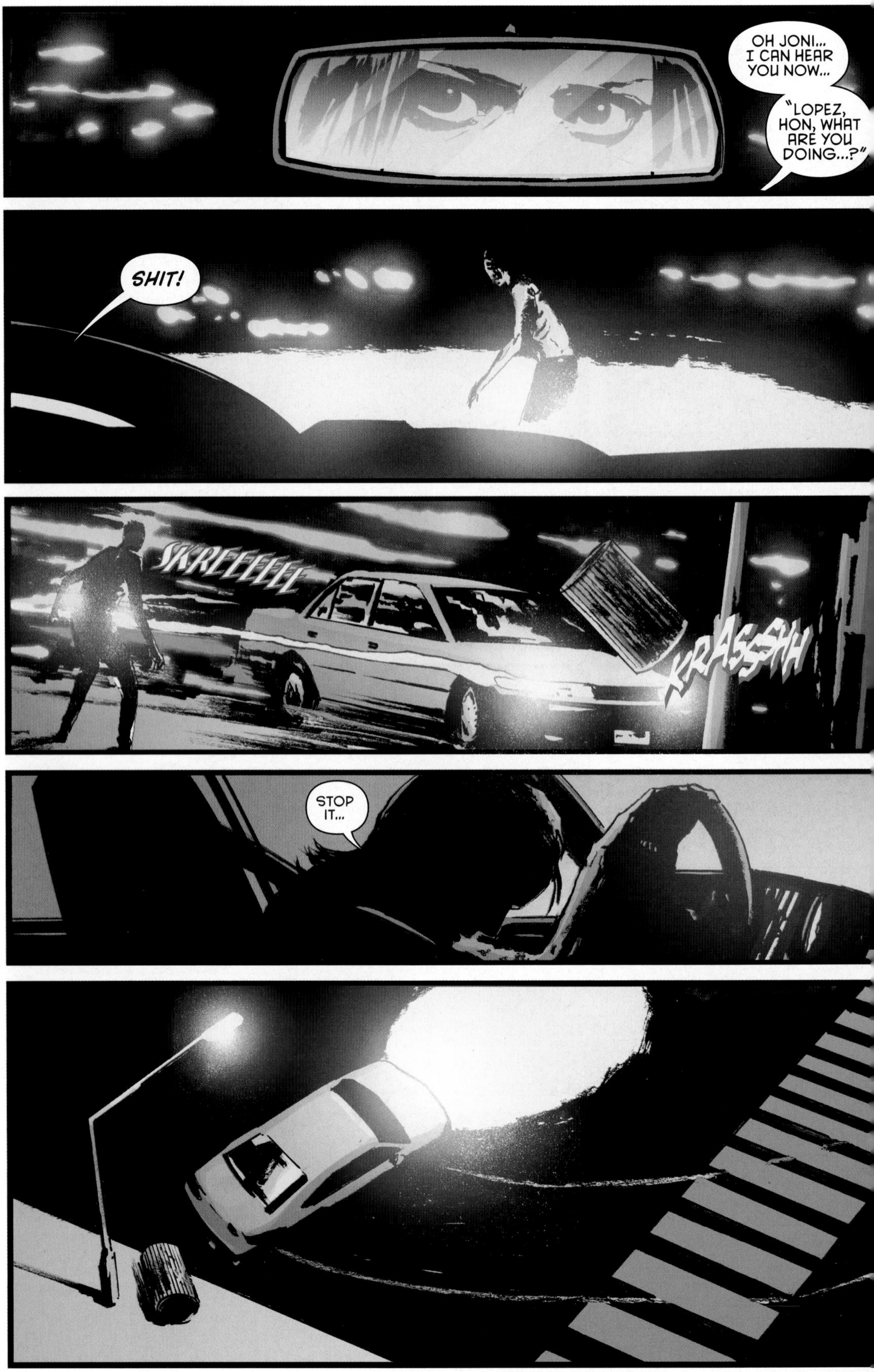
OH JONI... I CAN HEAR YOU NOW...
"LOPEZ, HON, WHAT ARE YOU DOING...?"
SHIT!
SKREEEEEEE
KRASSSHH
STOP IT...

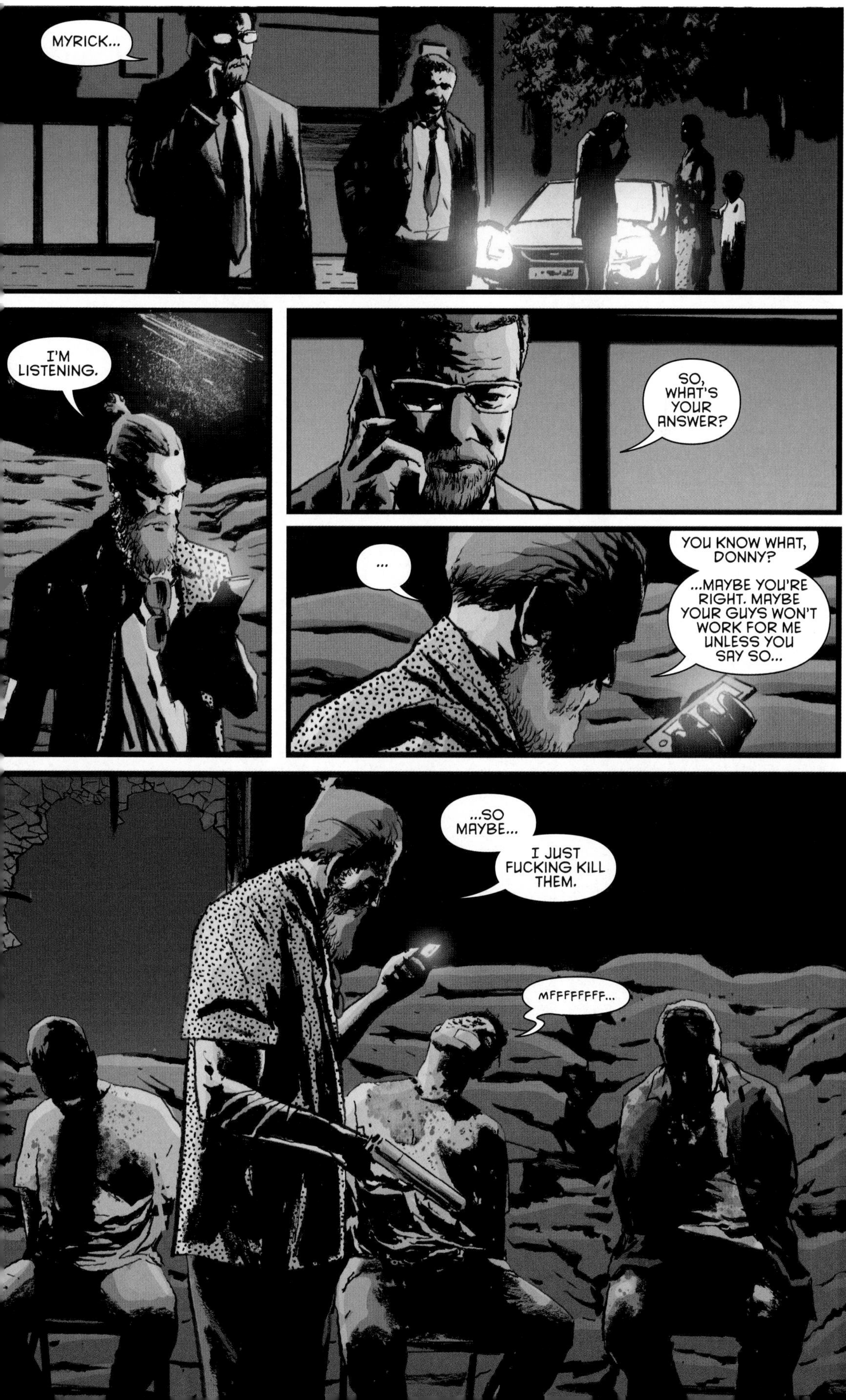
MYRICK...
I'M LISTENING.
SO, WHAT'S YOUR ANSWER?
...
YOU KNOW WHAT, DONNY?
...MAYBE YOU'RE RIGHT. MAYBE YOUR GUYS WON'T WORK FOR ME UNLESS YOU SAY SO...
...SO MAYBE...
I JUST FUCKING KILL THEM.
MFFFFFFFF...

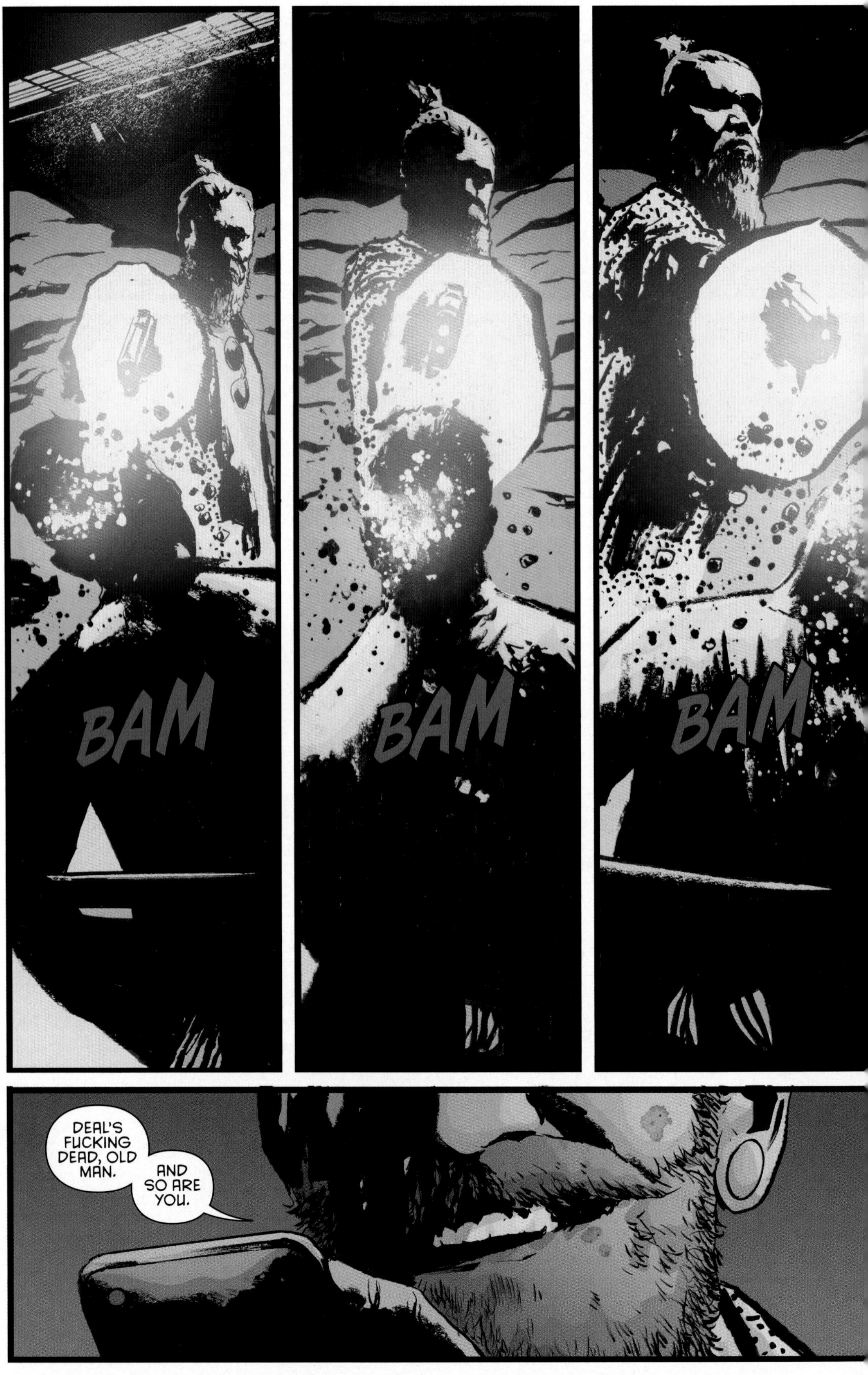
BAM
BAM
BAM
DEAL'S FUCKING DEAD, OLD MAN.
AND SO ARE YOU.

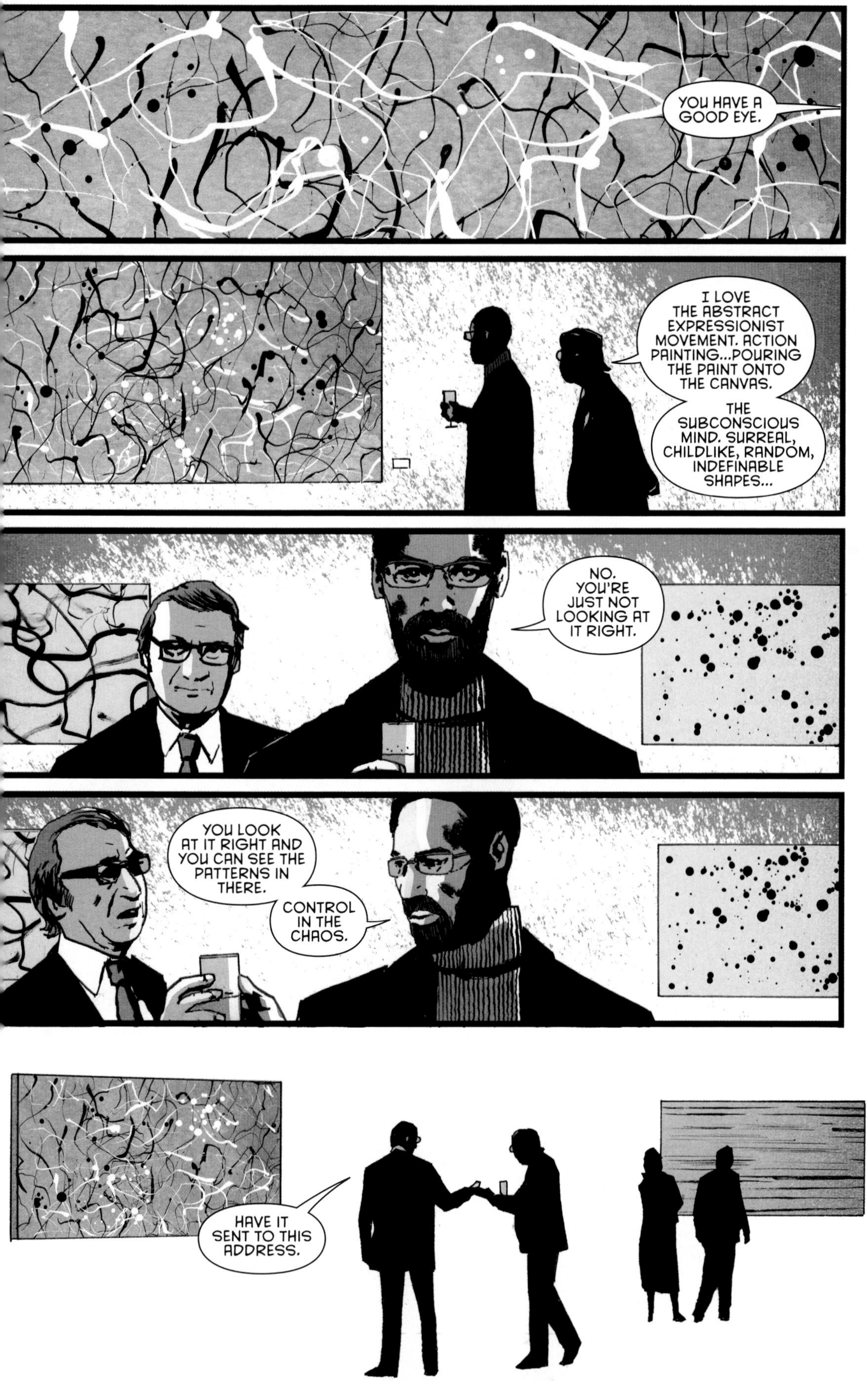
YOU HAVE A GOOD EYE.
I LOVE THE ABSTRACT EXPRESSIONIST MOVEMENT. ACTION PAINTING...POURING THE PAINT ONTO THE CANVAS.
THE SUBCONSCIOUS MIND. SURREAL, CHILDLIKE, RANDOM, INDEFINABLE SHAPES...
NO. YOU'RE JUST NOT LOOKING AT IT RIGHT.
YOU LOOK AT IT RIGHT AND YOU CAN SEE THE PATTERNS IN THERE.
CONTROL IN THE CHAOS.
HAVE IT SENT TO THIS ADDRESS.

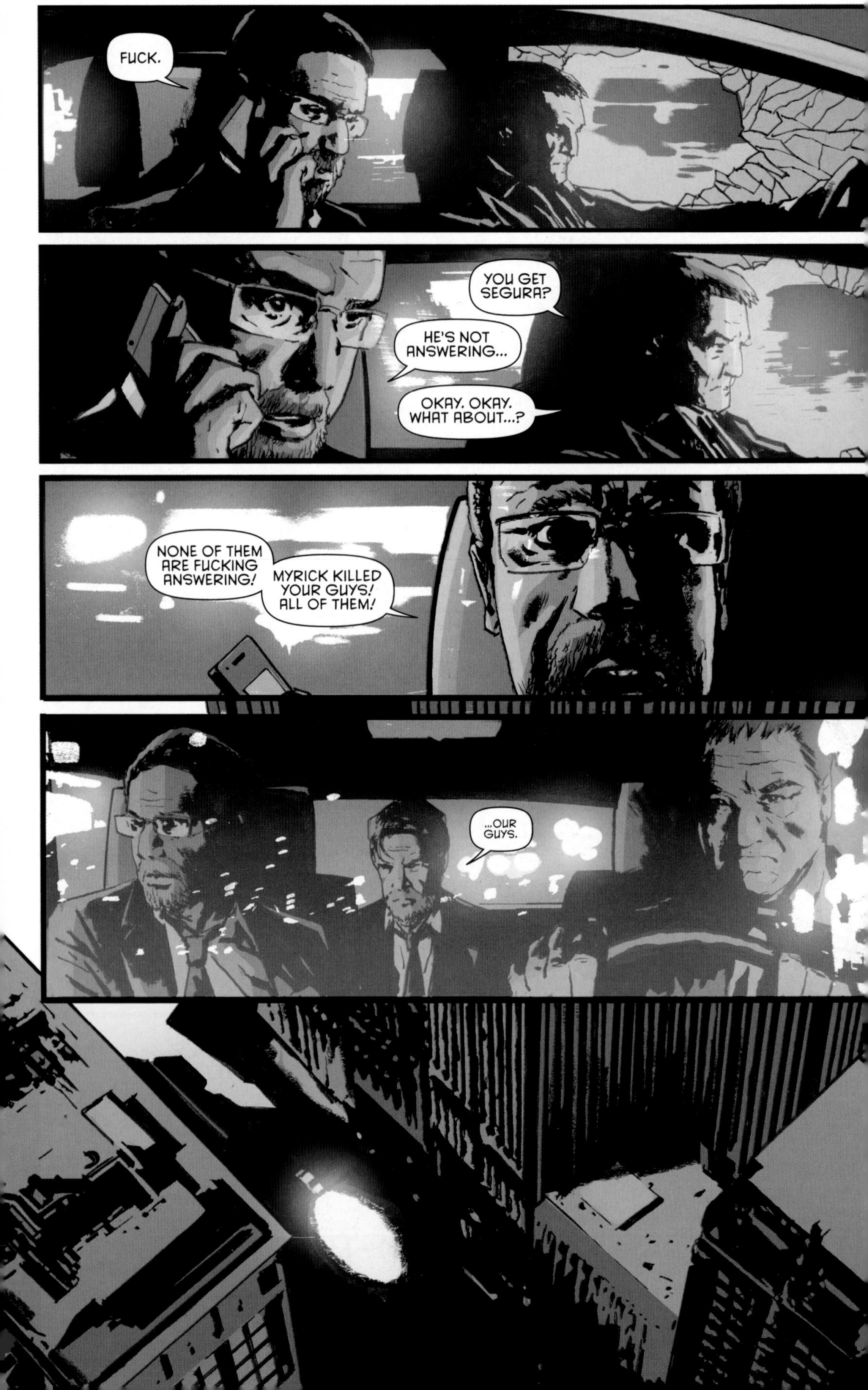
FUCK.
YOU GET SEGURA?
HE'S NOT ANSWERING...
OKAY. OKAY. WHAT ABOUT...?
NONE OF THEM ARE FUCKING ANSWERING!
MYRICK KILLED YOUR GUYS! ALL OF THEM!
...OUR GUYS.

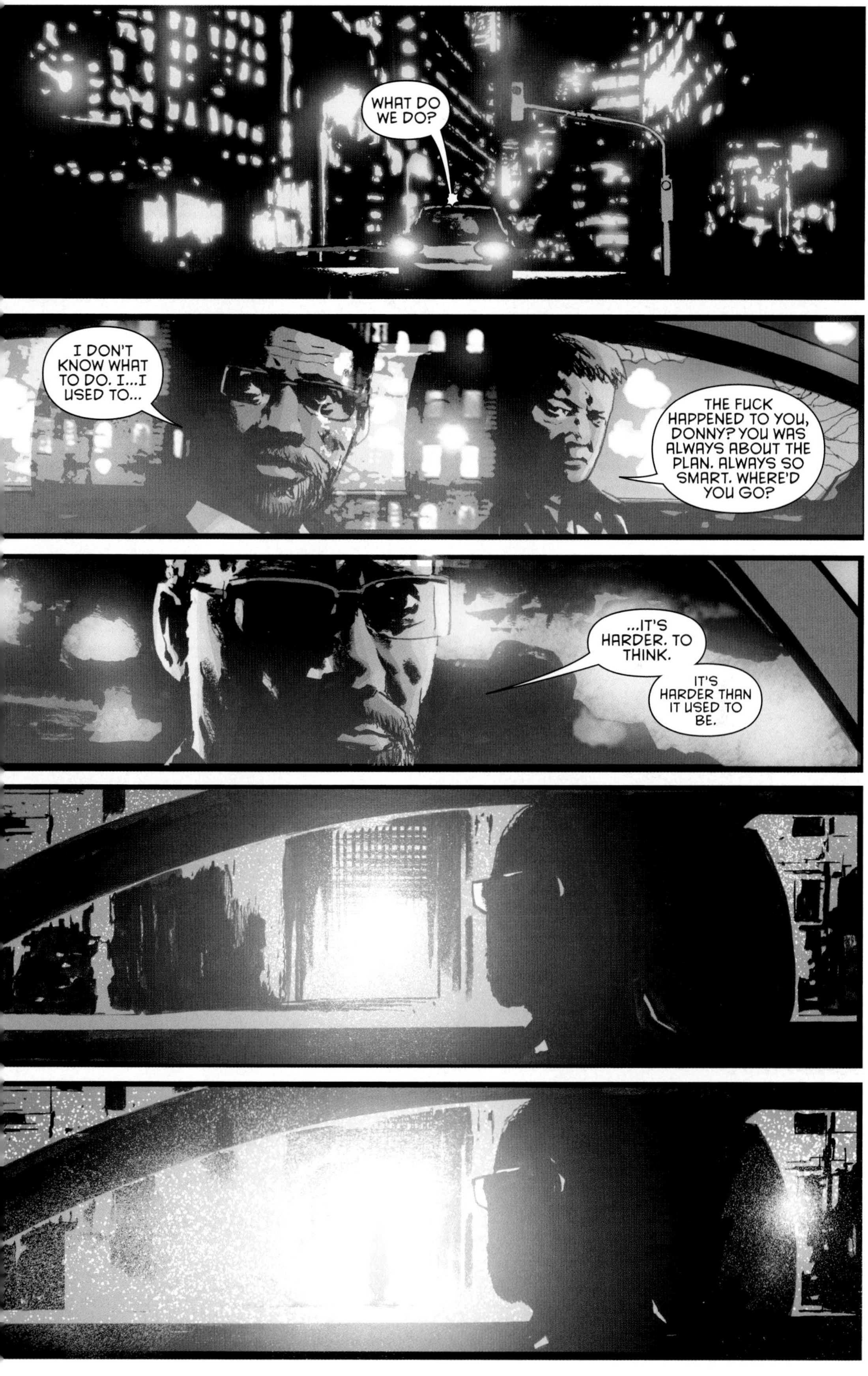
WHAT DO WE DO?
I DON'T KNOW WHAT TO DO. I...I USED TO...
THE FUCK HAPPENED TO YOU, DONNY? YOU WAS ALWAYS ABOUT THE PLAN. ALWAYS SO SMART. WHERE'D YOU GO?
...IT'S HARDER. TO THINK.
IT'S HARDER THAN IT USED TO BE.

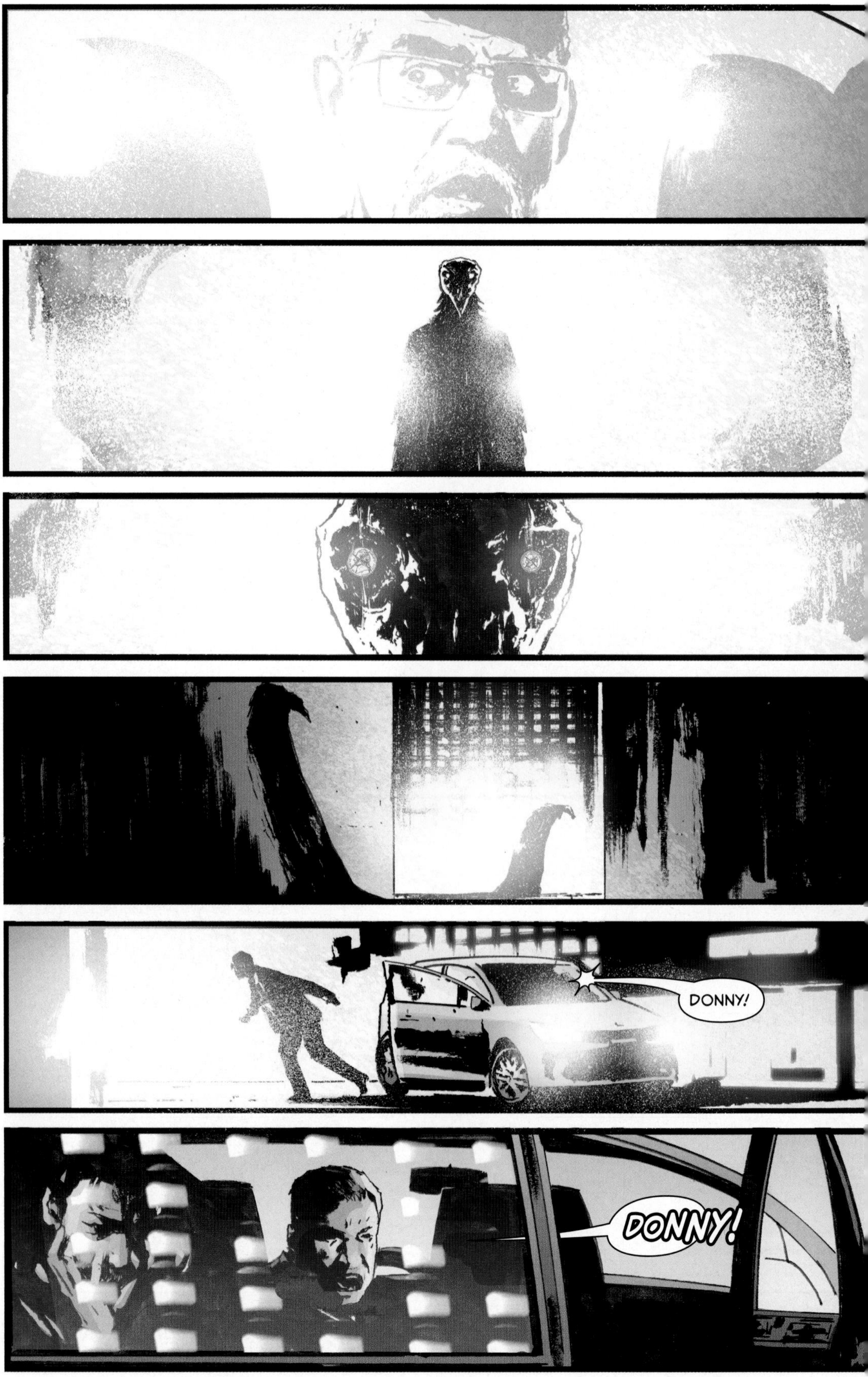
DONNY!
DONNY!

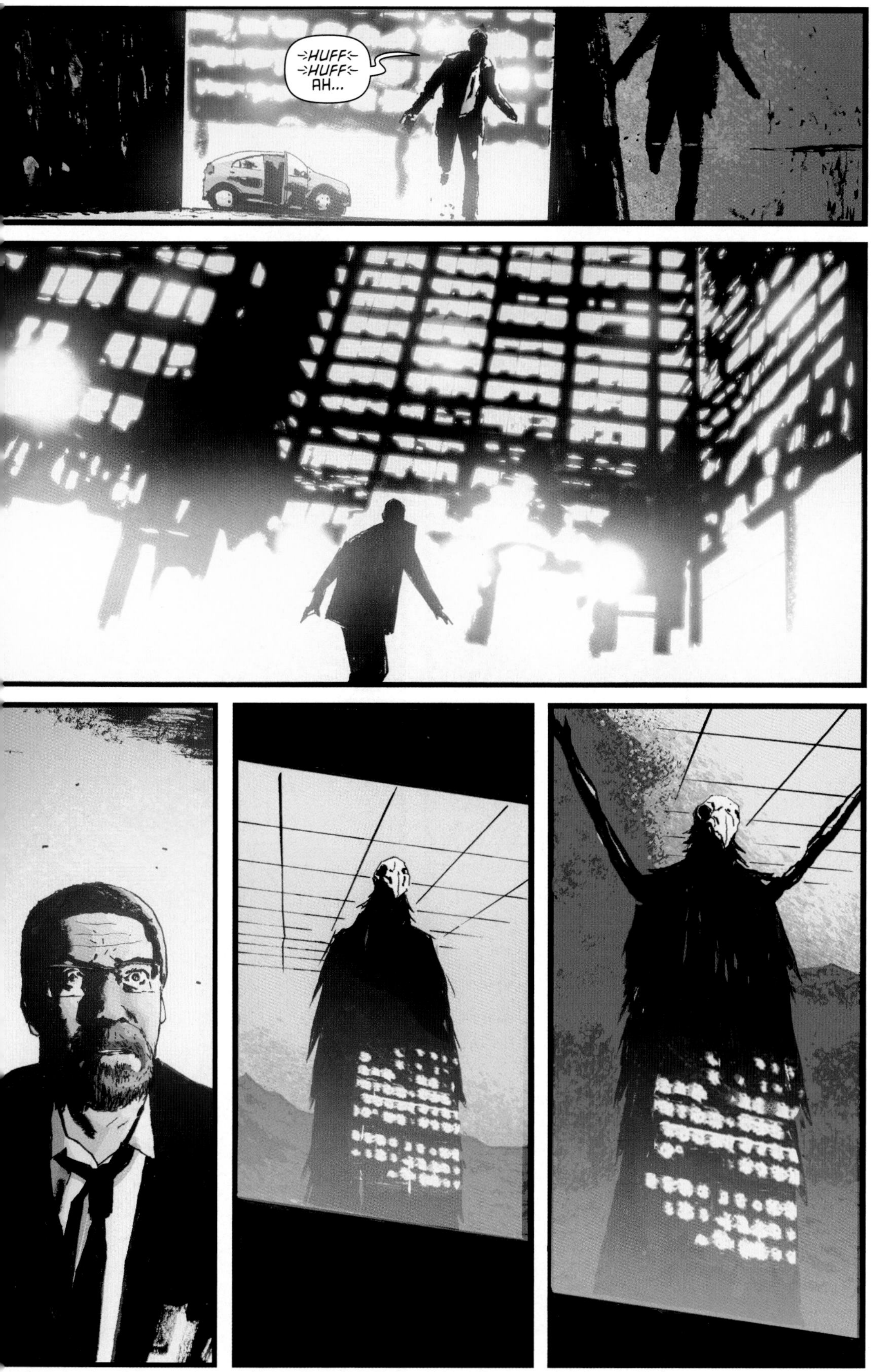

=HUFF= =HUFF= AH...

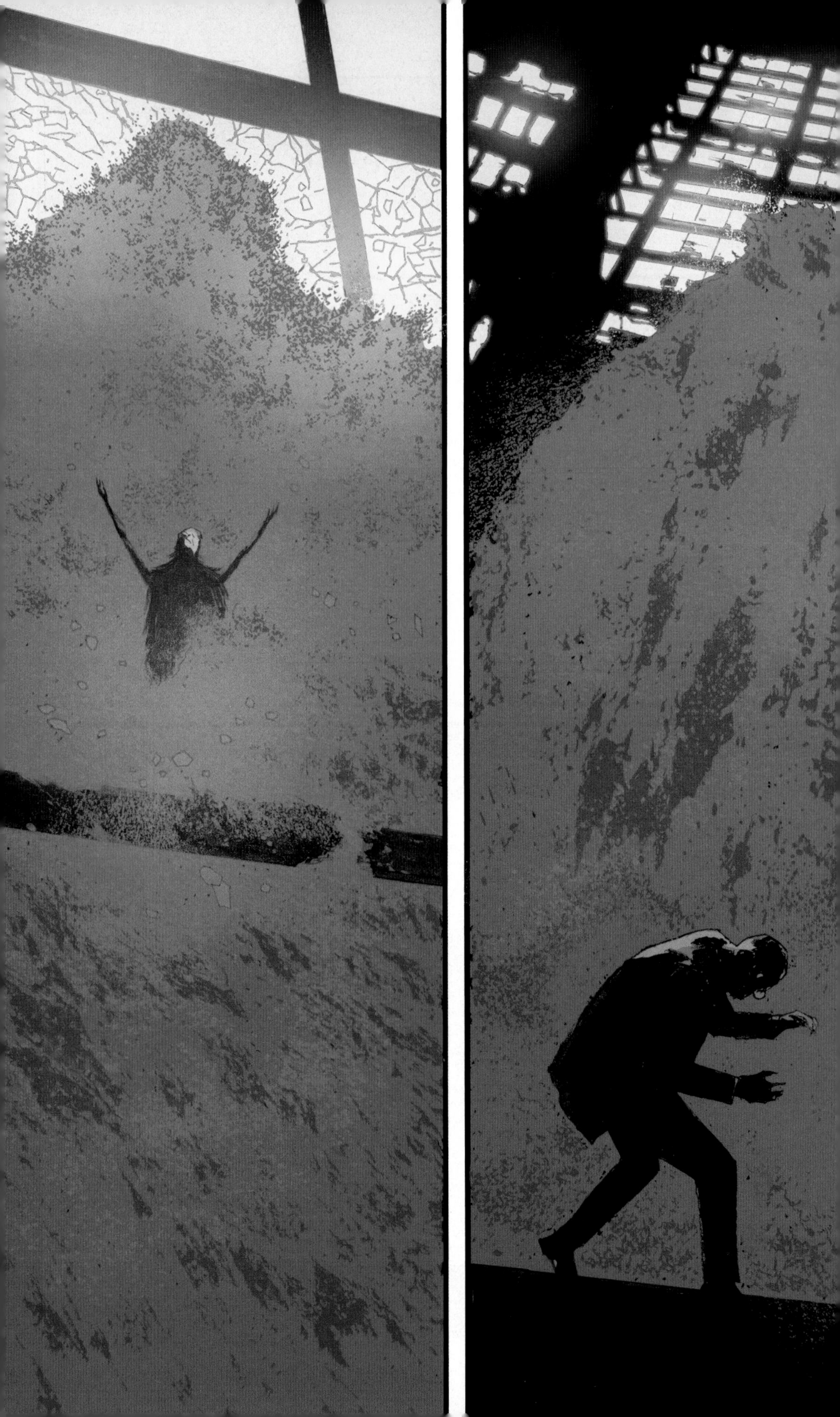

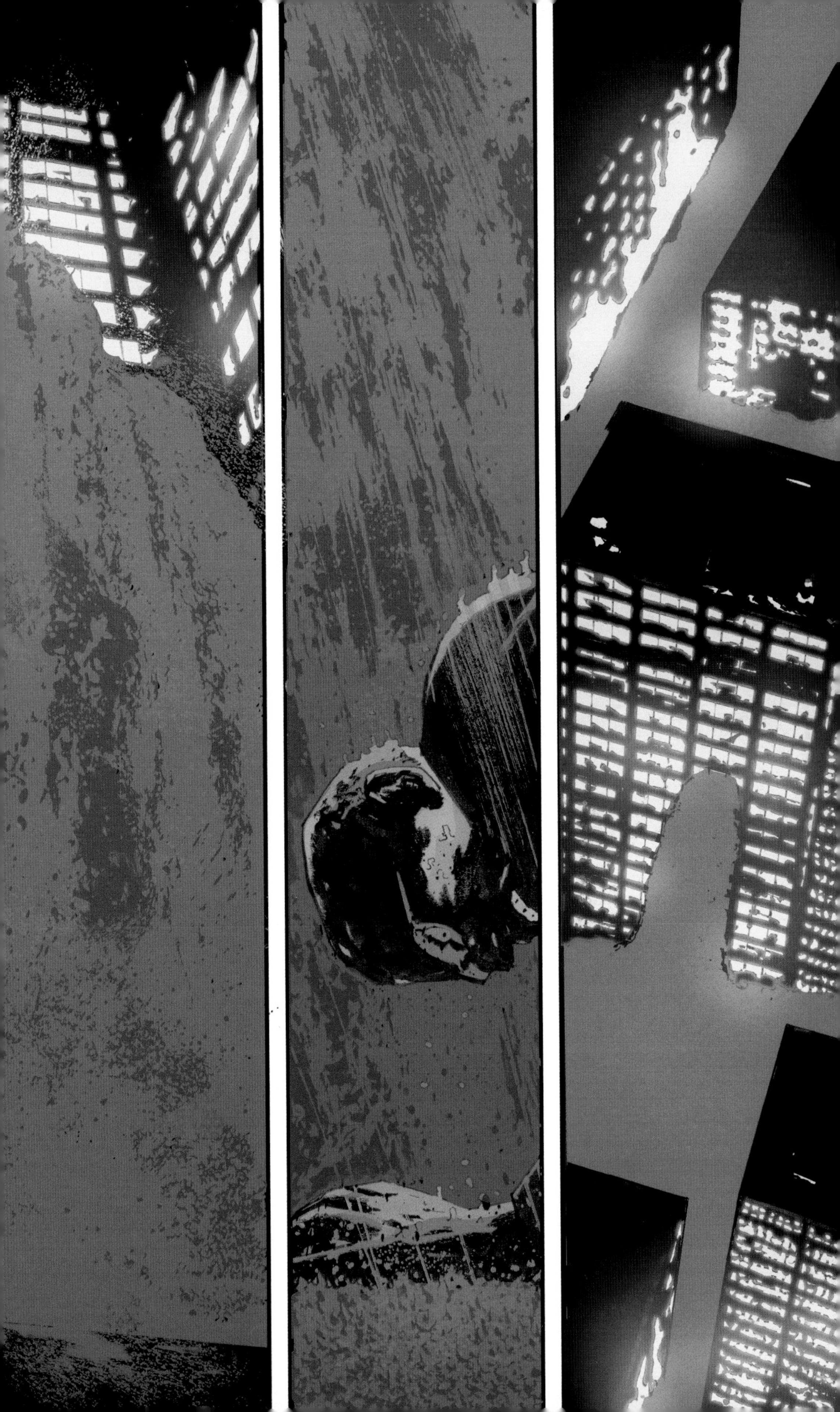

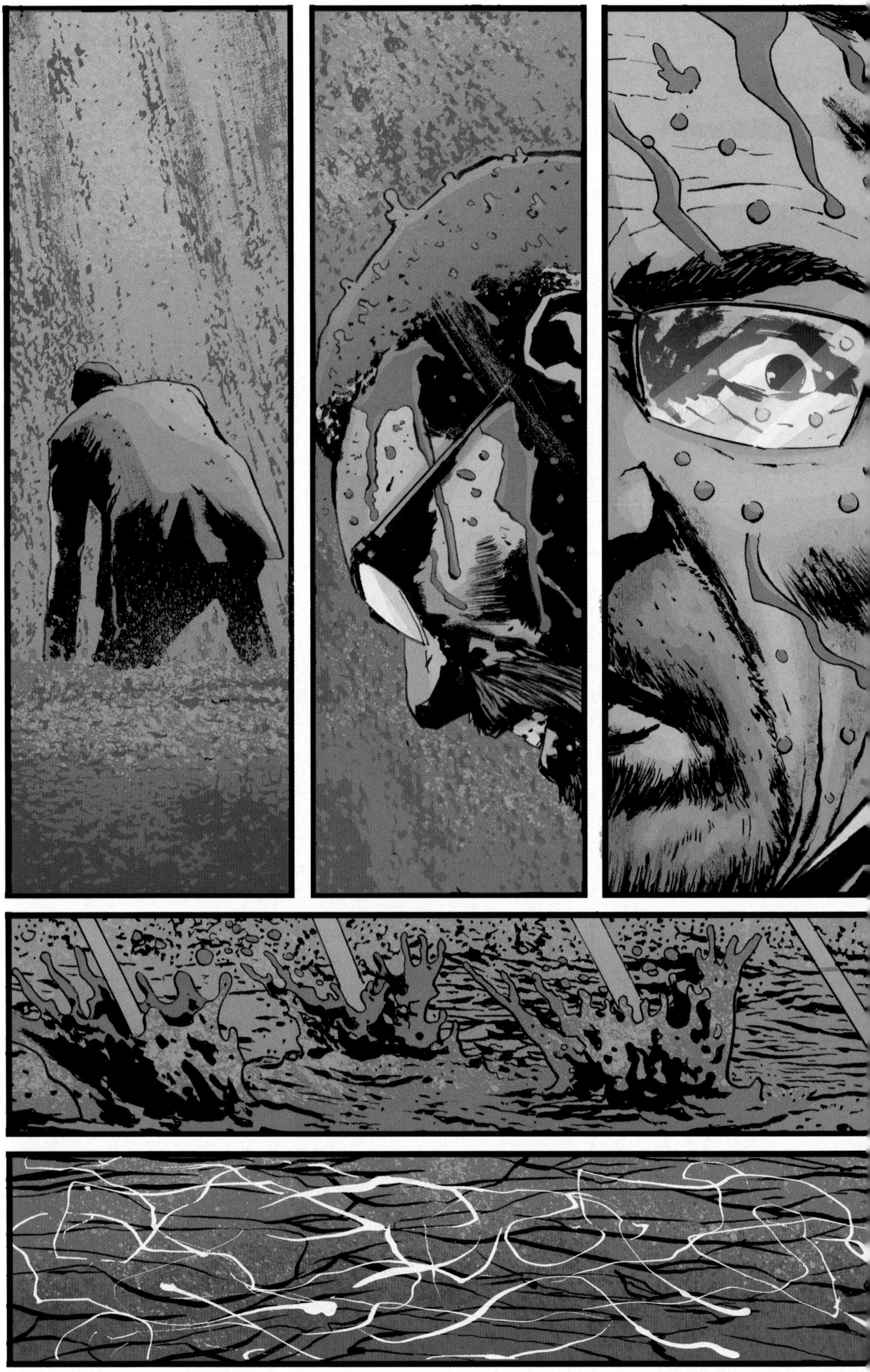

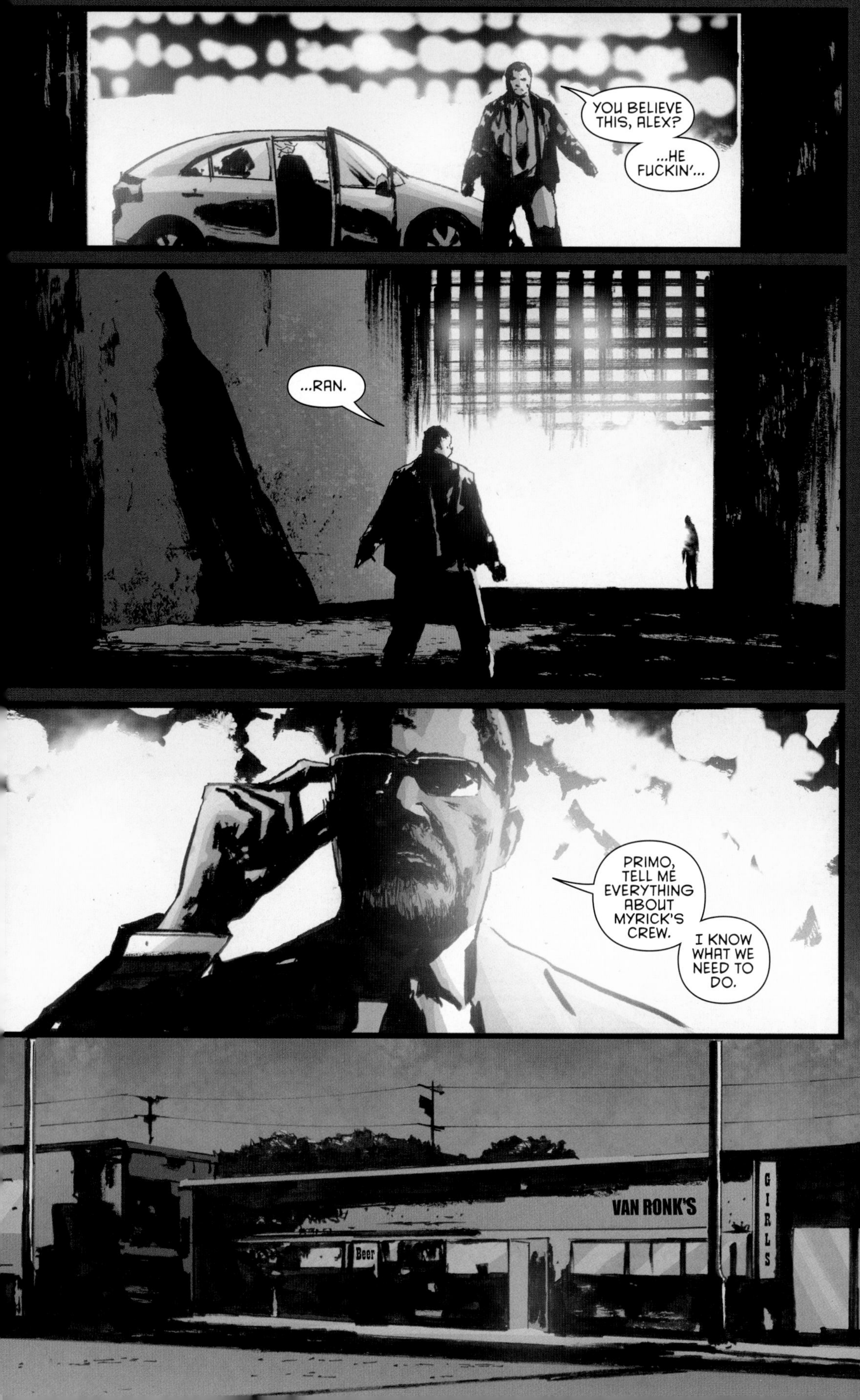
YOU BELIEVE THIS, ALEX?
...HE FUCKIN'...
...RAN.
PRIMO, TELL ME EVERYTHING ABOUT MYRICK'S CREW.
I KNOW WHAT WE NEED TO DO.
VAN RONK'S
Beer
GIRLS

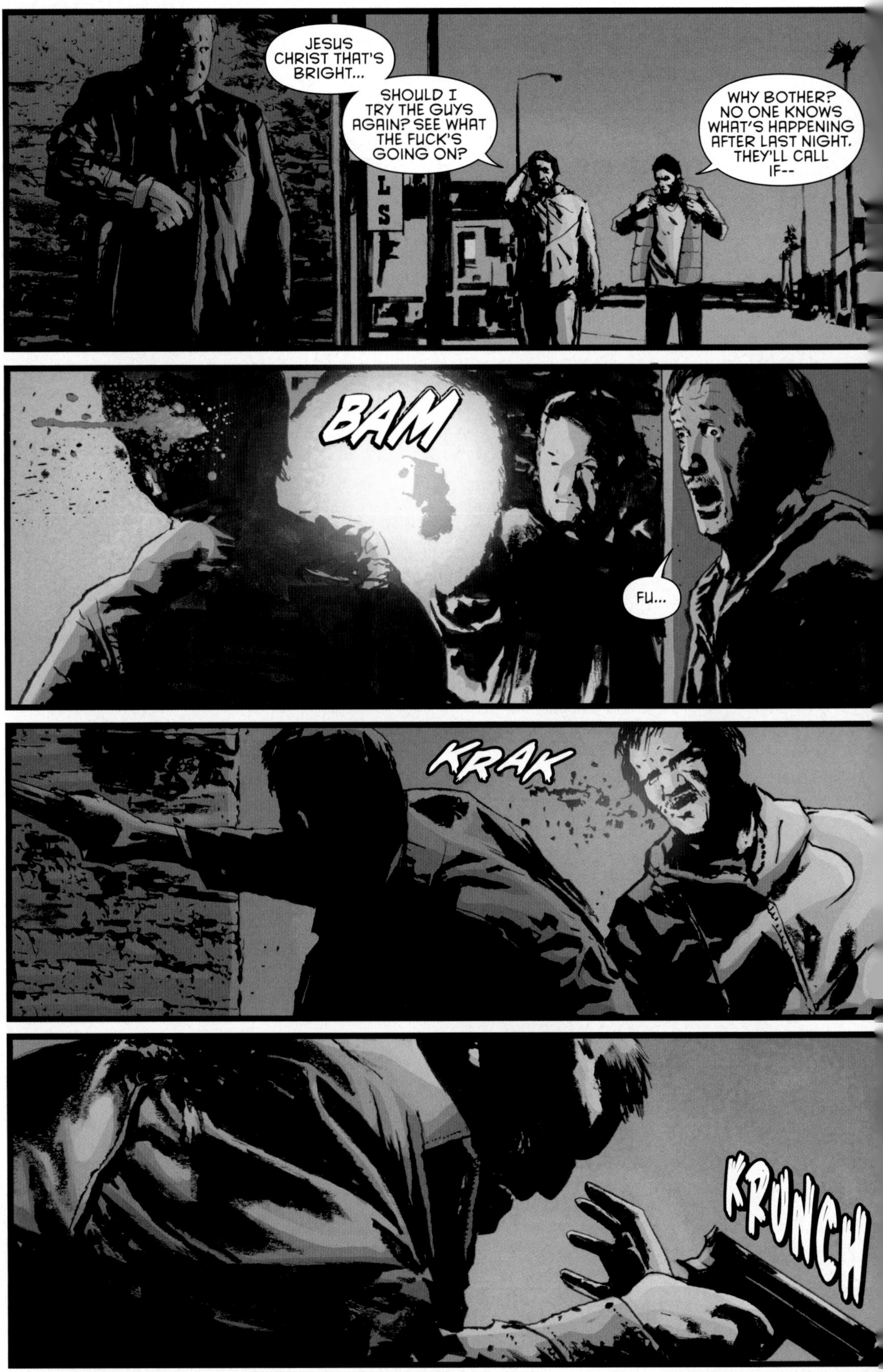
JESUS CHRIST THAT'S BRIGHT...
SHOULD I TRY THE GUYS AGAIN? SEE WHAT THE FUCK'S GOING ON?
WHY BOTHER? NO ONE KNOWS WHAT'S HAPPENING AFTER LAST NIGHT. THEY'LL CALL IF--
BAM
FU...
KRAK
KRUNCH

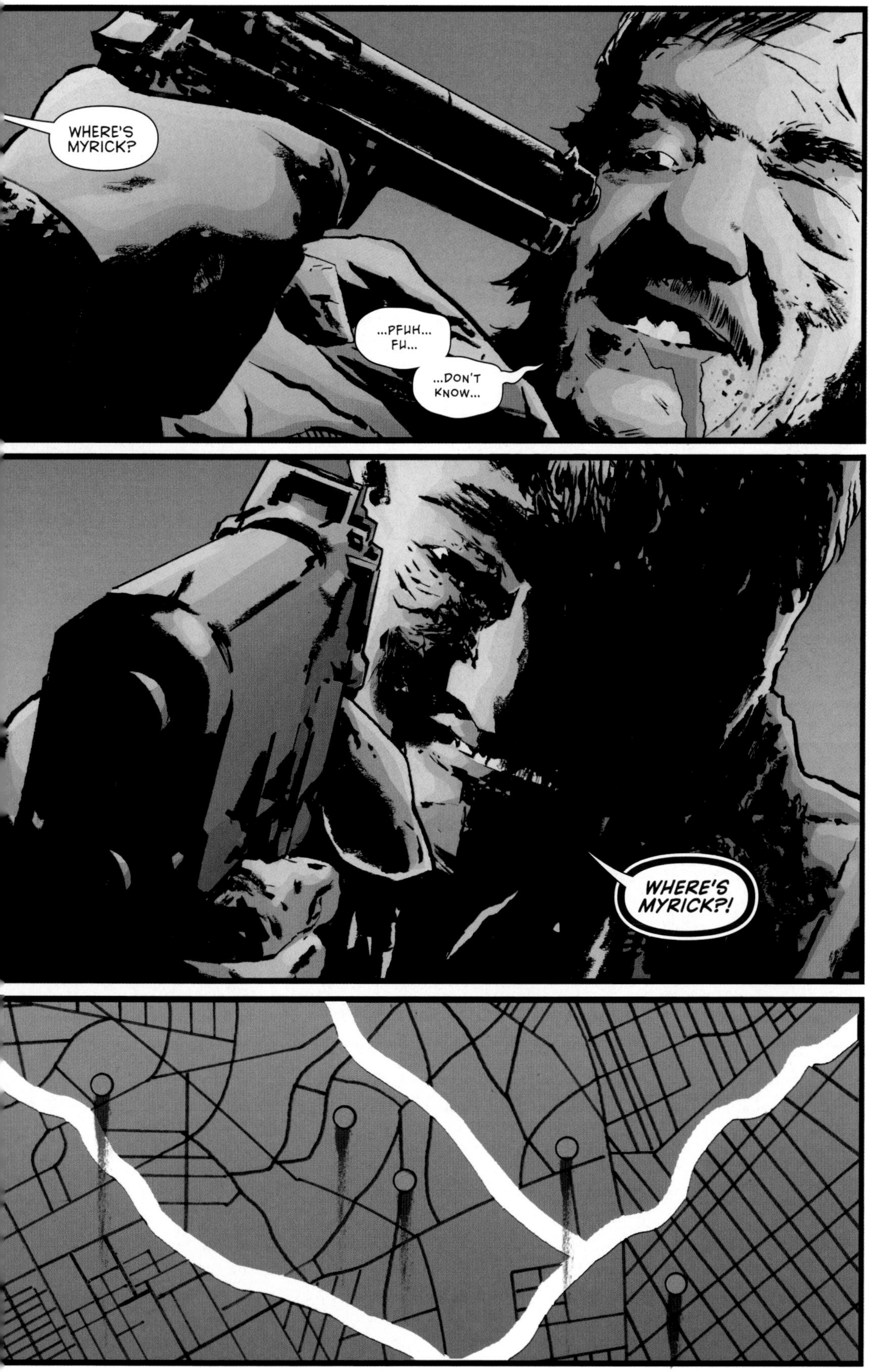
WHERE'S MYRICK?
...PFUH... FU...
...DON'T KNOW...
WHERE'S MYRICK?!

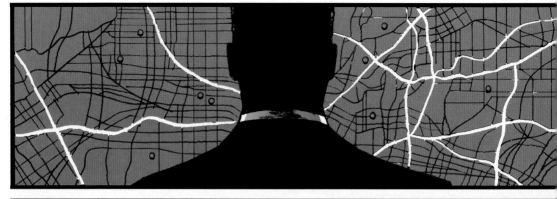

BEEP
BEEP

PRIMO? NOTHING? OKAY, JUST KEEP MOVING DOWN THE LIST.

WHERE THE FUCK ARE YOU, MYRICK?

THERE'S SOMETHING I CAN'T SEE HERE...

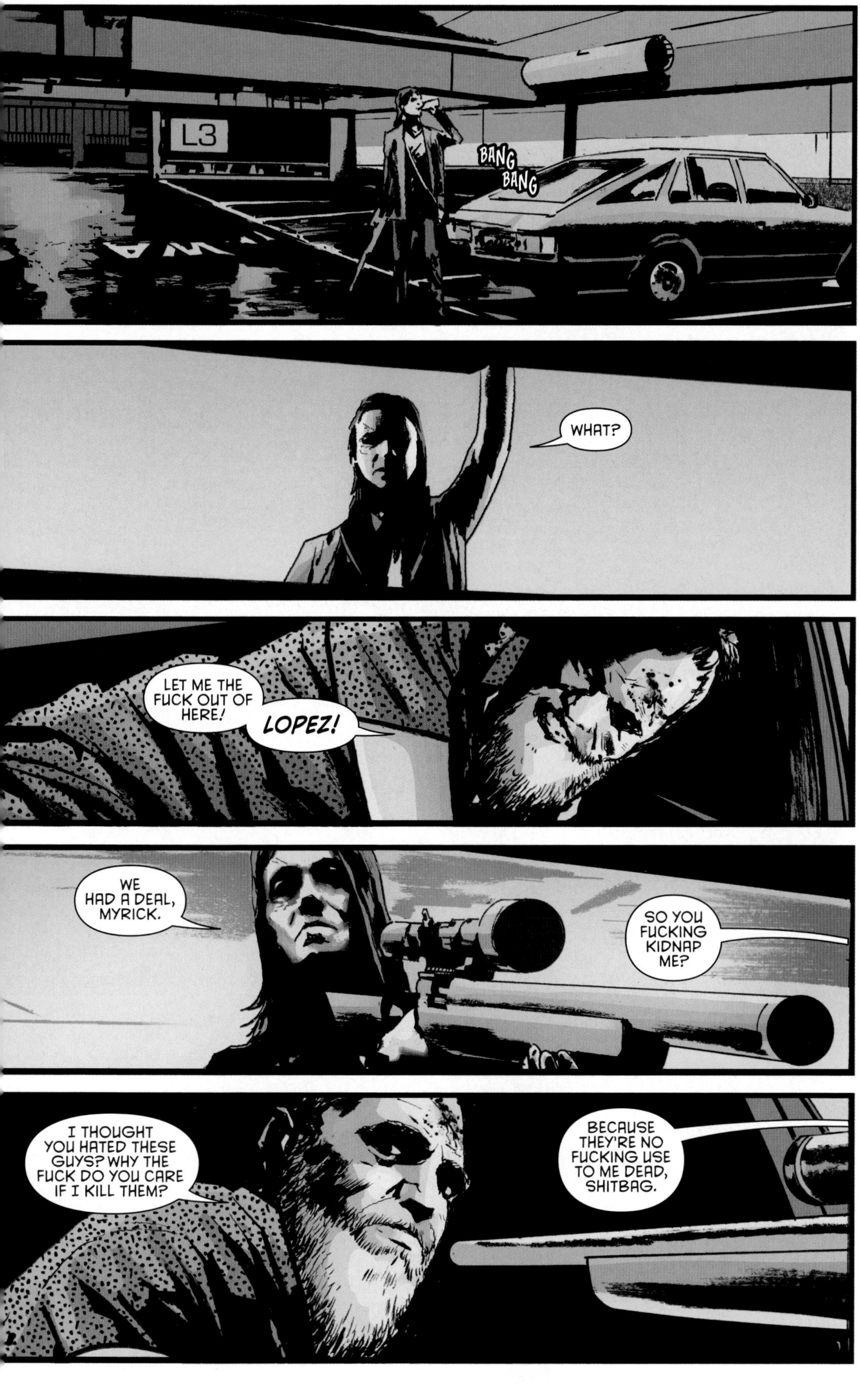
L3
BANG
BANG
WHAT?
LET ME THE FUCK OUT OF HERE!
LOPEZ!
WE HAD A DEAL, MYRICK.
SO YOU FUCKING KIDNAP ME?
I THOUGHT YOU HATED THESE GUYS? WHY THE FUCK DO YOU CARE IF I KILL THEM?
BECAUSE THEY'RE NO FUCKING USE TO ME DEAD, SHITBAG.

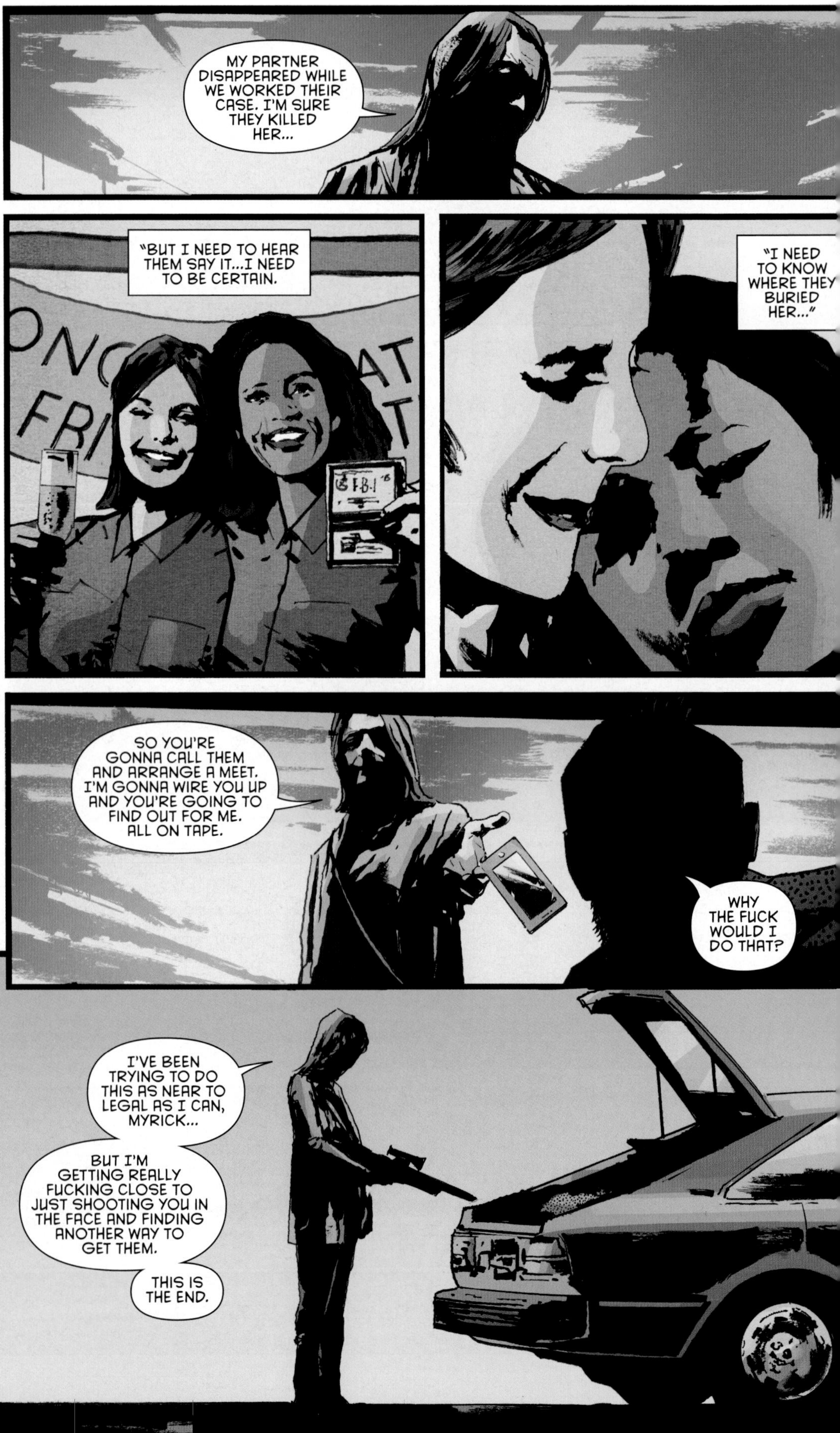

MY PARTNER DISAPPEARED WHILE WE WORKED THEIR CASE. I'M SURE THEY KILLED HER...
"BUT I NEED TO HEAR THEM SAY IT...I NEED TO BE CERTAIN.
F.B.I
"I NEED TO KNOW WHERE THEY BURIED HER..."
SO YOU'RE GONNA CALL THEM AND ARRANGE A MEET. I'M GONNA WIRE YOU UP AND YOU'RE GOING TO FIND OUT FOR ME. ALL ON TAPE.
WHY THE FUCK WOULD I DO THAT?
I'VE BEEN TRYING TO DO THIS AS NEAR TO LEGAL AS I CAN, MYRICK...
BUT I'M GETTING REALLY FUCKING CLOSE TO JUST SHOOTING YOU IN THE FACE AND FINDING ANOTHER WAY TO GET THEM.
THIS IS THE END.

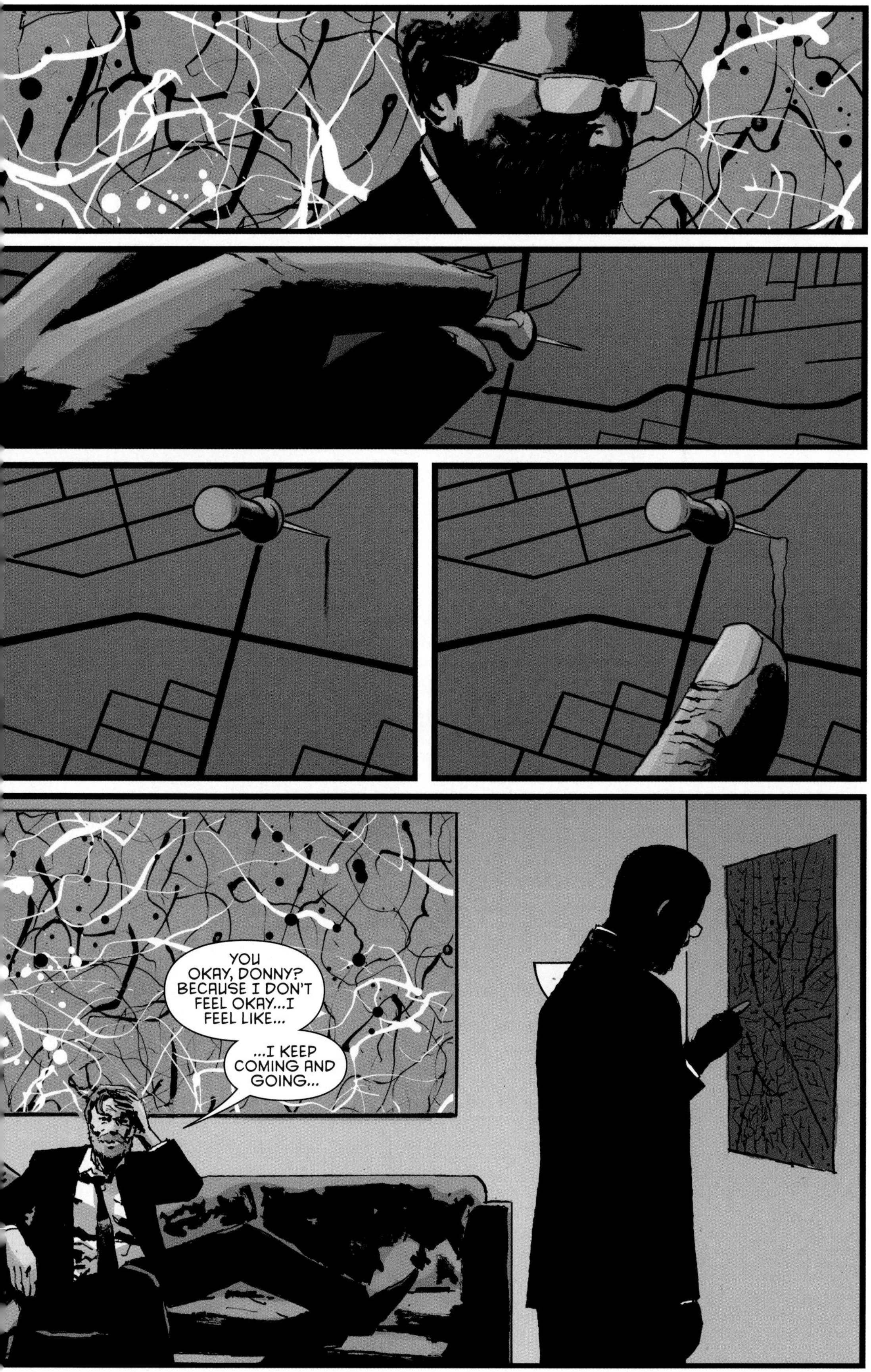
YOU OKAY, DONNY? BECAUSE I DON'T FEEL OKAY...I FEEL LIKE...
...I KEEP COMING AND GOING...

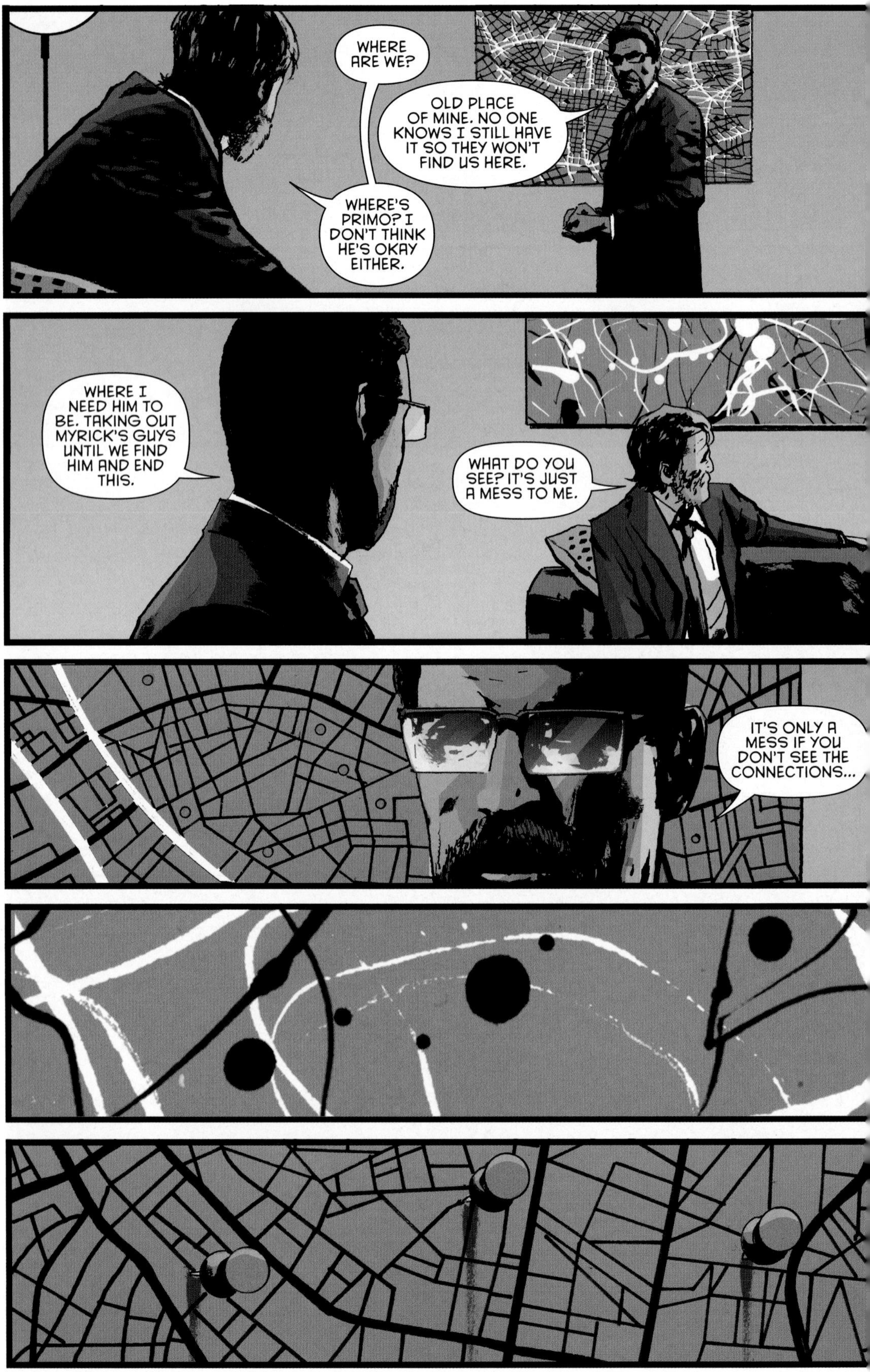
WHERE ARE WE?
OLD PLACE OF MINE. NO ONE KNOWS I STILL HAVE IT SO THEY WON'T FIND US HERE.
WHERE'S PRIMO? I DON'T THINK HE'S OKAY EITHER.
WHERE I NEED HIM TO BE. TAKING OUT MYRICK'S GUYS UNTIL WE FIND HIM AND END THIS.
WHAT DO YOU SEE? IT'S JUST A MESS TO ME.
IT'S ONLY A MESS IF YOU DON'T SEE THE CONNECTIONS...

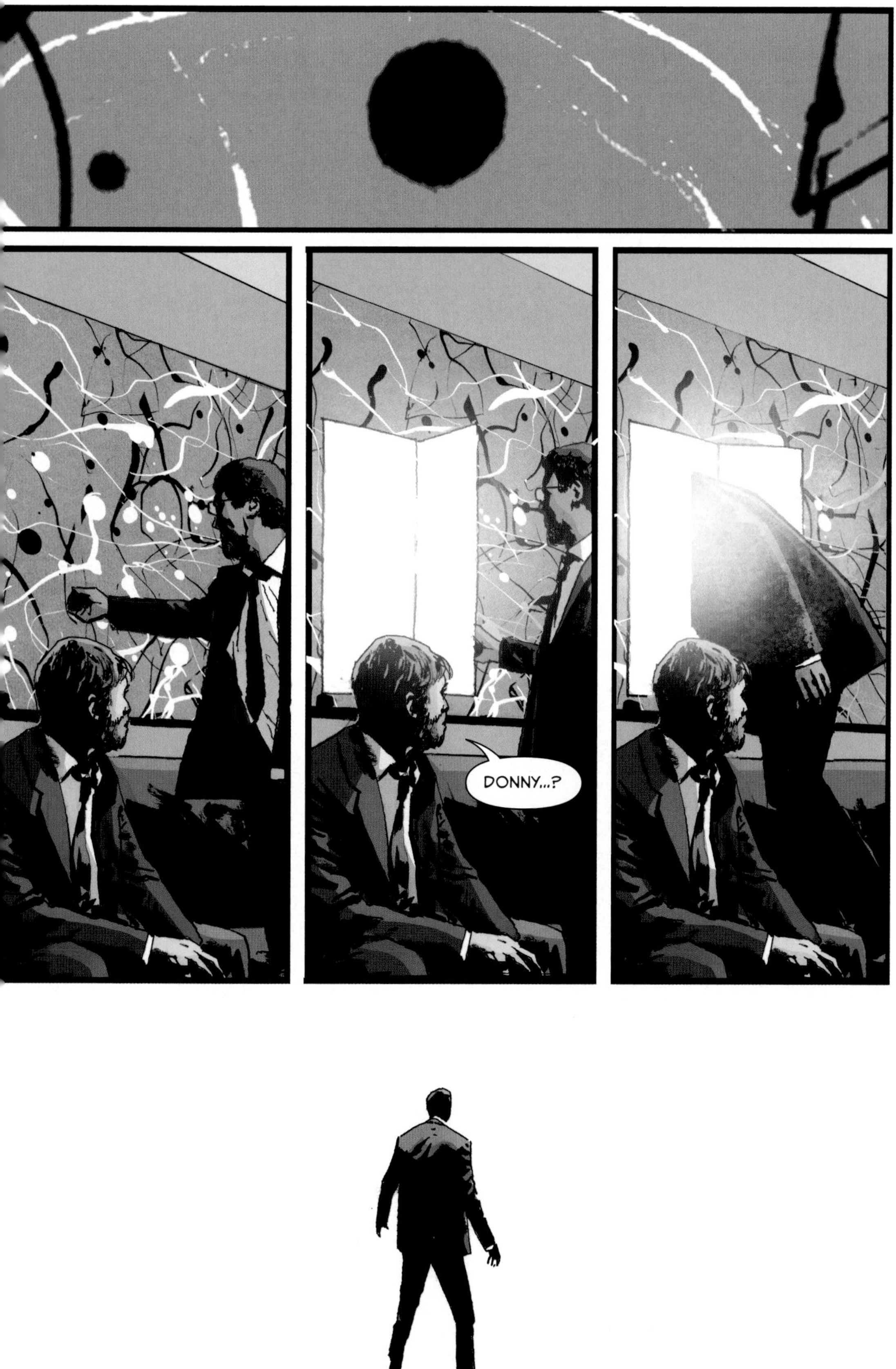
DONNY...?

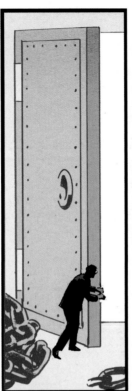

--WORKING WITH THE D.E.A., YOU'RE DOING A GOOD THING HERE, DONNY.

NO, I GOT CAUGHT WITH TEN KILOS... IT'S THE SMART THING...

IF YOU TAKE A STEP BACK AND LOOK AT IT ALL, THERE'S NO OTHER WAY IT CAN WORK. IT'S GOT TO BE THIS.

THE GUYS CAN'T KNOW THOUGH. THEY CAN NEVER KNOW.

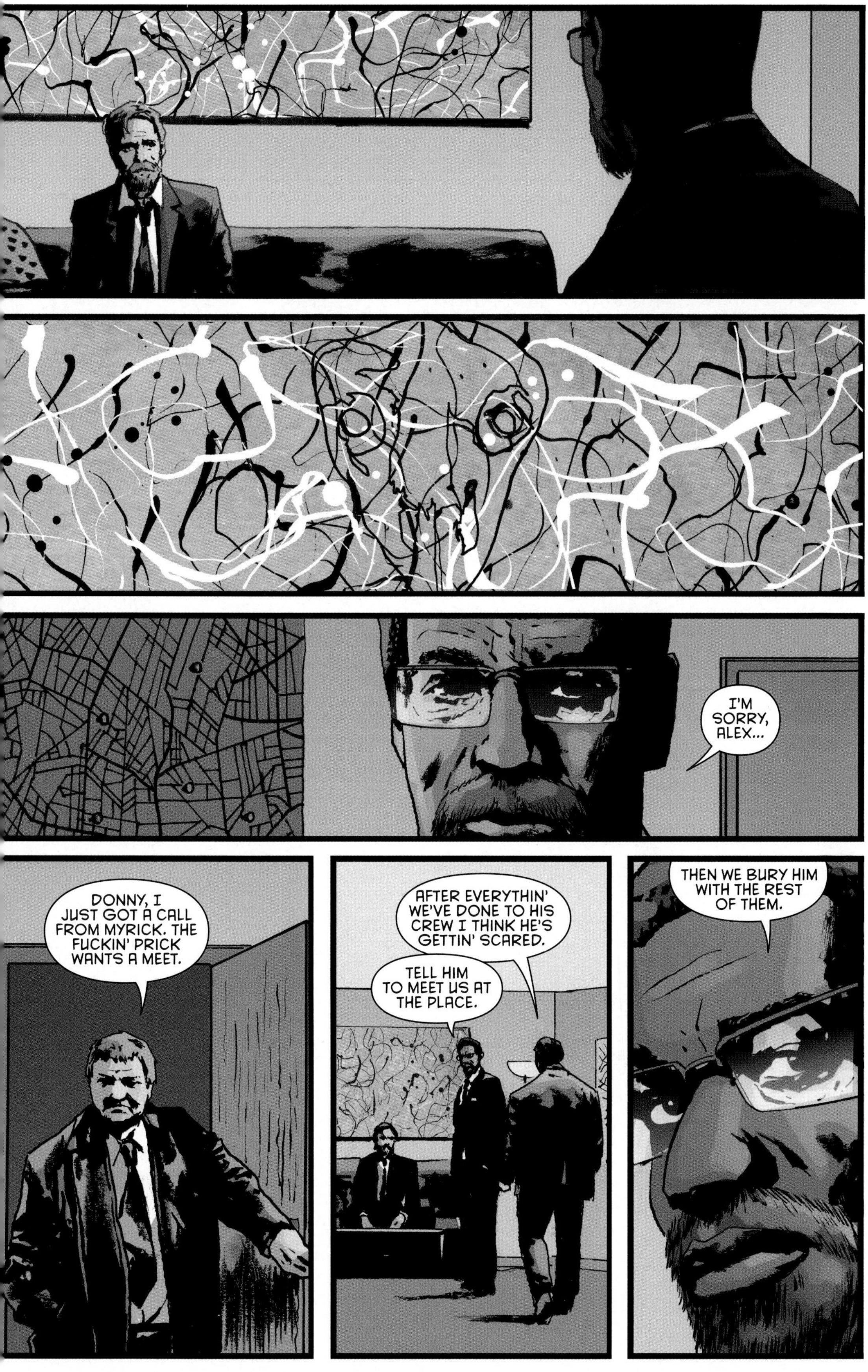
I'M SORRY, ALEX...
DONNY, I JUST GOT A CALL FROM MYRICK. THE FUCKIN' PRICK WANTS A MEET.
AFTER EVERYTHIN' WE'VE DONE TO HIS CREW I THINK HE'S GETTIN' SCARED.
TELL HIM TO MEET US AT THE PLACE.
THEN WE BURY HIM WITH THE REST OF THEM.

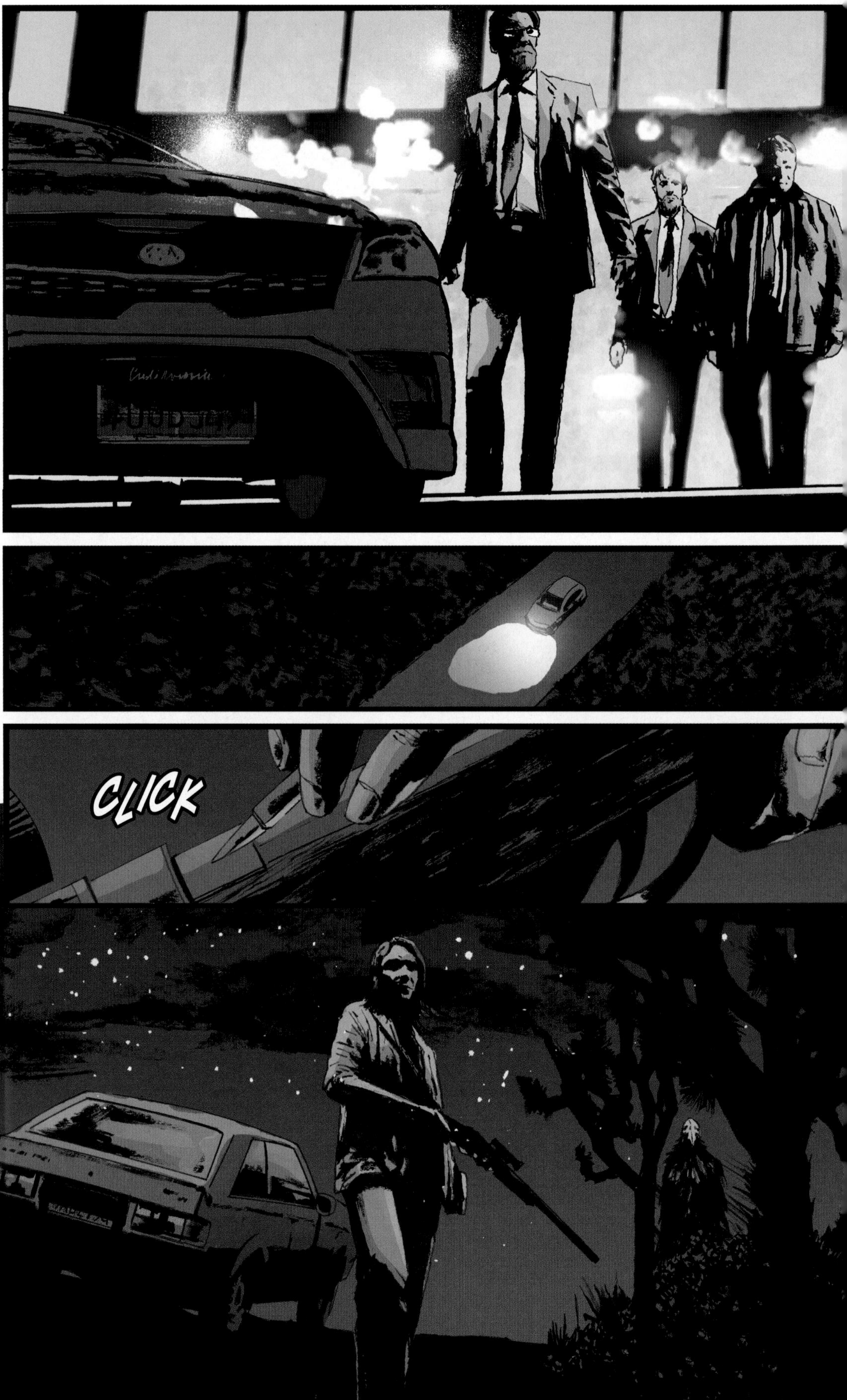
CLICK

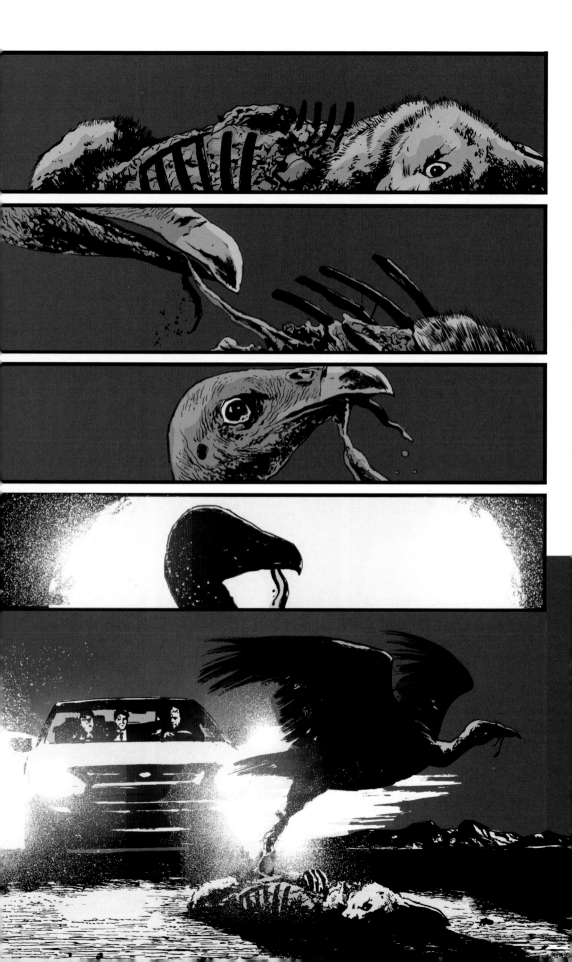

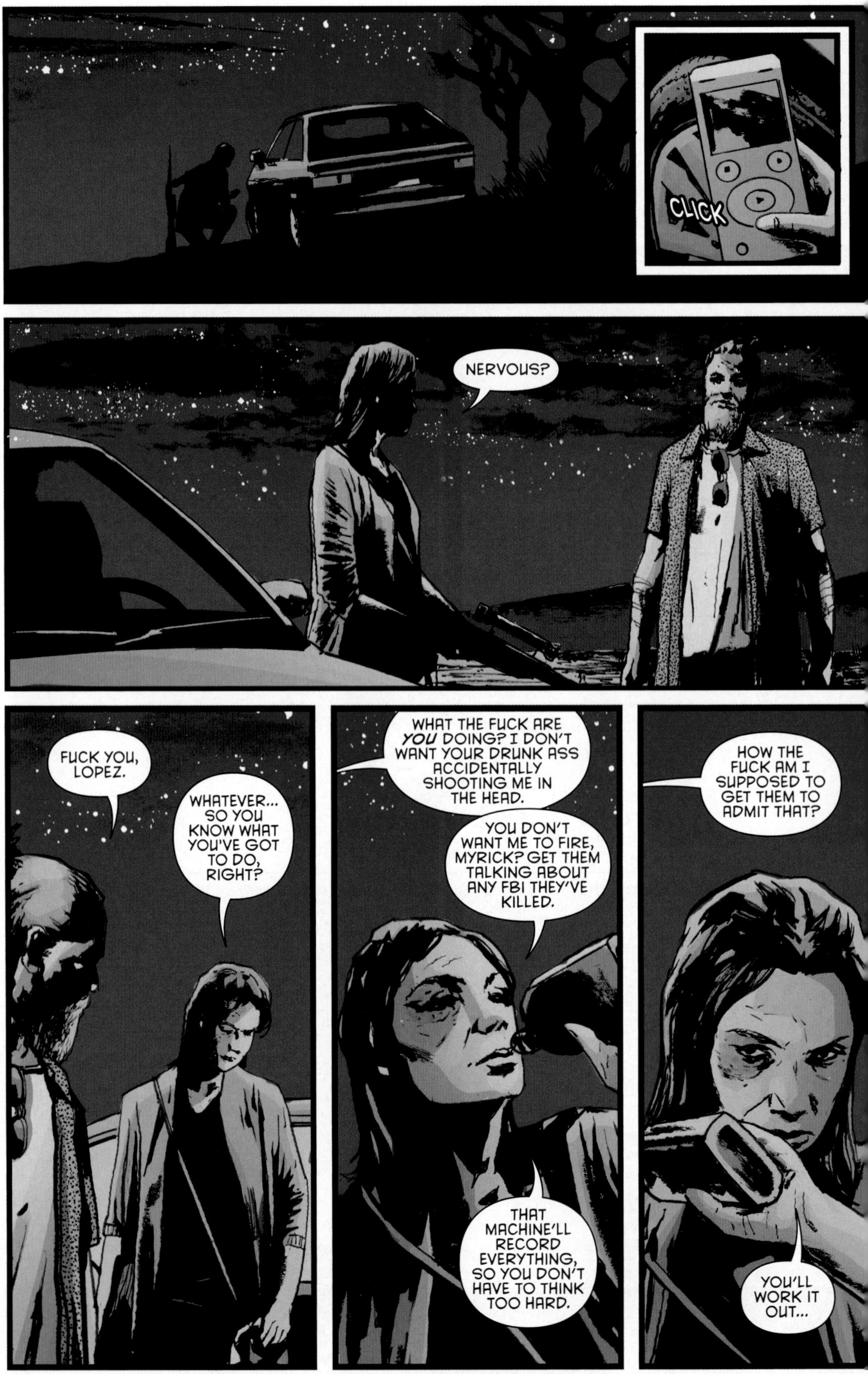
CLICK
NERVOUS?
FUCK YOU, LOPEZ.
WHATEVER... SO YOU KNOW WHAT YOU'VE GOT TO DO, RIGHT?
WHAT THE FUCK ARE *YOU* DOING? I DON'T WANT YOUR DRUNK ASS ACCIDENTALLY SHOOTING ME IN THE HEAD.
YOU DON'T WANT ME TO FIRE, MYRICK? GET THEM TALKING ABOUT ANY FBI THEY'VE KILLED.
THAT MACHINE'LL RECORD EVERYTHING, SO YOU DON'T HAVE TO THINK TOO HARD.
HOW THE FUCK AM I SUPPOSED TO GET THEM TO ADMIT THAT?
YOU'LL WORK IT OUT...

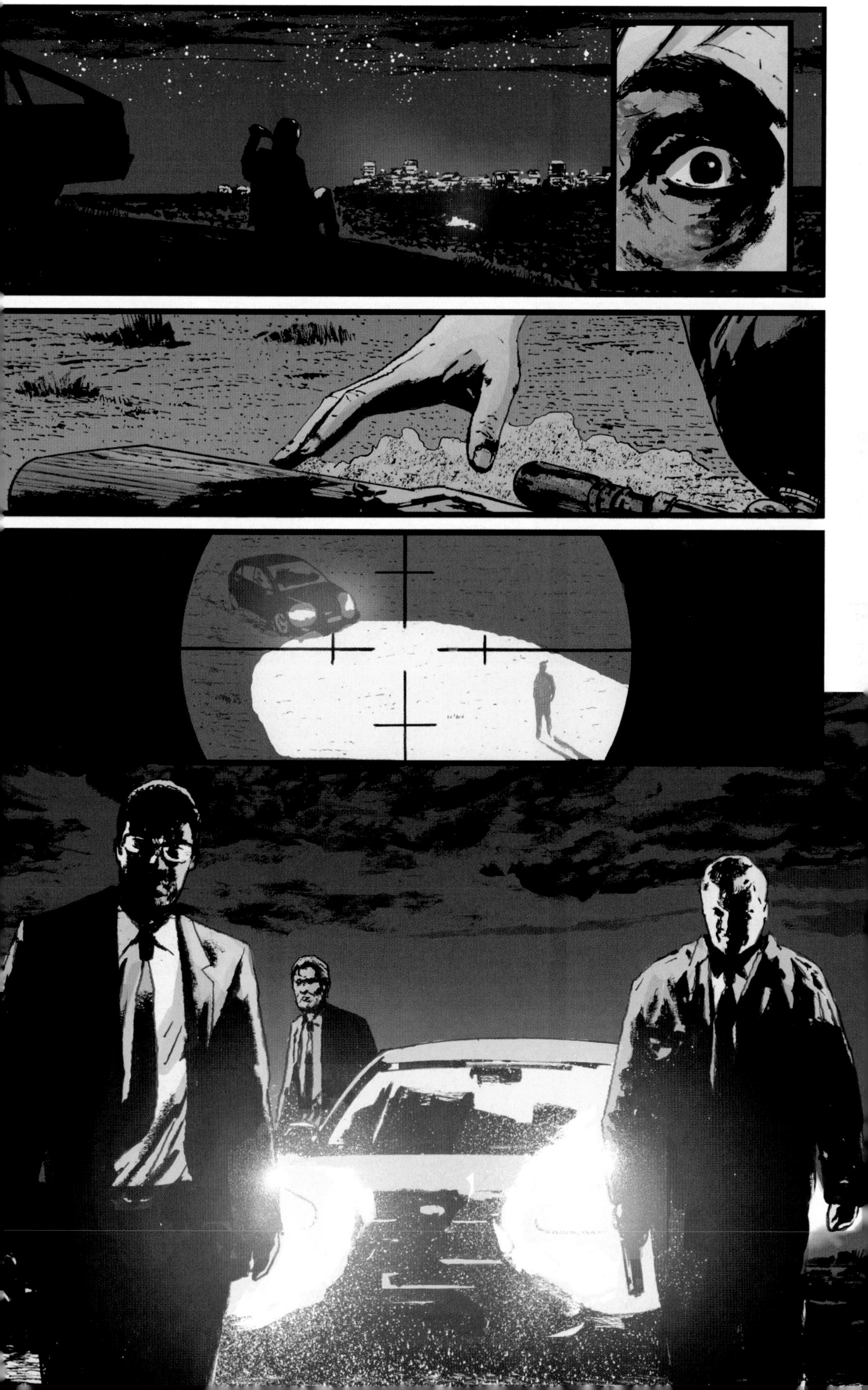

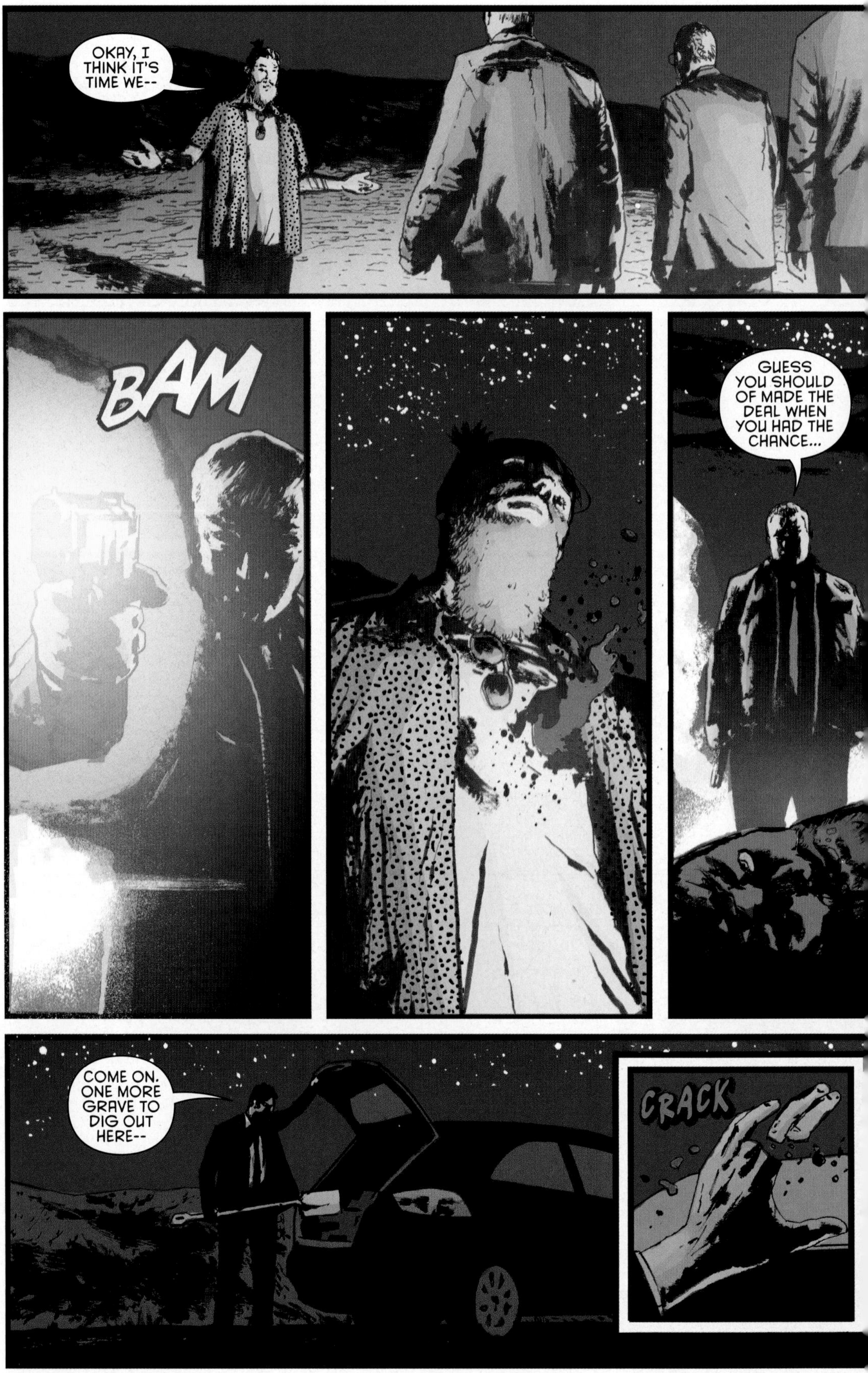
OKAY, I THINK IT'S TIME WE--
BAM
GUESS YOU SHOULD OF MADE THE DEAL WHEN YOU HAD THE CHANCE...
COME ON. ONE MORE GRAVE TO DIG OUT HERE--
CRACK

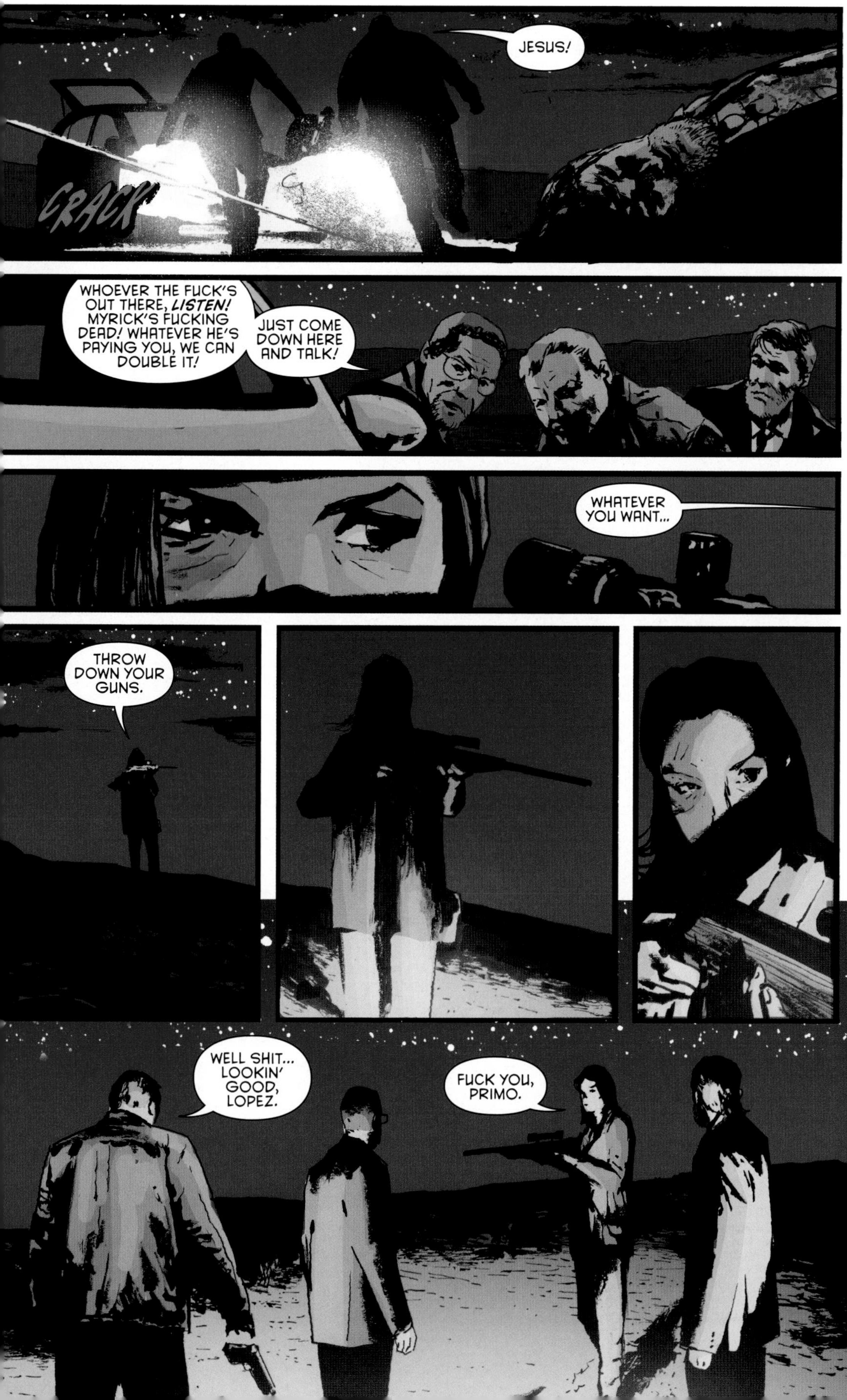
JESUS!
CRACK
WHOEVER THE FUCK'S OUT THERE, LISTEN! MYRICK'S FUCKING DEAD! WHATEVER HE'S PAYING YOU, WE CAN DOUBLE IT!
JUST COME DOWN HERE AND TALK!
WHATEVER YOU WANT...
THROW DOWN YOUR GUNS.
WELL SHIT... LOOKIN' GOOD, LOPEZ.
FUCK YOU, PRIMO.

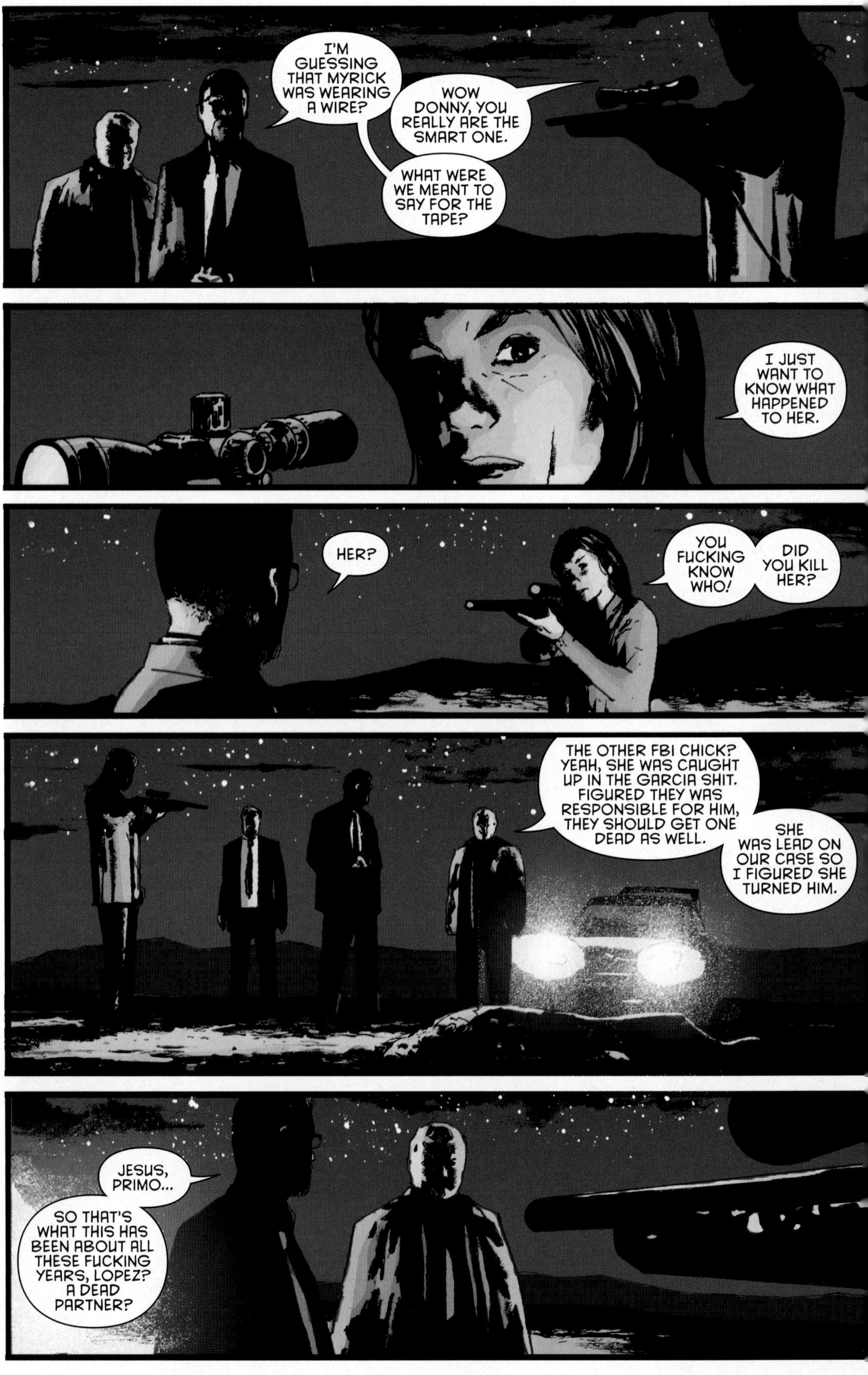
I'M GUESSING THAT MYRICK WAS WEARING A WIRE?
WOW DONNY, YOU REALLY ARE THE SMART ONE.
WHAT WERE WE MEANT TO SAY FOR THE TAPE?
I JUST WANT TO KNOW WHAT HAPPENED TO HER.
HER?
YOU FUCKING KNOW WHO!
DID YOU KILL HER?
THE OTHER FBI CHICK? YEAH, SHE WAS CAUGHT UP IN THE GARCIA SHIT. FIGURED THEY WAS RESPONSIBLE FOR HIM, THEY SHOULD GET ONE DEAD AS WELL.
SHE WAS LEAD ON OUR CASE SO I FIGURED SHE TURNED HIM.
JESUS, PRIMO...
SO THAT'S WHAT THIS HAS BEEN ABOUT ALL THESE FUCKING YEARS, LOPEZ? A DEAD PARTNER?

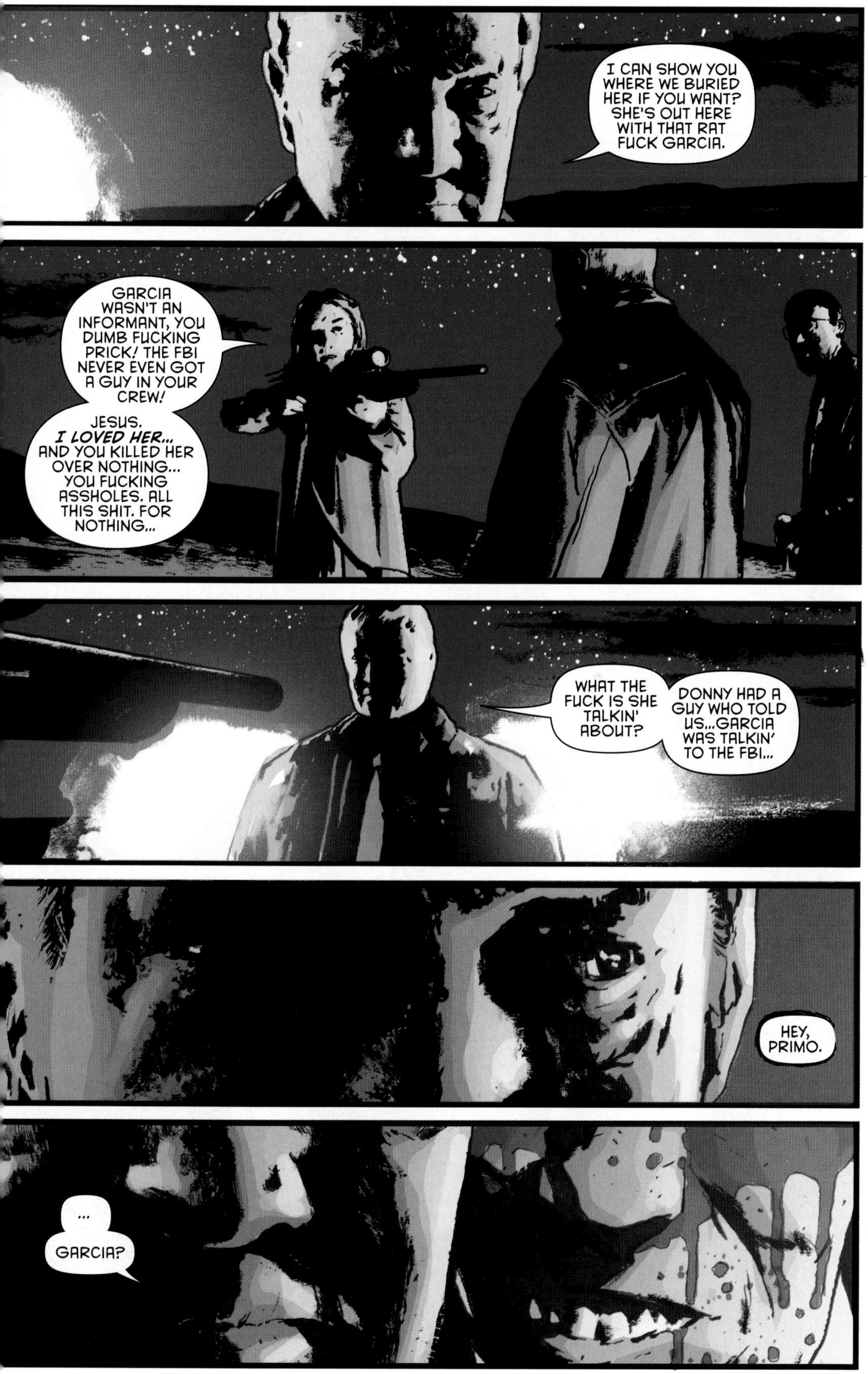
I CAN SHOW YOU WHERE WE BURIED HER IF YOU WANT? SHE'S OUT HERE WITH THAT RAT FUCK GARCIA.
GARCIA WASN'T AN INFORMANT, YOU DUMB FUCKING PRICK! THE FBI NEVER EVEN GOT A GUY IN YOUR CREW!
JESUS. *I LOVED HER...* AND YOU KILLED HER OVER NOTHING... YOU FUCKING ASSHOLES. ALL THIS SHIT. FOR NOTHING...
WHAT THE FUCK IS SHE TALKIN' ABOUT?
DONNY HAD A GUY WHO TOLD US...GARCIA WAS TALKIN' TO THE FBI...
HEY, PRIMO.
...
GARCIA?

YOU DIDN'T REALLY THINK I'D DIME ON YOU GUYS, DID YOU?

I DON'T FEEL SO GOOD.

COME ON, ALEX. HOLD IT TOGETHER THEN YOU CAN GET SOME REST.

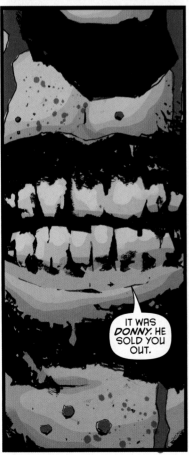

IT WAS *DONNY.* HE SOLD YOU OUT.

BUT HE HAD TO PUT THE SUSPICION ON SOMEONE ELSE...JUST IN CASE.

AND I WAS ALWAYS MORE OF A FRIEND OF *YOURS* THAN A FRIEND OF THEIRS...

...DONNY...

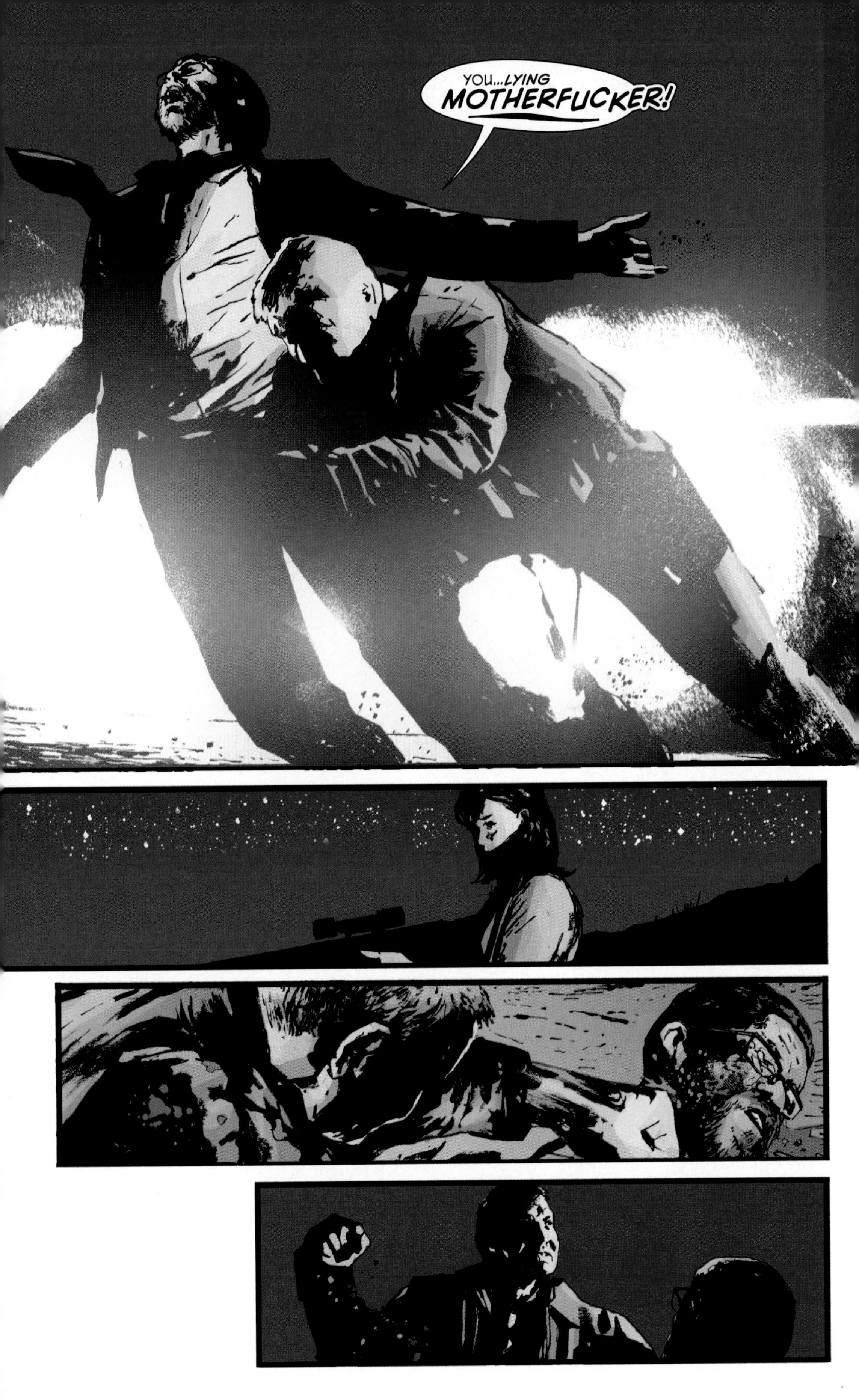
YOU...LYING MOTHERFUCKER!

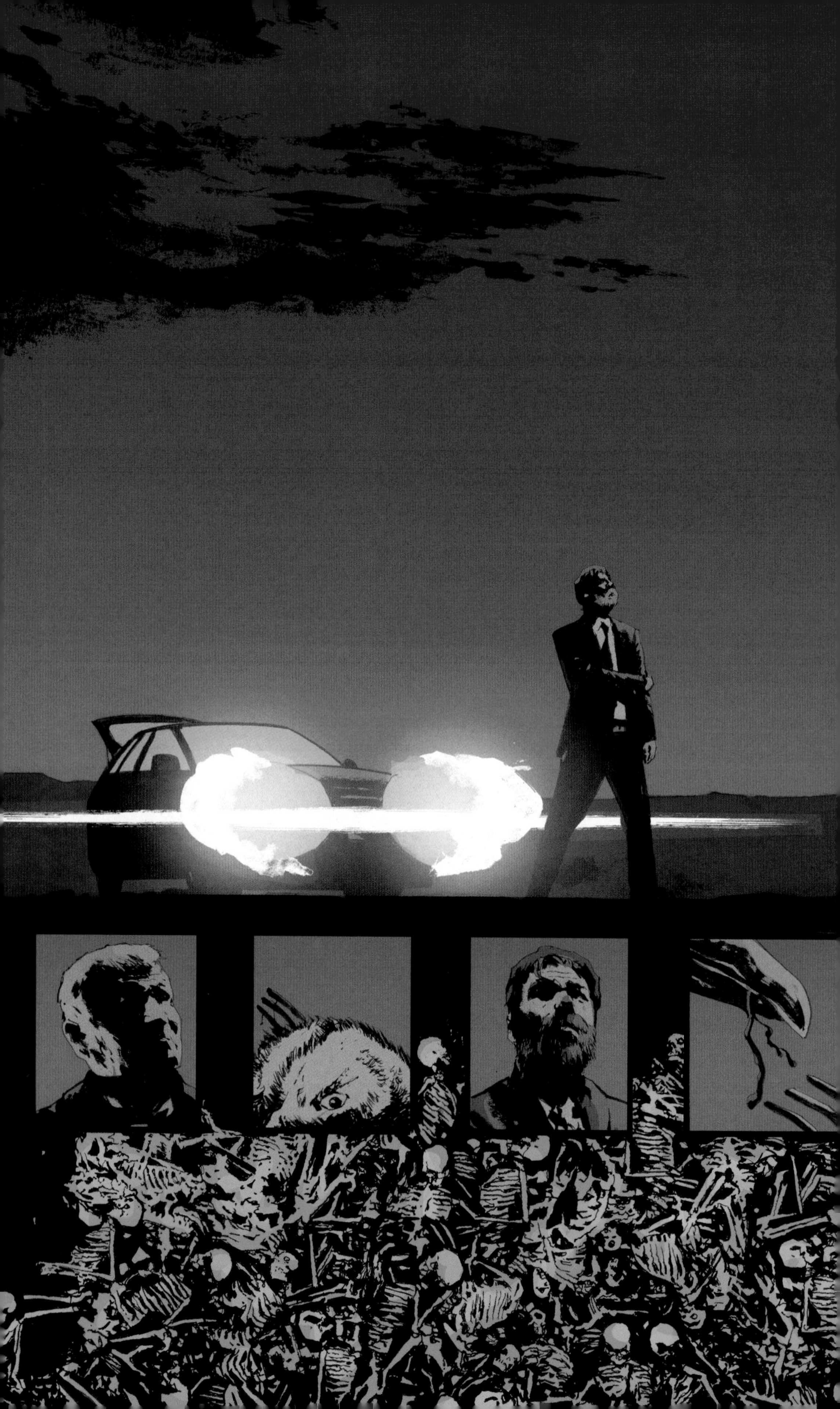

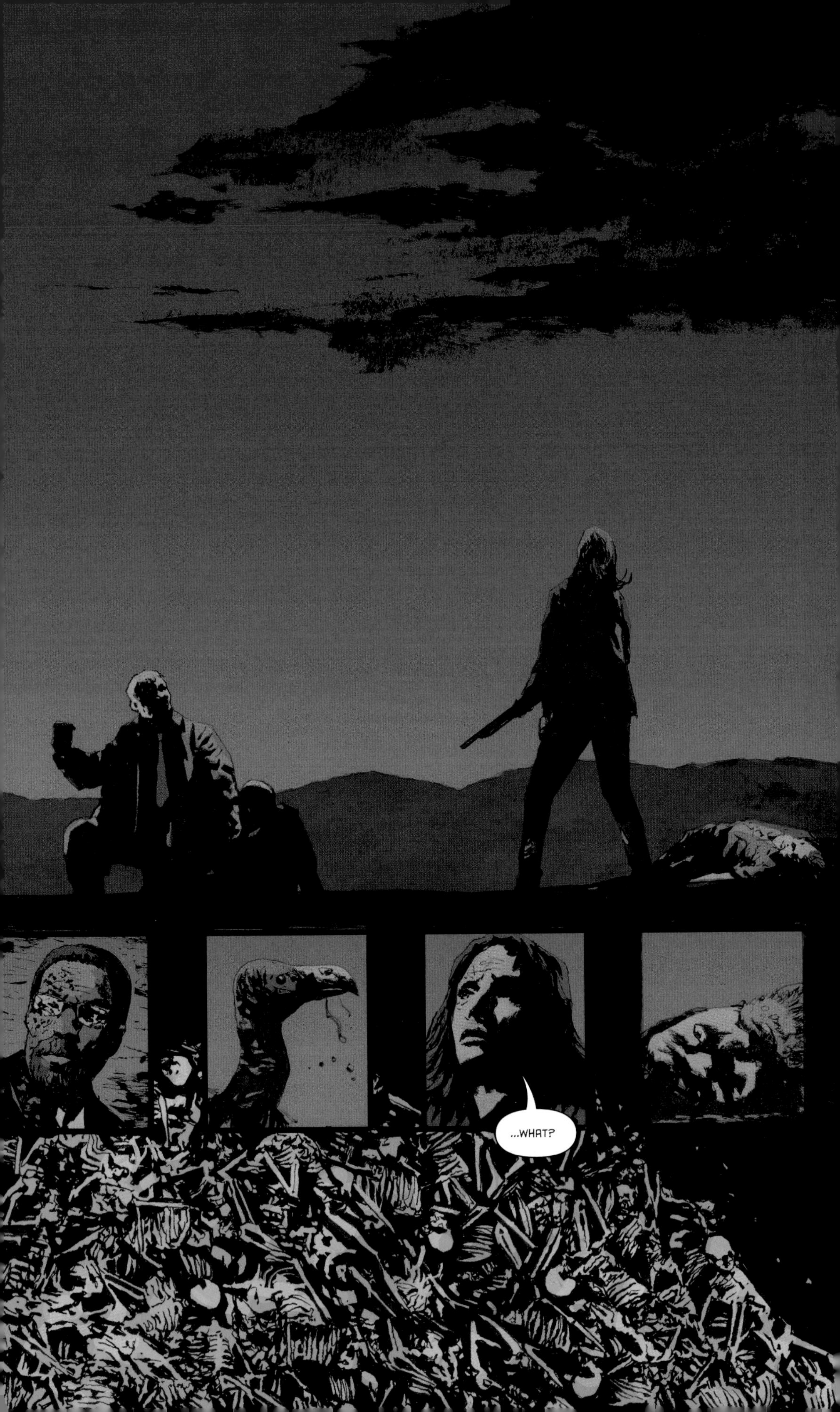
...WHAT?

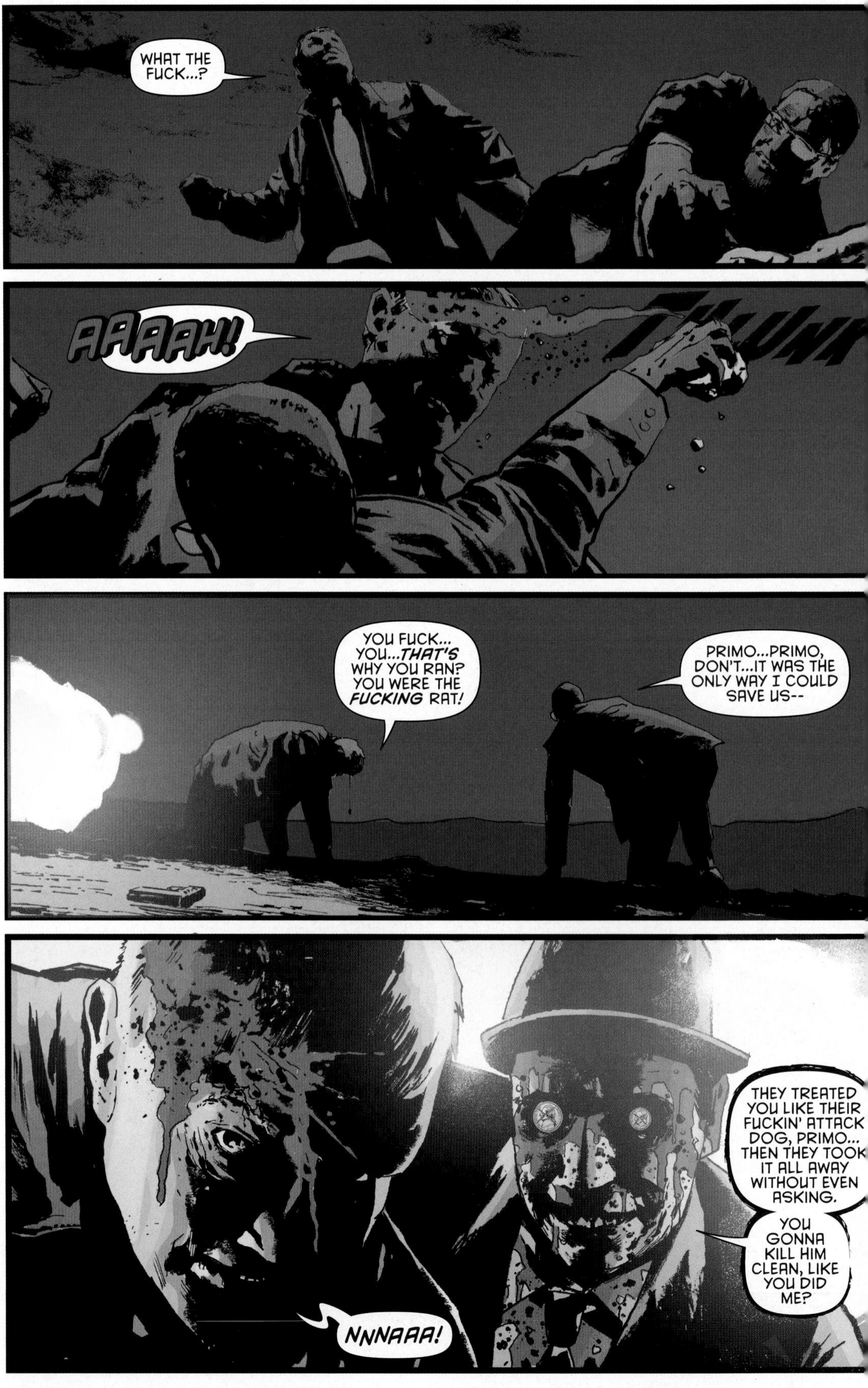
WHAT THE FUCK...?
AAAAH!
YOU FUCK... YOU...THAT'S WHY YOU RAN? YOU WERE THE FUCKING RAT!
PRIMO...PRIMO, DON'T...IT WAS THE ONLY WAY I COULD SAVE US--
THEY TREATED YOU LIKE THEIR FUCKIN' ATTACK DOG, PRIMO... THEN THEY TOOK IT ALL AWAY WITHOUT EVEN ASKING.
YOU GONNA KILL HIM CLEAN, LIKE YOU DID ME?
NNNAAA!

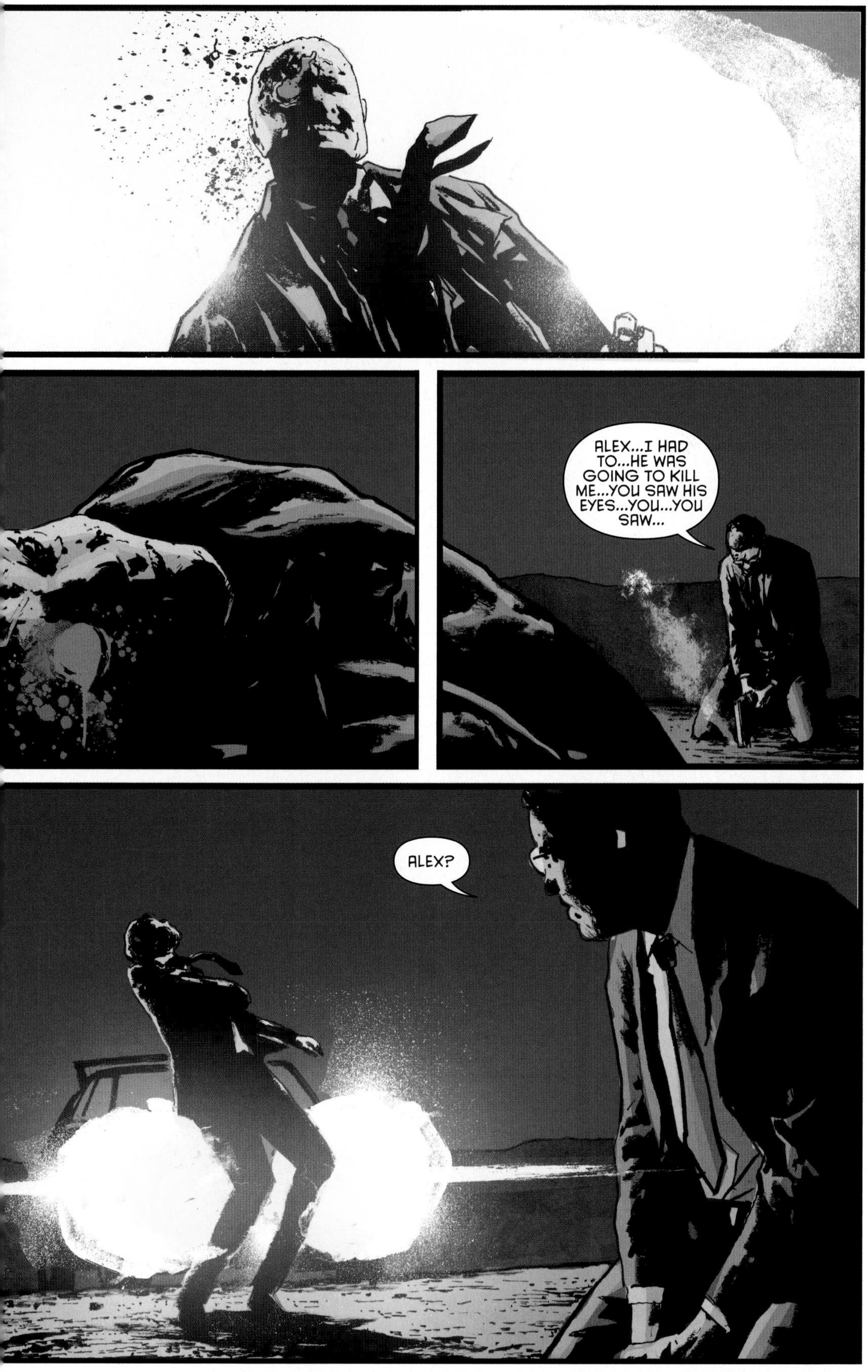
ALEX...I HAD TO...HE WAS GOING TO KILL ME...YOU SAW HIS EYES...YOU...YOU SAW...
ALEX?

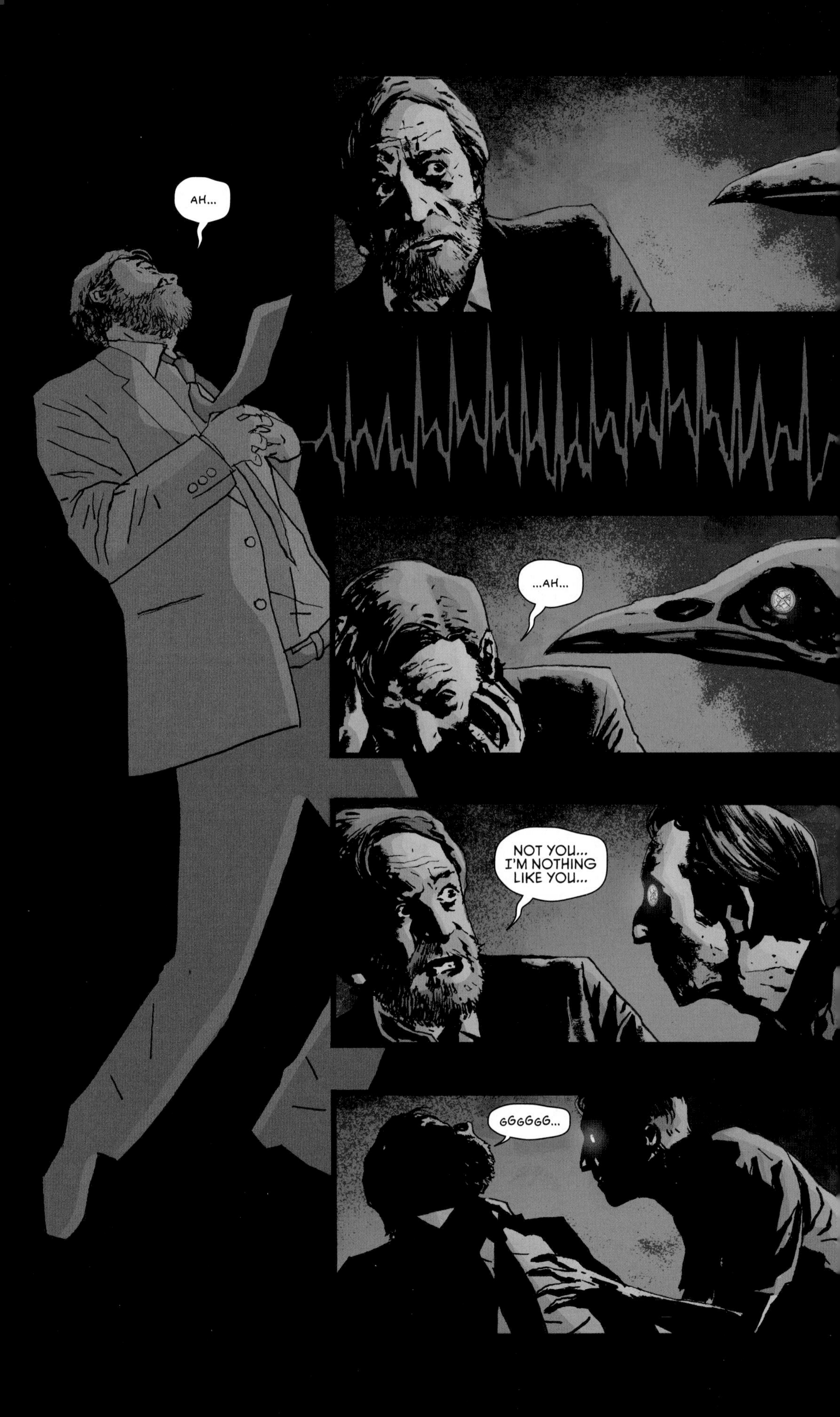
AH...
...AH...
NOT YOU... I'M NOTHING LIKE YOU...
GGGGGG...

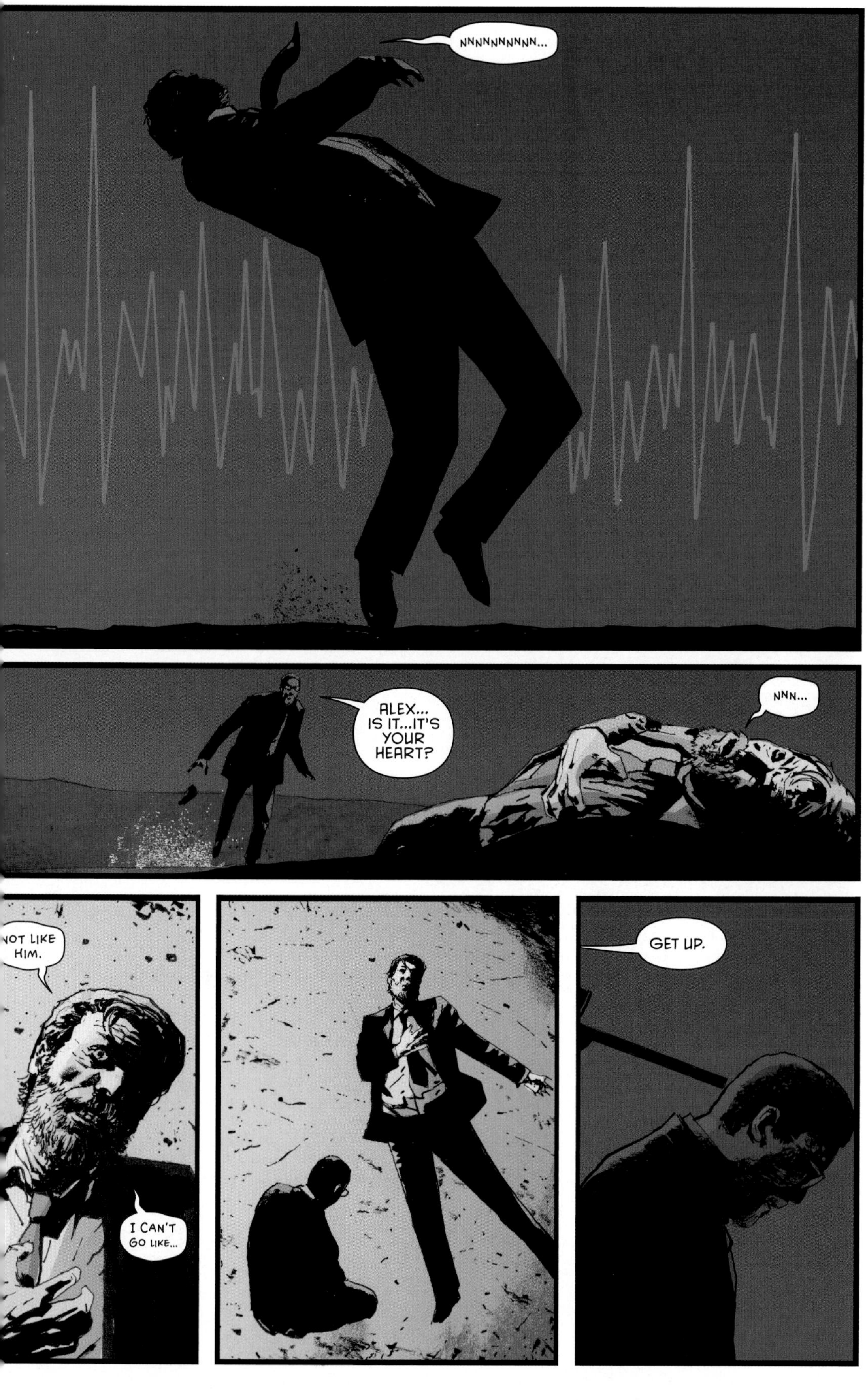
NNNNNNNNNN...
ALEX... IS IT...IT'S YOUR HEART?
NNN...
NOT LIKE HIM.
I CAN'T GO LIKE...
GET UP.

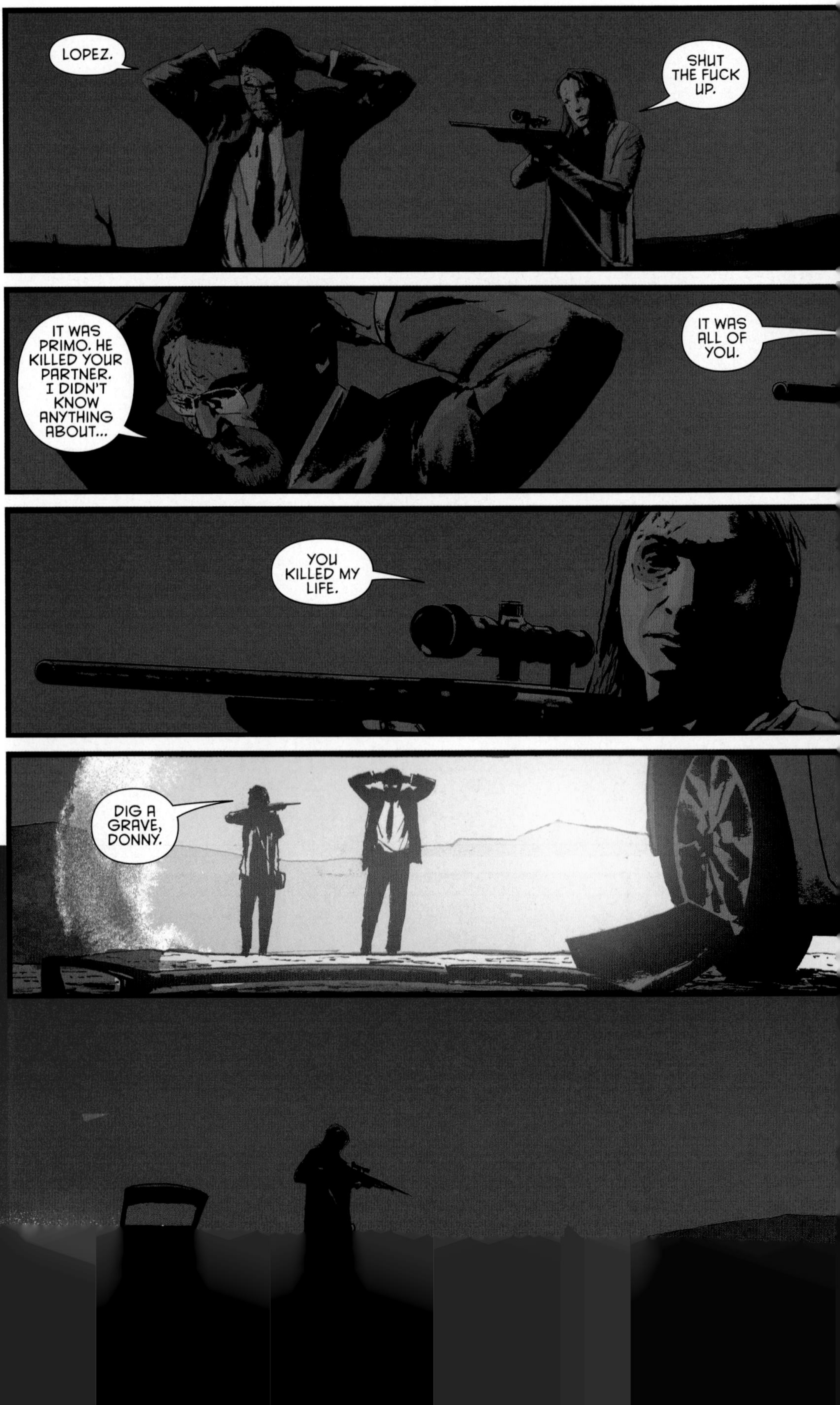
LOPEZ.
SHUT THE FUCK UP.
IT WAS PRIMO. HE KILLED YOUR PARTNER. I DIDN'T KNOW ANYTHING ABOUT...
IT WAS ALL OF YOU.
YOU KILLED MY LIFE.
DIG A GRAVE, DONNY.

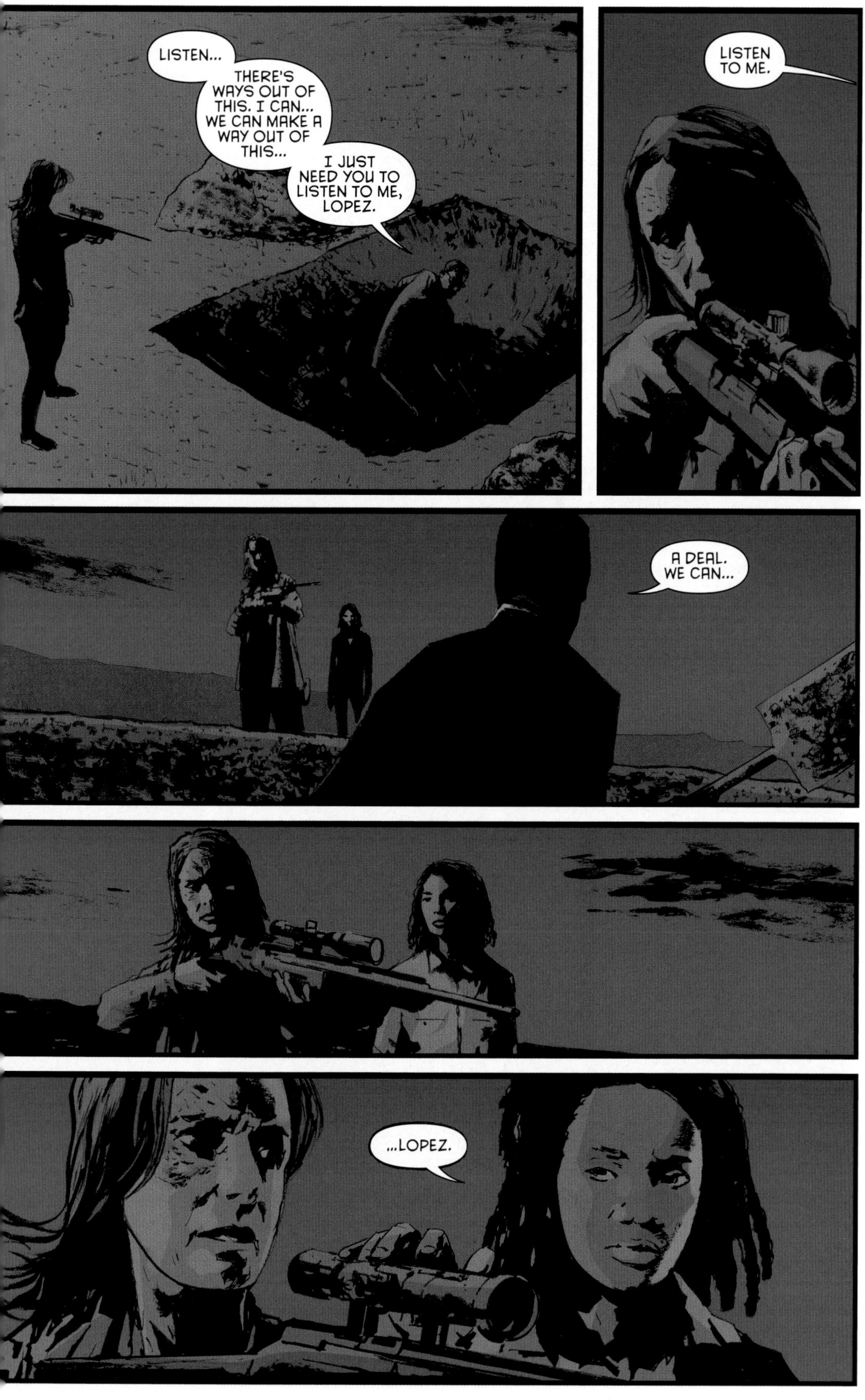
LISTEN...
THERE'S WAYS OUT OF THIS. I CAN... WE CAN MAKE A WAY OUT OF THIS...
I JUST NEED YOU TO LISTEN TO ME, LOPEZ.
LISTEN TO ME.
A DEAL. WE CAN...
...LOPEZ.

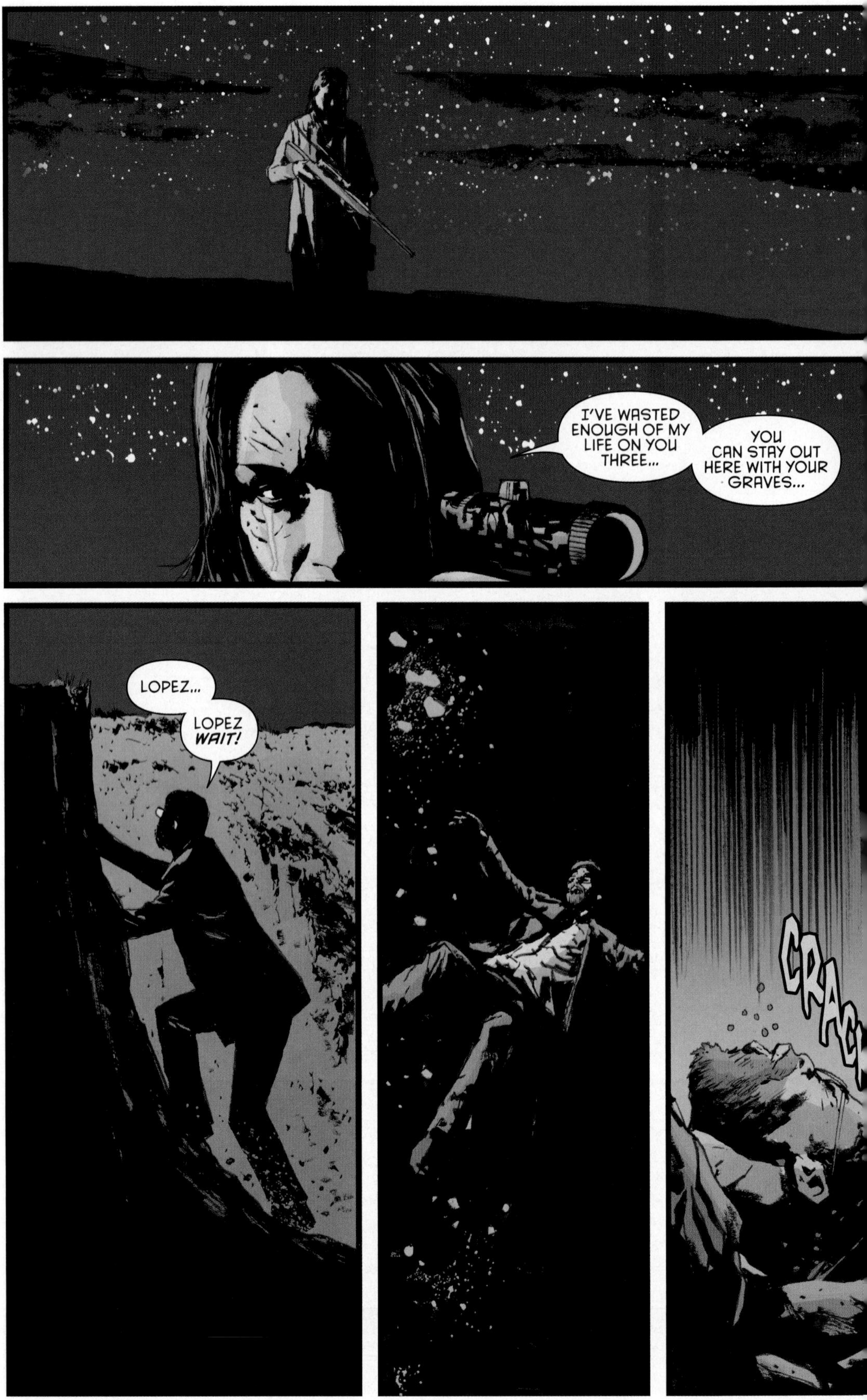
I'VE WASTED ENOUGH OF MY LIFE ON YOU THREE...
YOU CAN STAY OUT HERE WITH YOUR GRAVES...
LOPEZ...
LOPEZ WAIT!
CRACK

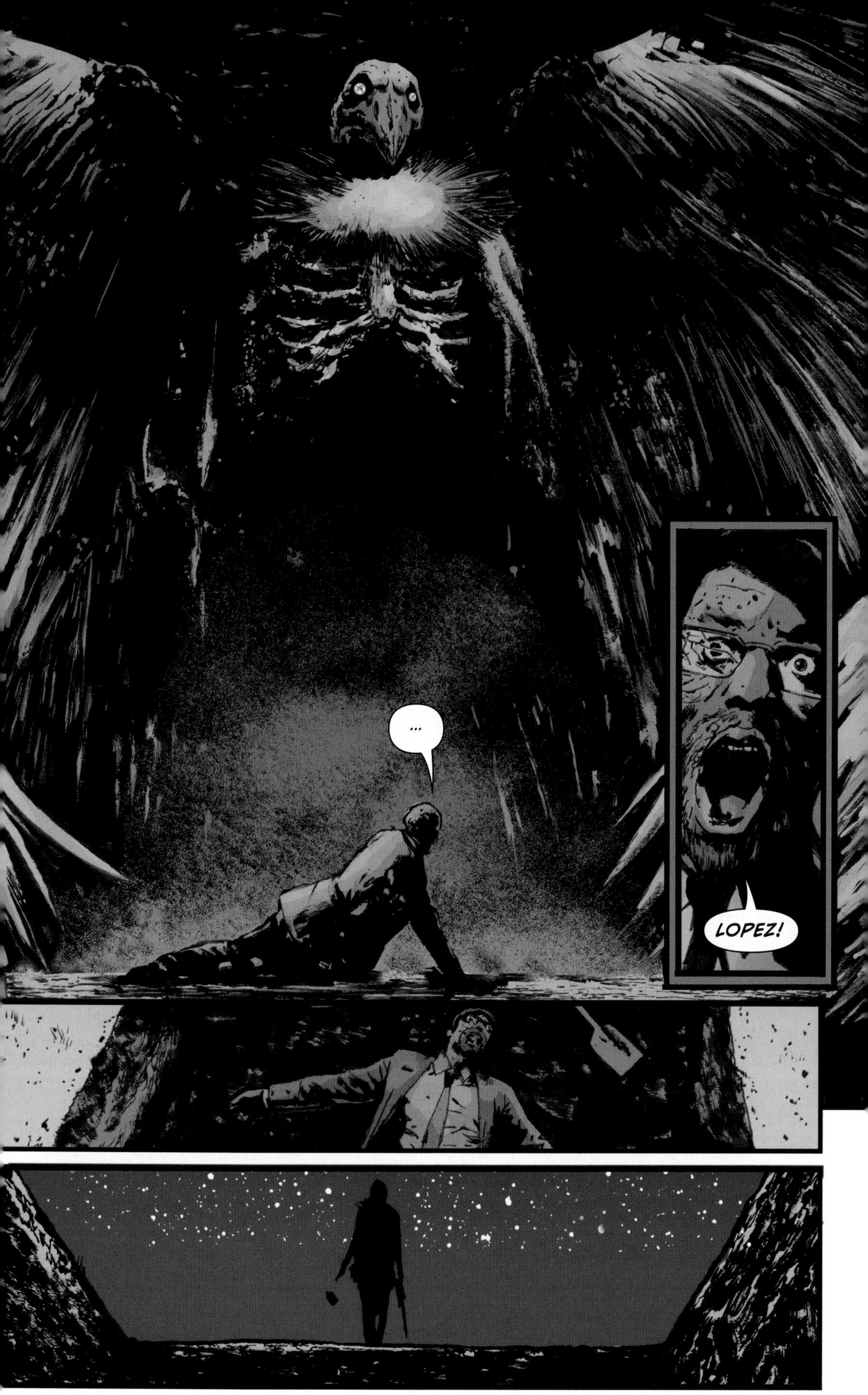
...
LOPEZ!

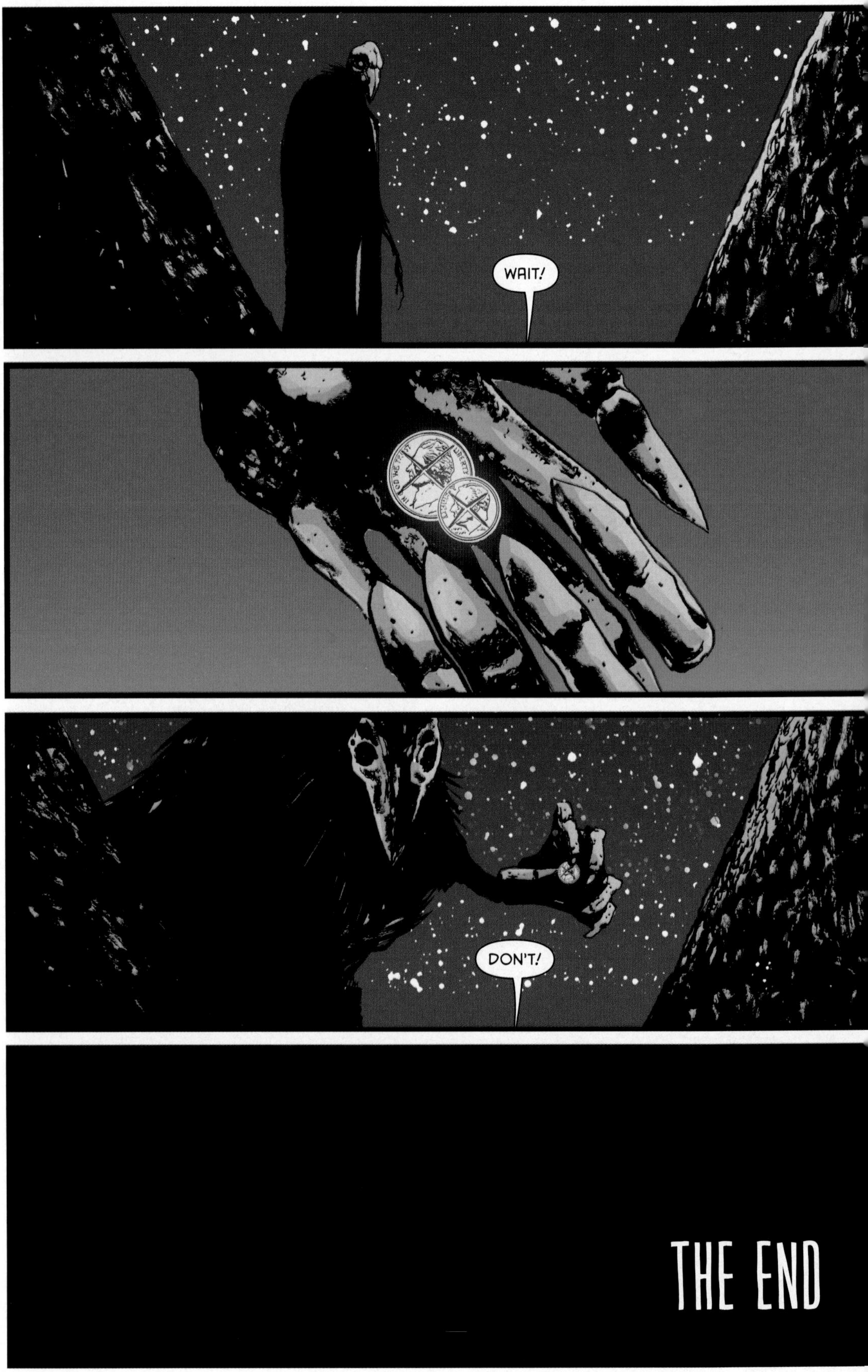
WAIT!
DON'T!
THE END

ETTERS FROM THE WRITERS OF

OLD HAUNTS

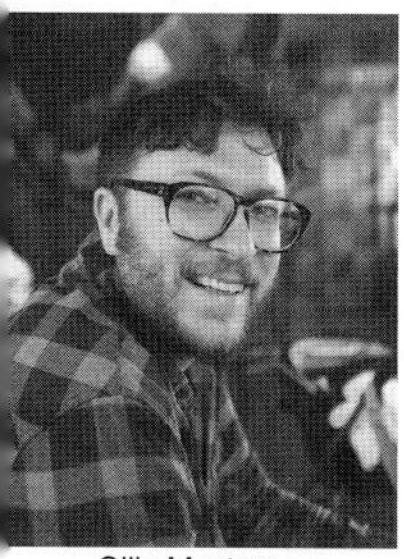

Ollie Masters

Kubrick thought that ghost stories were fundamentally hopeful. He said that "ghost stories appeal to our craving for immortality. If you can be afraid of a ghost, then you have to believe that a ghost may exist. And if a ghost exists, then oblivion might not be the end."

But what if the ghosts are there to remind you f all the terrible things you've done? What if the hosts are manifestations of your own guilt? Guilt r a life of crime that caused huge amounts of vionce, death and pain. Guilt for the people you beayed in that life. Guilt for the mistakes you made…

What if oblivion would actually be the better opon? What if the ghosts are just proof that you'll ever escape the guilt? That there's no running from e bad things you've done. Or rather, you can run ut the chase will only ever end in them catching ou. No escape. Not ever…

I don't think ghosts are real. As far as I know (and be fair, that's not a lot) physics says ghosts are npossible and all available evidence shows that hosts don't exist. Or maybe a more accurate way f saying it is, all available evidence doesn't show hosts exist.

But then, they don't need to be real for people to elieve in them…

Old Haunts.

What if the ghosts are there to remind you of all the terrible things you've done?

Ghosts don't have to exist for a place to be haunt-d. In our minds, the bad memories and associaons from our past can be imprinted onto a place. he bad memories and associations can place a uge 'do not enter' sign above certain doors we on't want to open, while others see nothing but n entrance. We all have places we'd rather not go.

Three old gangsters, closer to death than they ant to admit, in a city haunted by the bad things

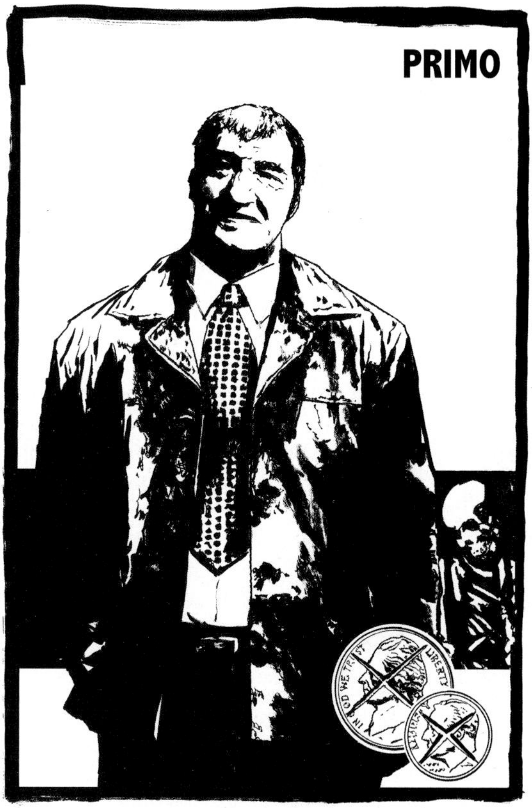
PRIMO
IN GOD WE TRUST
LIBERTY

they've done. When you get older, when there's a lot more past behind you than future ahead, it's easy to spend more time looking back than forward. For our main characters, Alex, Donny and Primo, there's a lot of blood and death in their past. A lot of ghosts haunting those memories.

Each of them, in their own way, have been running from those memories. But now they can't escape them. They can keep running, but the past is coming for them…

The past, in the form of the vulture, is after them. Vultures are scavengers. They don't let the dead rest in peace; they pick away at their flesh until there's nothing left but bones. Like a guilty mind, picking away at the memories of past misdeeds, refusing to let them die. Refusing to let them go and move on.

The vulture, not hunting, but following and waiting. Waiting for the right moment to pick away until there's nothing but bones.

In Alex, Primo and Donny's world of crime, you can't succeed without hurting people. You can't reach the top without leaving a trail of bodies in your wake. Enemies who stood in your way. Associates who turned rat. An innocent person who just happened to be in the wrong place at the wrong time and saw something they wish they hadn't. That's a lot of bodies…a lot of bones to be picked over.

When Kubrick suggested his theory on ghost stories to Stephen King, King replied, "But what about hell?" Kubrick's reply? "But I don't believe in hell."

Maybe hell is like ghosts: it doesn't matter if it's real or not. Hell doesn't need to be real for you to believe in it, and if you do and if you did the kind of shit Alex, Donny and Primo did? Well…where else would you think you were going?

We know the evidence (or lack of evidence) in our real world about ghosts, but do they exist in the world of *Old Haunts*? Does it matter? While writing the comic, Rob and I knew…but isn't the ambiguity more terrifying? The not knowing. The uncertainty of it all.

Is there hope in every ghost story? You'll just have to read to find out.

- Ollie Masters

LITTLE ALEX

Rob Williams

Scariest movie experience of my life was going to see *Jacob's Ladder* in 1990. It's an unnerving, hallucinogenic, bad trip movie anyway. The cinema's a quarter full, if that. I'm healthily creeped out by the demon people Tim Robbins' PTSD-scarred Vietnam vet might be seeing on the streets of his city (or might not).

Then, three-quarters of the way through, I get the strange feeling that someone's watching me. I turn my head and standing at the end of the aisle, staring right at me, is a small girl with long blonde hair. I jump out of my skin and let out a little strangled scream. She giggles and runs up the aisle and out of the cinema. I turn to my friends, heart beating out of chest, and whisper: "Did you see that little girl?" "See what?" is the reply. From all of them.

Jacob's Ladder was one of the touchstones for *Old Haunts* going in. Basically, we wanted to freak people out.

Stories don't tend to appear out of thin air. You sort of drop a load of touchstones into a (bloody) blender and come up with something all of your own, weave a narrative around them. I'm a big fan of Elliott Smith and there's a song on *Either/Or* called "Angeles" that I always wanted to write a movie for —if that makes sense. It feels like it should be in a movie. "Sign up for evil, Angeles?" goes the lyric. And the opening lines: "Someone's always coming around here / Trailing some new kill…"

The song ends on a repeating refrain: "No one's gonna fool around with us / No one's gonna fool around with us." A gang. A gang of killers. Maybe one of them's having doubts. One day, I thought, I'll write something this can be a soundtrack for. I just didn't know when.

It's a song that feels like it should play over a car driving through Los Angeles in the early hours of the morning when the streets are empty. A haunted driver, fried out on lack of sleep, sanity stretched. One of those moments when it feels like the universe is far more fragile than our certainties usually allow. When you can feel your structures flex and wobble.

> Something that picks off their memories one by one. That feasts on their regrets. Something that only they can see. Maybe they're crazy, maybe they're not...

Touchstones again. There's a scene in Michael Mann's *Collateral*, which I love (Tom Cruise's best role! Come at me). Jamie Foxx's terrified taxi driver is driving Cruise's hitman around L.A. in the early hours and, while stopped at a traffic light, a coyote pads across the busy road. An alien presence. It shouldn't be there. It looks at them, a spiritual incursion in our world, just for a second. If that's what you choose to believe. Or maybe it's just a coyote? The important thing is what it means to you. Subjective ethereal experiences that might be real or

LOPEZ

DONNY

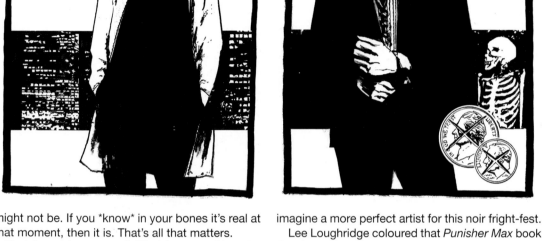

might not be. If you *know* in your bones it's real at that moment, then it is. That's all that matters.

Fast forward to me and Ollie Masters talking shit on a Skype call. Ollie and I had tried to write a totally different story that didn't quite coalesce. Now, whether I remember this correctly, Ollie can dispute, but we were talking story ideas and we found out we both had the same basic premise in our notebooks: "A bunch of old gangsters get haunted by their past crimes, literally."

Old Haunts. Perfect title.

"A ghost story in a city." We start talking about how ghost stories always seem to be set in old houses in the country. How about we do one in a modern metropolis? Spirits between the neon lights.

Retiring gangsters, who have profited hugely from the life and are now selling up for a peaceful, moneyed autumn period. But their past isn't buried that deep. Older characters are more interesting. More lines on those faces, more crimes, more regrets.

Ollie had been talking to Axel Alonso about maybe pitching something for Axel's new venture, AWA. "Shall I pitch him *Old Haunts*?" Axel liked it and off we went.

I've worked with Laurence Campbell quite a few times previously. In fact, Laurence and I did a book for Axel years ago when he was at Marvel—*Punisher Max*: *Get Castle*. I still think it's one of the best things I've ever done.

Laurence is brilliant. His art is cinematic, menace, deep mood. He would be perfect for this. He's one of my best friends, he's also very good friends with Ollie. Axel loves his work and wants him onboard. Fortunately for us Laurence is finishing up his long run on *B.P.R.D.* soon and we get him. It's difficult to

imagine a more perfect artist for this noir fright-fest.

Lee Loughridge coloured that *Punisher Max* book that Laurence and I did together. Lee's terrific and suits this down to the ground. The city lights of L.A. at night reflecting off glass. Strange, terrifying faces looking back.

Something coming for these men. Something that crawls up out of the desert burial ground and flies into the city. Something that picks off their memories one by one. That feasts on their regrets. Something that only they can see. Maybe they're crazy, maybe they're not…

Touchstones again. Kubrick and *The Shining*, obviously. Kubrick and *2001*. The less you explain, the more the audience fill in the gaps with their own experience. And Ollie and I want this to be a cinematic script. Sparse. Silent panels. Mood. Keep the dialogue to the minimum. Let Laurence's visuals tell a lot of the story.

Ollie and I both love Nick Cave. He and the Bad Seeds are in here somewhere. The line from "Jubilee Street": "I'm transforming / I'm vibrating / I'm glowing / I'm flying / Look at me now." Barriers breaking. I mean, if *Old Haunts* ever becomes a movie, a Cave/Warren Ellis score would be something we'd be very down with. A world that was sleek and paid off so well suddenly scarring and clawing, like an Ellis violin line scratching across your turntable.

Like something you're not quite sure that you really did just see. Something that shouldn't be here. Something like getting the shit scared out of you by a weird blonde child who shouldn't be in a cinema.

-Rob Williams

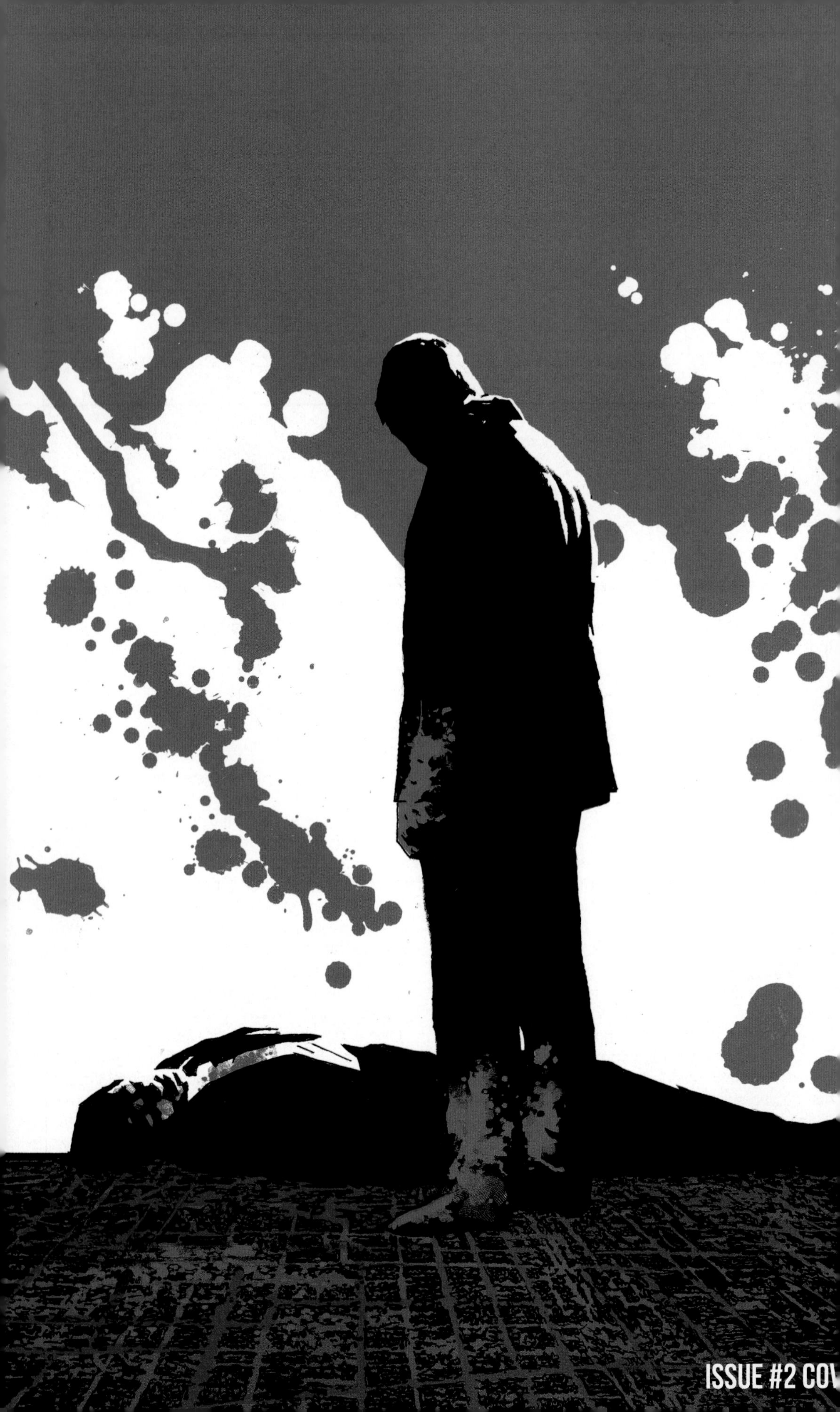

ISSUE #2 COV

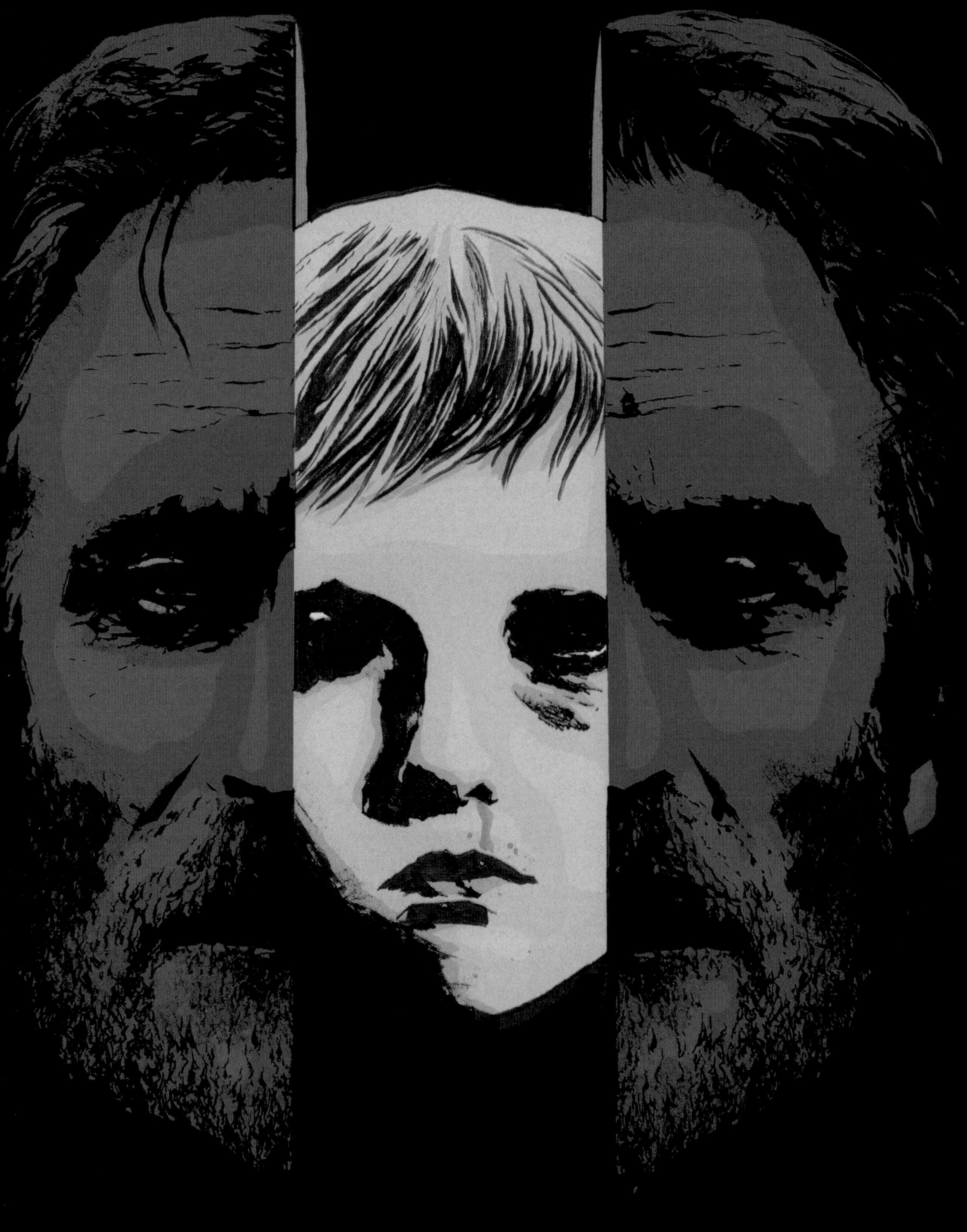

ISSUE #3 COVER

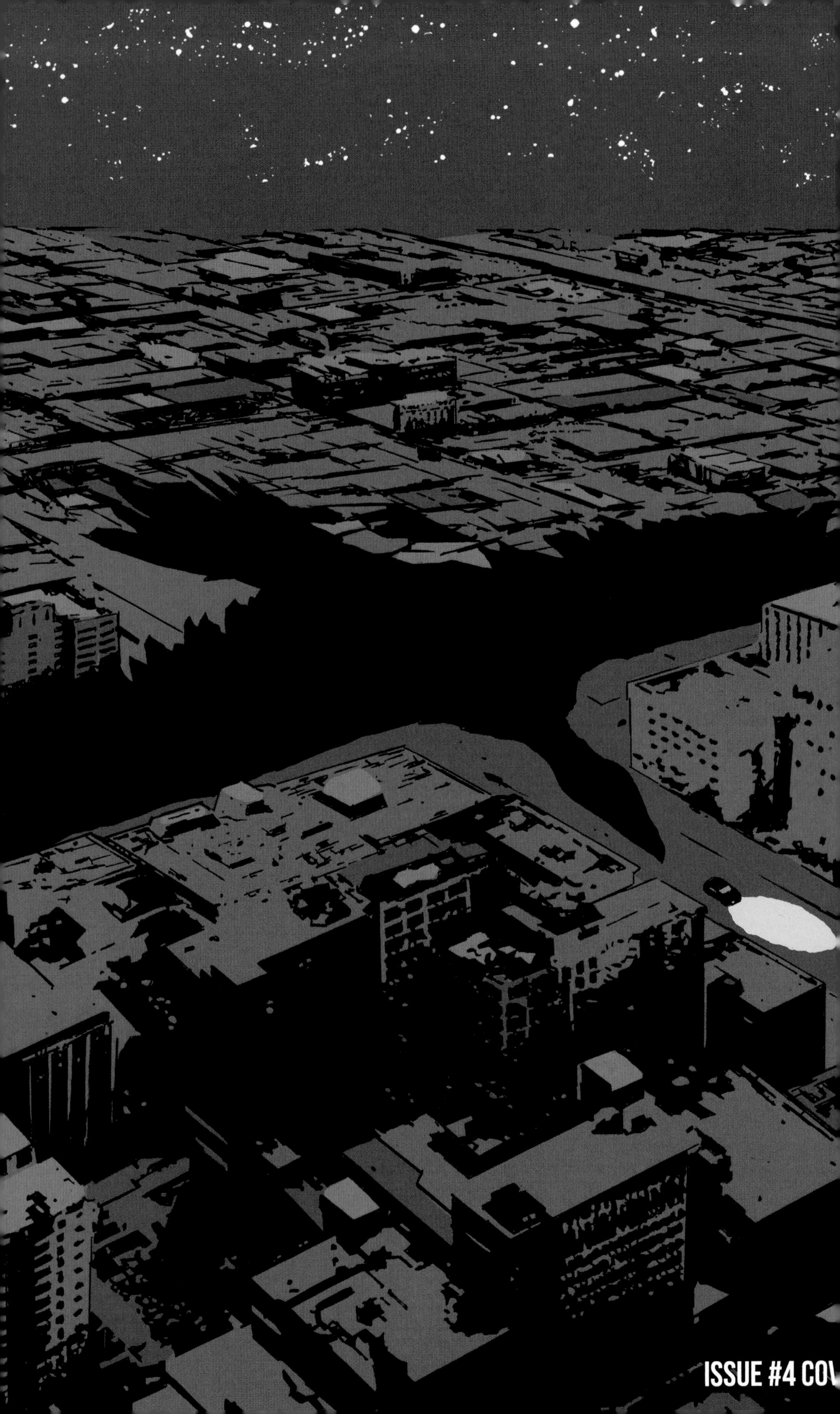

ISSUE #4 COV

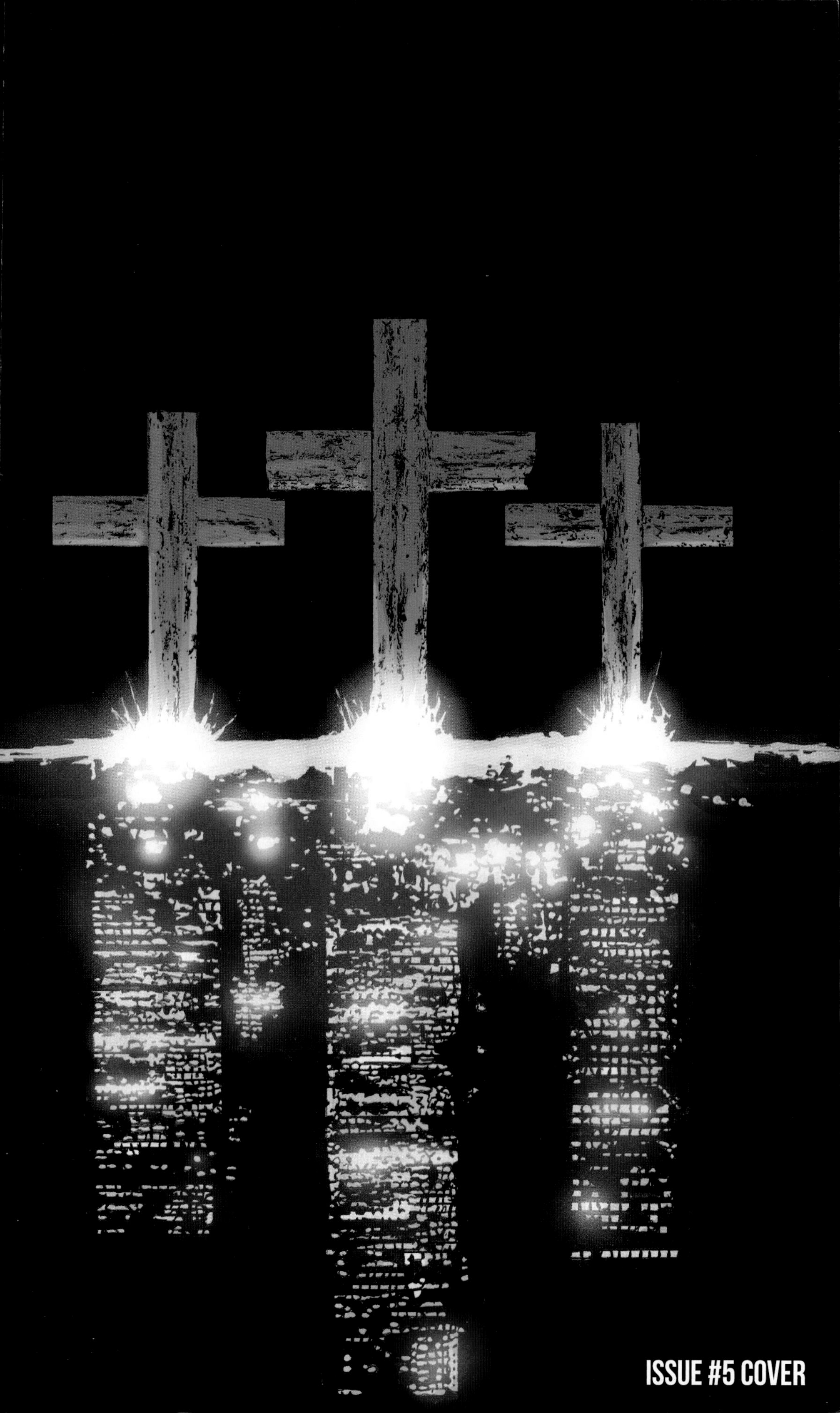

ISSUE #5 COVER

PANEL 1

CUT TO: Exterior shot of a plush, moneyed Los
Angeles home. Up on a hill. Laurence, I fucking
love this Julius Shulman picture of LA. Maybe crib
this, but with none of the furniture, and put Primo
there, looking out. He looks pensive, troubled. And
in this shot he's like a wild animal in a zoo. The
wild outside. He's wearing a vest and trousers. In
amazing shape for his age. Plainly works out. White
strapping on his hands. He's getting older but he's a
boxer at heart. He has a whiskey tumbler in his
hand.

PRIMO   Everything I want...

PANEL 2
Panels Two, Three, Four... Three small silent panels. Primo's eyes. This is a hard fucking man. He
looks angry, even when he's not.
NO DIALOGUE

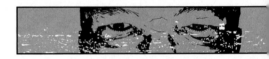

PANEL 3
He places the whiskey tumbler (neat) on the table,
his hands strapped for the boxing ring.
NO DIALOGUE

PANEL 4
He clenches his fists. Mean fists, battered fists over
the years. Fists that have beaten a lot of people to
death.
NO DIALOGUE

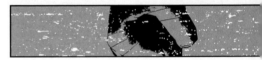

PANEL 5
Wide shot now. We're behind Primo as he walks
into the house, and there is virtually no furniture.
No sign of family or a life. No warmth of happiness
here. Hanging from the ceiling is a PUNCHBAG
on a chain. That's it in this big room. He has the
house of dreams and all he can think to do with it is
exactly what he would have done had he just had a
crummy garage.

PRIMO   Yeah... Thanks Alex.

PANEL 1

CUT TO: Alex. He's stood in front of a full-length mirror, killer rich suit. He looks cool and moneyed and the epitome of success. He's done it. Achieved everything he could ever want. But there's a sadness in his face, he carries all his pain in the dark shadows under his eyes.

PAT (OFF PANEL)   There's my silver fox.

PANEL 2

Alex looks around. In the doorway to the bedroom, his wife. PATRICIA. She's in her forties. Great looking. She's not joining him. They're good. Pretty solid. A lot of shit under the bridge over the years but they've stayed afloat, somehow, and love each other. She doesn't resent him here. She genuinely thinks he looks really hot.

ALEX   I really need a drink.

PANEL 3

Pat pulls his tie, flirtatiously towards her but Alex is thinking about other things.

PAT   Look at how far you've come.

ALEX   How far I've come...You know, I first saw it about twenty years ago. I looked in the mirror and I saw him looking back at me.

ALEX   Now he's all I see in that fucking glass...I came all this way but still can't escap him.

PANEL 4

Repeat of the last panel but Alex kind of freezes when he hears this. Pat knows what this means to him.

PAT   You're not your father Alex. He could never of done what you've done.

PANEL 5

Pull back at a distance, like someone's watching them. They hug. Maybe this takes place in background of scene. A bottle of whiskey in foreground on a table. Alex will be drinking that soon enough.

ALEX   I love you.

PANEL 1
CUT TO: Hotel Room.
Front onto Donny. Naked. Haunted. He looks wor-
ried, staring at nothing.
NO DIALOGUE

PANEL 2
Donny turns. Looks at the prostitute who's getting
dressed on the bed. Donny looks like he's forgotten
she was even there.

DONNY   Money's on the
                         sidetable.

PANEL 3
She picks up the roll of cash as she goes. Donny
watches her.

PROSTITUTE   Got it. You in town
                         long? If you want,
                         we could work out
                         something for the
                         week --

DONNY   Just the night...

PROSTITUTE   You know, it's pretty
                         common for guys your
                         age--

DONNY   I've got things I need
                         to do.

PANEL 4
CUT TO: Donny, fully dressed. In a suit. Heading
out of the revolving doors of an expensive hotel in
Downtown.

PANEL 5
Donny's head flips around when he hears his name
called from off panel.

PRIMO (o/s)   Hey, fuck face!

DONNY   Huh

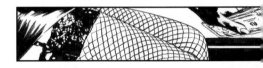